MANIFESTING FROM ONENESS

The Book of Yoga & Manifestation

RAINER PERRY

 **KRI**

A KUNDALINI RESEARCH INSTITUTE PUBLICATION

Kundalini Yoga as taught by Yogi Bhajan

© 2025 RAINER PERRY
PUBLISHED BY THE KUNDALINI RESEARCH INSTITUTE
TRAINING • PUBLISHING • RESEARCH • RESOURCES
PO BOX 1819
SANTA CRUZ, NM 87532
WWW.KUNDALINIRESEARCHINSTITUTE.ORG
ISBN: 979-8-9886160-7-8

EDITOR: MARIANA LAGE
AUTHOR: RAINER PERRY
ILLUSTRATOR: JANIS SOUZA
DESIGN AND LAYOUT: FERNANDA MONTE-MÓR
REVIEWERS: SIRI NEEL KAUR KHALSA AND DIANA NANU
PROOFREADING: CARLOS ANDREI SIQUARA
EDITORIAL ASSISTANT: ANTONIO LARA SILVA

The diet, exercise, and lifestyle suggestions in this book come from ancient yogic traditions. Nothing in this book should be construed as medical advice. Always check with your personal physician or licensed care practitioner before making any significant modifications to your diet or lifestyle to ensure that the changes are appropriate for your personal health condition and consistent with any medication you may be taking. For more information about Kundalini Yoga as taught by Yogi Bhajan®, please see www.kundaliniresearchinstitute.org.

This publication has received the KRI Seal of Approval. This Seal is given only to products that have been reviewed for accuracy and integrity of the sections containing the 3HO lifestyle and Kundalini Yoga as taught by Yogi Bhajan®.

REUNITING ANCIENT YOGIC & MODERN MANIFESTATION TECHNOLOGY FOR NEXT-LEVEL PRACTICE AND RESULTS

A complete guide on how to integrate yoga and manifestation for success for practitioners, teachers, therapists, and coaches at all levels.

EDITOR'S NOTE

—

Welcome to *Manifesting From Oneness: The Book of Yoga & Manifestation.* We are proud to present to you this one-of-a-kind book that knowledgeably merges yoga and manifestation teachings and practices. As you will see throughout these pages, this is a comprehensive guide that bridges ancient yogic wisdom and modern manifestation techniques, providing a unique and transformative approach for next-level success and well-being.

Drawing from a wide range of spiritual traditions, this book goes beyond the teachings of Kundalini Yoga as taught by Yogi Bhajan, reaching back to the ancient texts of the *Patanjali Sutras* and the *Bhagavad Gita* while also exploring common threads in Buddhism, Christianity, and Hinduism. Here, yoga and manifestation are presented as two ancient soulmates — deeply interconnected yet often separated in modern practice. Through this book, you will explore how these practices can come together to create powerful results.

This work is the result of extensive research and long, consistent practice, as well as a deep commitment to both the yogic and manifestation traditions. While the Kundalini Research Institute (KRI) traditionally publishes works that focus solely on the teachings of Yogi Bhajan, we recognize the importance of clearly identifying when practices drawn from his teachings are included here. For this reason, you will see "Kundalini Yoga" labeled at the beginning of practice titles, such as "Kundalini Yoga Meditation" or "Kundalini Yoga Kriya." Other practices, like "Buddhist Meditation: Sympathetic Joy," will be labeled according to their respective traditions, but not all practices will have this designation. As with all Kundalini Yoga practices, we suggest you observe a few points before you begin your yoga or meditation session (see below in "Before You Begin").

We are honored to present this synthesis of spiritual wisdom that offers a more profound understanding of how yoga and manifestation can work together to create lasting transformation in your life.

Mariana Lage
(HariShabad Kaur Khalsa)

Before You Begin

If you're new to Kundalini Yoga, note that it's always a good practice to tune in before you begin your yoga each day. Here, we share key points to be aware of when doing the practices below.

TUNING IN

Every Kundalini Yoga session begins with chanting the Adi Mantra[1], "Ong Namo Guru Dev Namo." By chanting it with the right pronunciation and projection, the student becomes open to their higher self, the source of all guidance, and accesses the protective link between himself or herself and the consciousness of the divine teacher.

Sit in a comfortable cross-legged position with the spine straight. Place the palms of the hands together as if in prayer, with the fingers pointing straight up, and then press the joints of the thumbs into the center of the chest at the sternum. Inhale deeply. Focus your concentration on the Third Eye Point. As you exhale, chant the entire mantra in one breath. Chant this mantra at least three times before beginning your Kundalini Yoga practice.

MENTAL FOCUS

Meditation requires concentration. To receive the benefits of each meditation, you will need to mentally focus. To assist you, the instructions for each meditation will tell you where to focus your concentration with your eyes. Unless you are directed to do otherwise, close your eyes and focus on the Third Eye Point. It is located between the eyebrows, where the root of the nose meets the skull bone. Mentally locate this point by gently turning your eyes upward and inward.

ENDING A YOGA PRACTICE

To close up a yoga practice, sit up straight and put the palms together, with the thumbs pointing up and resting against the sternum. Inhale deeply and chant the mantra SAT NAAM three times ("Sat" lasts 7 seconds, "Naam" 1 second). The mantra means "Truth is my name" or "my true identity." This mantra connects you with your soul and your destination.

---

1   "Adi" means primal or first. Thus, Adi Mantra is the first, or primal, mantra.

TABLE OF CONTENTS

MEDITATIONS INDEX

—

INTRODUCTION

—

I practiced yoga for over a decade before I become interested in manifestation. Right away, I observed similarities between manifestation techniques and yoga principles. I noticed no contradictions between them and found that I could merge both effortlessly into a single spiritual practice. I started seeing yoga and manifestation as long-lost siblings more and more, even though they are mostly taught separately. Ashtanga and Vinyasa yoga are considered serious and highbrow practices for enlightenment, while teachings like The Secret or Law of Attraction are seen as more popular and focused on material wealth. The truth I found is that combining them enhances their power together — a classic synergy. This book is about exploring this synergy and making it work for you.

Nothing has prepared me better for successful manifestation than my yoga practice. I can apply everything I have learned from yoga to manifestation, and vice versa. If you already practice yoga, you know it can improve every aspect of your life, and I am here to tell you that adding yoga to manifestation is no exception. It is a simple and seamless combination that has brought tremendous benefits to my life.

I've been practicing and teaching yoga since 2006, and it has transformed my life and the lives of my students, clients, and friends. My yoga practice now focuses explicitly on manifesting improved states — physical, mental, and spiritual — and it has elevated everything to another level. Achieving my goals becomes simpler, new blessings constantly appear, and fears dissolve as I comprehend my agency in shaping my reality and the world. More than ever, I understand that the quality of my consciousness is the main variable in the quality of my life. When I run my mind's power with clarity and focus, manifestations occur with astonishing speed and accuracy, and when my mind is scattered or I am lazy behind the wheel, I sit in traffic and wait for the lights to change like everyone else. Yoga improves the quality of my consciousness immensely so that I can manifest on a higher level.

Manifestation techniques focus on the importance of positive feelings, and generating them in any situation is crucial for successful manifestation. Simply put, yoga is a technology for making your life positive. The key message I have for you is that nurturing positive feelings consistently is a worthwhile investment of your time and energy, as it creates a better reality for yourself and others. Yoga practice based on manifestation techniques is the best method and incentive I've found for feeling good. Combined with manifestation, yoga is the source of renewable, clean energy that powers the creation of the world we want to live in. Please join me on a journey to next-level manifestation through yoga.

WHAT THIS BOOK IS AND WHAT IT ISN'T

When I told a friend that I had written a yoga book, she was supportive but also said: "There are already so many yoga books. It's surprising they would publish another." She's right. There's an infinite number of books that explain what yoga is and how to do it. The main difference between all of them is the style in which the information is presented. Most yoga books, whether scholarly or lighthearted, personal or general, predominantly textual or graphic, revolve around the same ancient teachings. That's understandable. What else can you do with revered yoga sources like the Upanishads, the various Sutras, or the Bhagavad Gita other than try to interpret them for today's life in the best way you know? It's no wonder the core of every yoga book never strays far from these ancient teachings.

But what if you could expand the teachings without changing them? What if there are other profound teachings and methods that are very aligned with yogic philosophy but exist mostly separate from them? Manifestation teachings are like that. They have ancient roots, yet we don't think of them as coming from the same vein. Rather than inventing a new type of yoga, this book fuses popular manifestation with existing yoga techniques to create a potent synergy.

The book is not named "The Yoga of Manifestation," but instead "Yoga and Manifestation," highlighting the value of combining the two. There is no iconoclasm, the kind that is very common in publishing today and aimed at turning everything upside down, as in "Everything you've ever learned about coffee, personal finance, romantic relationships, or how to be happy is wrong." This is not that kind of book. This book aims to enhance what you already know and feel to be true. Discovering common ground between seemingly separate things is a common experience for yogis, who aim to find oneness in everything through their practice. I discovered the connections weren't just in my own experience but also in the similarities of the teachings, wording, concepts, and applications.

Yoga is a method to enhance the beauty of your life, and there's no quicker path to a beautiful life than the ability to manifest exquisite things through your own power of consciousness. And I don't just mean material things; I mean situations, relationships, environments, and whole worlds. Manifestation takes the abstract concept of creating our own realities, which most yogis believe in, and makes it more concrete and applicable to our lives.

Although I refer to specific traditions and publications, the overall view is broad. There are no unnecessary fillers in this book. I will repeat basic manifestation concepts only to look at them through the lens of yoga and with an expanded consciousness. The intention behind this book is to combine ancient yoga teachings and popular manifestation techniques — yoking them — and apply them to modern life. In simple language, I want to show the deep roots that yogic and manifestation teachings share, that their objectives are identical, and that practicing both is a synergy, not a split. I not only want to remove the mystery and complexity from manifestation but also the weirdness, because so often manifestation seems to border on hocus-pocus. This book blends the idea of humans engaging in the universe's manifestation using yogic teachings in both explicit and implicit ways.

What I want the most is for everyone to rediscover their powers of manifestation. Yoga, for me, has always been about developing my agency by connecting to my true nature, all the while the power of manifestation is an inherent agency of every human being. This book shifts the premise from mystical to basic human capacity, placing it in your lap to facilitate wholeness, just like a solid yoga practice would. The book is also an attempt at a larger application of the basic yogic principle that says that wholeness achieved in the inner world creates wholeness in the outer world. As we reunite yogic teachings with manifestation teachings, we become whole and healthy, and our powers to heal and grow ourselves and others will develop.

Like yoga awakens our true selves, we can also awaken to our true nature as manifestors. Whether we know it or not, we are always manifesting. Yoga is not only about exercise but also about becoming aware. Understanding our powers of manifestation is equally important to understanding any other aspect of our lives because our manifestations shape our reality and the quality of our lives. This book helps you, your students, and your clients become conscious manifestors through yoga. The practical application of yoga is at the heart of it and can change your life more significantly than anything else you've done in your yoga practice.

Above all, I want to show the hidden existence of manifestation in yogic philosophy. I have found that, like scripture and religion, yogic teachings might also have enigmatic aspects that involve manifestation. If the purpose of yoga is to awaken you to a conscious being connected with the universe, then an awakened being can actively take part in the creation process.

WHO IS THIS BOOK FOR

This book is ideal for anyone interested in yoga or manifestation: yoga practitioners, yoga teachers, therapists, healers, and health practitioners who integrate yoga into their work. If you or your students and clients are at ease with yoga but struggle with manifestation, this can be particularly helpful. Many doubt the simple truth that everyone is inherently a creator. Now it's time to overcome these mental limitations.

You will discover how to present ancient and established concepts in a new way that is easy to understand and accepted by everyone. You will find bridges between ideas that may have seemed impossible to unite before. One example we will discuss is talking about faith as a tool, not an identity. Our approach is to be flexible and promote harmony when dealing with belief systems, instead of being rigid and confrontational. Most importantly, we will reveal the hidden trails that connect yoga and manifestation and the immense pleasure of walking on them. If you are interested in creating new solutions and well-being for yourself and others, this book is for you.

The main objectives of this books are to

- » Introduce fresh terminology on manifestation within the context of yoga and meditation.
- » Deliberately blend modern and ancient manifestation technologies with yoga practices.

» Create experts in next-level manifesting to advance conscious manifestation abilities in humans.
» Remove obstacles and resistance to accepting and leveraging your inherent power of manifestation.
» Eliminate spiritual barriers such as doubt, ambiguity, self-criticism, and skepticism.
» Convince yourself and others about your own capabilities and the immense rewards of conscious manifestation.
» Upgrade popular approaches to ignite fresh energy in yoga practice.
» Highlight the parallels between manifestation teachings and modern, quantum science.
» Find answers to lingering questions.
» Be equipped with answers for when clients, students, and peers inquire.

HOW TO USE THIS BOOK

Whether you're a beginner or advanced, this book can support your study and application of yoga and manifestation. Every chapter combines theory and practice, giving you the opportunity to apply what you learn through exercises and plans. Teachers and coaches can find inspiration for their classes and sessions by using the yogic tools described in each chapter. For example, you can use some of the physical yoga practices throughout the book to prepare for meditation and then guide your students through a specific meditation for personal manifestations.

If you read the book from start to finish, you'll establish a strong foundation for achieving better outcomes in all related pursuits. You can also explore any chapter individually or search for keywords in areas where support is necessary for yourself and your associates, ranging from grasping fundamental ideas to aligning belief systems and attitudes. By doing so, you can hone practical skills, such as concentration and creativity, or surpass states to cultivate desired outcomes. Once more, use it as you prefer to support your study and application of yoga and manifestation. You will find the support needed here.

PART 1 QUALIFYING MANIFESTATION TECHNIQUES AND UNDERSTANDING THE BASICS

CHAPTER 1

MANIFESTATION IN ANCIENT TEACHINGS

You and the people you work with will encounter doubt about the validity of manifestation techniques and teachings. These doubts are fueled by the notion that the techniques have no basis in ancient texts and scriptures and are mostly fabricated. Nothing could be further from the truth. This chapter shows the history of manifestation teachings using examples from ancient texts, scholars, and accepted sources. This will help you and the people you work with to build a foundation of trust.

PATANJALI'S SUTRAS. IT'S ALL ABOUT THE PSYCHE

I have never heard the Patanjali's sutras mentioned in any context of manifestation, even though an entire section of the sutras is devoted to it. Even spiritual teacher Alan Watts, who is usually effortless in explaining spiritual teachings with precise references that he seems to pull out of his vast memory at the drop of a hat, says this in one of his lectures: "To understand yoga, you need to get hold of a good translation of Patanjali's Yoga Sutras. I don't know which is the best translation; there are so many albums."[2] Coming from him, that doesn't bode well for our introductory study of the Sutras. But don't despair; I'll give you the basics to kick-start our discussion on manifestation, and later on, you may want to pick up a good translation as you deepen your practice. Hopefully, it will encourage you to read the entire text.

Many people consider Patanjali's Yoga Sutras to be the classic textbook on yoga as a spiritual journey to the union of body, mind, and soul. This makes the sutras a good starting point for exploring how their teachings relate to manifestation.

Patanjali's Yoga Sutras are a collection of 196 short statements written by Patanjali in the second to fourth centuries BC. Each sutra is step-by-step advice on how

---

2 Alan Watts, "The World as Self," (lecture, Esalen Institute, Big Sur, CA, 1965).

to practice yoga to achieve liberation. The sutras are divided into four books, and Patanjali devoted the third book entirely to the development of superpowers, including manifestation. Keep in mind that the sutras are written for anyone, not some privileged few chosen for superhuman tasks, and that your liberation does not depend on luck or outside influences but on your own practice and discipline.

The actual sutras are short and cryptic. The 196 sutras are all concise, as you'll see in the examples later. So, theoretically, you could read the entire book quickly. But doing that would probably not get you very far. Sutra means "holding together," like something that is stitched up as with a medical suture (same word root), like a knot or a flower bud, and when it opens, a whole new world or being appears. In other words, when you read a sutra, a lot of information may come out, and when your mind starts interacting with it, processing the data might become overwhelming or at least difficult. Usually, not just one interpretation of a sutra is possible, and you might struggle to find a meaning within the words that feels unequivocal. This is intentional because your understanding of the sutras will depend on your level of experience and frame of reference. Reading the sutras as a young yogi can give you a basic understanding. However, as you explore more yogic concepts and practice, your comprehension will grow and become more profound. That's why it's a good idea to read the sutras again and again, and, as you do, you'll almost certainly get a clearer perspective on your own progress each time.

The first time I read the sutras, I hardly enjoyed them. I found the language archaic, and the wisdom was not easily accessible. However, when I read the sutras today as a much more experienced yogi, I find them opening up inside of me like flowers watered with the knowledge and experience I have gained over the years. If you continue practicing yoga, you'll likely have a similar experience.

Manifestation as an achievable human power is clearly mentioned in the Sutras. As you will see, several sutras explain techniques for manifestation, both directly and indirectly. One sutra even names the ability to manifest: Isatva, "ability to create anything." This alone strengthens the argument that manifestation is an essential part of yoga teachings and has always been included.

You won't find asanas in the Sutras, and there are certainly no instructions on how to do a proper downward dog or warrior pose. It might surprise you that a standard text about yoga is mostly concerned with a person's mind and spirit. Specifically, the four books of the Sutras talk about disciplining the mind and the results that come from such advanced mind management, including the ultimate result: liberation. One of the first sutras confirms this clearly: "The restraint of the modifications of the mind-stuff is Yoga."[3]

This sutra makes yoga sound like something similar to Buddhist meditation practices, which often lack instructions for the physical body. For our mission — establishing the inclusion of manifestation in yoga — such a focus on the psyche would imply that the power of manifestation, too, is a result of the focused application of psychic energy. We find the clearest references to this in Book 3, which covers the power of manifestation, besides other superpowers. Patanjali's third book is all about attaining extraordinary powers, also called "Siddhi," which are rarely discussed in modern yoga writings. In 55 sutras and very blunt language, the origins of superpowers are described, and you can take this literally. According to Patanjali's principles, intense yoga can help you achieve extraordinary abilities like invisibility, precognition, and past-life recall — all through applied focus. It's all in the following sutra:

> "From that comes attainment of anima and other siddhis, bodily perfection, and the non-obstruction of bodily functions by the influence of the elements." – Patanjali, Yoga Sutras[4]

According to the author of this translation of Sutra 46, Swami Satchidananda, the following eight siddhis are alluded to here:

- » Anima (to become very small)
- » Mahima (to become very big)
- » Lagima (to become very light)
- » Garima (to become very heavy)
- » Prapti (to reach anywhere)
- » Prakamya (to achieve all one's desires)
- » Isatva (ability to create anything)
- » Vasitva (ability to command and control everything)[5]

---

3 *The Yoga Sutras of Patanjali*, sutra 1.2 (Ashland: Integral Yoga Publications, 2002).

4 *The Yoga Sutras of Patanjali*, sutra 3.46.

5 *The Yoga Sutras of Patanjali*, sutra 3.46.

Throughout history, there have been many instances of yogis with siddhis. In the book *Autobiography* of a Yogi by Paramahansa Yogananda, one of the best-known yoga books, superpower-like abilities are mentioned, such as teleportation, levitation, and healing. I primarily studied the Kundalini Yoga that Yogi Bhajan taught. I never met him in person, but I've heard many stories from those who knew him about his abilities, like controlling rain and raising the kundalini energy by touch. He taught and published meditations that supposedly grant superpowers, but he also warned against pursuing the wrong objectives. Yoga aims for liberation, not gaining *siddhis*. While these abilities are tempting, especially for a new practitioner; they don't truly advance yogic goals. Similarly, Buddhism views such skills and phenomena as distractions from self-realization and liberation, so it doesn't encourage them.

Then comes the question: Is manifestation a superpower? If super means above others, then no, because manifestation is not an exclusive power. If super means extraordinary, that's closer, because from what I see, very few people work with the basic power of manifestation consciously or even believe in it. Everyone can manifest, but some do it better than others. "Skill" is a better word than "power," and "basic human skill" is even closer to the truth. Manifestation is the innate ability we all have to shape our environment using our thoughts, often without realizing it. As our consciousness grows, we see more and more how we are responsible for what shows up in our lives. What's important to acknowledge is that manifestation is listed in Patanjali's Sutra among the siddhis that humans can develop and enhance through targeted yoga practice. Moreover, manifestation is only one of many fantastic powers that can be obtained, and an entire book of the sutras is devoted to the subject. Let's analyze the following sutra:

> "Mastery of the elements comes from perfectly concentrated meditation on their five forms: the gross, the elemental, the subtle, the inherent, and the purposive." – Patanjali, Yoga Sutras[6]

The elements are what everything in the universe is made of: matter with different degrees of density; earth, water, fire, air, and ether. The elements in this sutra are named in the five phases, which correspond to modern physics (gross = solid, elemental = liquid, subtle = gas, inherent = radiant, purposive = iconic). Radiant and iconic matter are ultra-gaseous states, so thin and subtle that they can be

---

6 *The Yoga Sutras of Patanjali,* sutra 3.44, trans. Charles Johnston (n.p., Prabhat Prakashan, 2021), page 136.

transmitted by radiation like electromagnetic energy, or maybe even by intention. "Mastery of the elements" means both understanding them and working with them skillfully. The understanding of an object is gained by a meditator through a laser-sharp focus on the object, and working with elements in this context means the application of mind energy for transformation.

The sutra explains that a focused mind, like the one-pointed mind of an advanced yogi, enters a relationship with matter by bringing a controlling and creative quality to it. When the mind gains access to matter, it can alter it according to the mind's energy. This is comparable to modern quantum science, which suggests that human attention can influence electrons and how they behave. It also corresponds to yogic and modern teachings about the mind. We'll see both topics later in different chapters. But, for now, do you remember from physics class how matter moves from one phase to another through the application of energy? For example, adding energy as heat to ice (solid) will turn ice into water (liquid) and eventually into mist (gaseous). For manifestation in the physical world, this would mean that mind energy can mix and move particles from highly gaseous states to more solid states. The mind can then create new forms that appear on the physical plane of your life.

> "Thereupon will come the manifestation of the atomic and other powers, which are the endowment of the body, together with its unassailable force." – Patanjali, Yoga Sutras[7]

This sutra confirms our assumption that a focused mind can cause manifestation, following the logic of the previous one. An atom is the tiniest part of matter. So, when something is a "manifestation of the atomic," it means it is at the most basic level, like the smallest particles in the physical world. That's clearly a power, and this power is "the endowment of the body," which is another way of saying that manifestation through a focused mind is a basic human capacity. This and the "unassailable force," which can be interpreted as your soul or spirit, imply that every human being has an invincible spirit and the power to manifest.

There's more: As mentioned above in the comments about Sutra 46, manifestation is not even the last power. As your consciousness, discipline, and techniques strengthen, a myriad of abilities can develop in a human being. This is a reminder that everything is in motion, develops, and evolves, and it also helps categorize manifestation as a

---

7   *The Yoga Sutras of Patanjali*, sutra 3.45.

normal human quality. Further information on the specific techniques can be found in subsequent chapters, but for now, we can be assured that manifestation is an integral part of yoga practice and accomplishment. Knowing this, let's look with an open mind at more references in the sutras relevant to the manifestation process, such as Sutra 2.23:

> "The association of the Seer (Purusha) with things seen (Prakriti) is the cause of the realizing of the nature of things seen and also of the realizing of the nature of the Seer." – Patanjali, Yoga Sutras[8]

What does this mean? At a simpler level, we can understand that, when someone looks at their surroundings and observes objects and phenomena, they can draw conclusions about them and their own nature. For example, they may wonder where these things come from or ask other questions such as, How did it become what it is? Will it stay the same or change? Will it last or die? What will happen to it after all that? And what does it mean for me? These are basic philosophical questions that most people will ask themselves at some point in their lives. However, seen through the lens of manifestation, this sutra tells something more. The word "realizing" is essential here. It's not just about comprehension; it's about realizing your own nature as a powerful and creative being. You realize your nature, the creative relationship with everything that is already in your world, and the potential for creating absolutely everything that is not there yet. Neville Goddard puts it this way:

> "It is I AM's concept of itself that determines the form and scenery of its existence. Everything depends upon its attitude towards itself; that which it will not affirm as true of itself cannot awaken in its world. That is, your concept of yourself, such as "I am strong," "I am secure," "I am loved," determines the world in which you live. In other words, when you say, "I am a man, I am a father, I am an American," you are not defining different I AM's; you are defining different concepts or arrangements of the one cause-substance — the one I AM. Even in the phenomena of nature, if the tree were articulate, it would say, 'I am a tree, an apple tree, a fruitful tree.'" – Neville Goddard[9]

Sutra 2.23 and Neville's explanation point to the importance of the relationship between human consciousness and the related manifestation. It describes a very particular and personal interdependence between the mind and the object it brings into the human cognitive space. Sutra 4.14 elaborates on this:

---

8   *The Yoga Sutras of Patanjali: The Book of the Spiritual Man*, sutra 2.23 (Dubai: DigiCat, 2022).

9   Neville Goddard, Chapter 1, in *The Power of Awareness*, (Summit: Start Publishing LLC, 2016), page 2.

"The external manifestation of an object takes place when the transformations are in the same phase." – Patanjali, Yoga Sutras[10]

Let's analyze it. A manifestation is something that you can perceive with your senses. However, if you can't pick it up with your senses, it is not manifested in your reality. To meet, you and the object need to tune into the same frequency, just like how you can only pick up a TV or radio broadcast when the receiver is set to the frequency of the transmission. Frequency is one way to explain the "transformations" in this sutra. The transformation is the vibratory translation of the nature of the object and of the particular frequency it gives off. And only if the person has the receiver to pick up this frequency can the person see or perceive the object. This is one explanation of the phenomenon of some people seeing things, e.g., auras, beings, colors, etc., that others don't. The receiver must have a certain level of development or sophistication to receive a manifestation. The receiver here is the human being, who is both hardware (the physical body and the senses with their specific attunements) and software (the mind and its particular quality and training, the thoughts and beliefs that create filters for items to be received or not). Yoga supports this development and the refinement of both a person's hardware and software for optimum receiving. We will revisit this idea and learn more about what a developed human system can do with specific frequencies in a later chapter about entering different states or universes. Let's now analyze manifestation teachings in other forms of yoga.

MANIFESTATION IN HATHA, RAJA AND ASHTANGA YOGA

"Hatha Yoga is a relatively late arrival in the evolution of yoga, dating back little more than one thousand years. Hatha Yoga is the most widely practiced branch of Hindu Yoga. Its traditional goal is self-realization and transcendence, and evolved into the asana-based practice that is commonly found in the West today. Some of the Hatha Yoga styles include: Iyengar Yoga, Ashtanga Yoga, Bikram Yoga, Integral Yoga, Kripalu Yoga, Sivananda Yoga, Ananda Yoga, and Kundalini Yoga." – Georg Feuerstein[11]

---

10 *The Yoga Sutras of Patanjali: The Book of the Spiritual Man*, sutra 4.14 (ed. Charles Johnston, New York City: Dover Publications, 2019), page 106.

11 Georg Feuerstein, *The Deeper Dimension of Yoga: Theory and Practice* (Boston: Shambhala, 2003), 53.

We can connect Hatha yoga to manifestation by going deeply into its essence. Hatha yoga is all about achieving balance and living in balance, and its name is a merger of the words for two essential energies, "Ha" (sun) and "Tha" (moon). The practice of Hatha yoga is then an effort to balance polarities and reach liberation within the balance and neutrality that come from being at the center, not on either side of a polarity. With a yogic disposition of engaging without being attached, of being in the world and not of the world, you float through life without being anchored or chained to anything.

Sun and moon are examples of opposing energies and polarities that anyone can relate to, and opposing energies and polarities are everywhere. In fact, they make up the entire universe and keep it in balance. And just like the universe balances itself with opposing energies, we humans too can sustain ourselves if we achieve a balance within the energies instead of getting pulled completely in one direction or another. Like the planet Earth, we can stay firmly between the sun and the moon to stay alive, connected, and not completely consumed by either. There, free and unattached, we can dance with the energies and enjoy the different rays that both shine on us. Hatha wants to bring this principle of conscious balance between polarities to all kinds of opposing energies we encounter every day: summer and winter, warm and cold, up and down, sad and happy, fear and love, expansion and contraction, relaxation and tension, etc. Our liberation lies in the balance of connection and independence as we float between them.

"Ha" also represents the mind, while "Tha" represents the body. In a broader sense, they represent our thoughts and our physical reality, what we think and embody, and Hatha aims for a balance between these two aspects as well. We can achieve balance by merging aspects and combining mind and earth energy into manifestations. As well-known yoga teacher and author Swami Anandakapila Saraswati states in his book *A Chakra and Kundalini Workbook,* "few realize that the base upon which Hatha Yoga rests is an implicit axiom stating that if the mind can influence the body (psychosomatics), then the converse is equally true. The body influences the mind (somatopsychics)." [12]

The swami's statement is crucial for our understanding of manifestation, so let's look at this Hatha quality in yoga practice more closely. He talks about an upside-

---

12 Jonn Mumford, *A Chakra & Kundalini Workbook: Psycho-spiritual Techniques for Health, Rejuvenation, Psychic Powers, and Spiritual Realization* (Woodbury: Llewellyn Publications, 1994), 3.

down approach to managing our energy. Usually, we feel that our environment dictates our feelings, but he suggests it can be reversed for different results. Let's take the effects of an argument as an example: you have an argument with someone in the morning, which brings you down emotionally, and for the rest of the day, your body reflects your mental state with hunched shoulders, a slow walk, and your head hanging. Through a conscious yoga practice, we try to reverse the negative mental state by switching to a physical posture that expresses a different, more desirable state and gets us from sadness to elevation: you pull up the shoulders, lift the chest, and bring the head high. You feel more positive inside and almost instantly, the world is looking brighter already. This subtle yet profound change in our experience is nothing less than a transformation of the universe from your perspective, and it teaches us that our surroundings can influence our feelings, but we also have the power to change our surroundings through our internal state. The implications for manifestation are profound as well. I think spiritual teacher and author Neville Goddard says it best in his book *Resurrection*. He explains the process of manifestation in one paragraph:

> "Assume the feeling of your wish being fulfilled and continue feeling that it is fulfilled until that which you feel objectifies itself. If a physical fact can produce a psychological state, a psychological state can produce a physical fact. If the effect (a) can be produced by the cause (b), then, inversely, the effect (b) can be produced by the cause (a)." – Neville Goddard[13]

Like Hatha, Raja yoga is a traditional branch of yoga and was already outlined in Paranjali's Sutras. Swami Anandakapila Saraswati defines in Raja Yoga as the science of controlling the conscious mind and quieting its fluctuations so that greater focus and concentration can take the mind to higher states to (manifest) greater awareness, inner peace, and spiritual expansion — and ultimately to spiritual enlightenment and a merger into the superconscious. Here, we see that Raja yoga, described as the "royal path," manifestation can be achieved through meditation, concentration, and, ultimately, through a disciplined mind.

About Ashtanga yoga, Swami Saraswati says the following:

> "Ashtanga Yoga, as Patanjali's book is often called, is a specific study of the inner or esoteric form of the limbs of Yoga. These four limbs are Pratyahara (sometimes considered a part of

---

13   Neville Goddard, Chapter 1, in *Prayer — The Art of Believing* (Altenmünster: Jazzybee Verlag, 2012), page 6.

Bahira-anga or as the transitory stage from Hatha to Raja), Dharana (concentration), Dhyana (contemplation or sustained concentration), and Samadhi (states of ecstasy, realization, and cosmic consciousness)." – Swami Anandakapila Saraswati[14]

As you can see here, Raja and Ashtanga Yoga are not only inseparable from the Yoga Sutras; they clearly focus on the mind activities that we are discussing in this book for manifestation. These mental activities are inseparable from manifestation. The connection of Raja and Ashtanga yoga to manifestation, for our purposes, gives an answer to the question: What can I do with my mind once I bring it under my control?

MANIFESTATION IN BUDDHISM AND HINDUISM

Yoga is inseparable from Hinduism and its side-by-side religions and systems, Buddhism and Jainism, as many consider yoga itself an esoteric part of Hinduism. Well-known philosopher and indologist Georg Feuerstein, who wrote many books on yoga, writes this in his book, *The Deeper Dimension of Yoga*: "Both the world and the concept of yoga are known to and used by India's three major cultural complexes — Hinduism, Buddhism, and Jainism. Yoga lies at their very heart. Thus, it is not only completely possible to speak of Hindu Yoga, Buddhist Yoga, and Jaina Yoga, but these cultural complexes do so themselves."[15]

Hinduism is not just a religion; it is also a cultural system that pervades all aspects of life. While Buddhism and Hinduism have many similarities, given their shared origins in India and the significant influence of Hinduism on Buddhism, there are also notable differences. One prominent distinction is that Buddha rejected the Hindu practices of scarification and the rigid social caste system. He also did not recognize the Vedas, the spiritual texts at the core of Hinduism, as the authority. Instead, he believed in the agency of the individual rather than relying on a god or higher authority. This is reflected in his famous quote: "Work out your own salvation. Do not depend on others." All his instructions, summarized in the Four Noble Truths and the Eightfold Path, assume instead the authority of the self. The Eightfold Path, a route to enlightenment, can be seen as a set of instructions for manifestation, ultimately

---

14 Jonn Mumford, *A Chakra & Kundalini Workbook: Psycho-spiritual Techniques for Health, Rejuvenation, Psychic Powers, and Spiritual Realization* (Woodbury: Llewellyn Publications, 1994), 49.

15 Georg Feuerstein, *The Deeper Dimension of Yoga: Theory and Practice* (Boston: Shambhala, 2003), 32.

leading to a state of enlightenment. All eight steps, which are presented as the "right" way, or "Samma," include: right understanding, right directed thought, right speech, right action, right livelihood, right effort, right mindfulness, and right concentration. In this way, Buddhism shares with manifestation the belief that you are at the center of what your life becomes and what you manifest.

This attitude towards self-responsibility of spiritual development and life management is essential in yoga, and for the rest of this chapter, we'll focus on the yogic teachings of Buddhism and how they relate to manifestation. By the way, the Dalai Lama, the leader of one of the major schools of Buddhism, the Gelug school, is widely considered a great yogi. In his book *Virtue and Reality*, Lama Zopa Rinpoche says this: "His Holiness, the Dalai Lama and his own teachers, who themselves are enlightened beings, [are] accomplished scholars, and, even to the ordinary view, great yogis."[16]

BUDDHISM AND MANIFESTATION

Although both yoga and meditation developed around the same time in human history and in ancient India[17], they are not identical, but they share many similarities in the way the yogic teachings and buddhadharma[18] understand the laws of the universe as they relate to human existence, and both look at it in a method-focused, scientific way. One major similarity is their focus on the mind as the cause of human suffering and their attempts to provide remedies, classifying them as ancient psychological sciences.

Two terms that easily come to mind when you think of contemporary Buddhist meditation are mindfulness and loving-kindness. Mindfulness is about becoming aware of your experiences to better understand yourself and your interactions with the world. Loving-kindness is about replacing anger with love in your heart and in the world around you. It's common to think that becoming calm and compassionate is the ultimate goal, but there's a bigger picture. The principal goal

16 Kelsang Geshe Gyatso, *Understanding the Mind* (New York City: Tharpa Publications, 2002), 4.

17 Buddha was born in the 5th century B.C. in northern India, and Patanjali's Yoga Sutras are said to have been written between the 4th and 2nd centuries B.C.

18 Buddhadharma is broadly defined as the teachings of the Buddha and a life lived according to the teachings.

of Buddhist practice and the declared goal of its founder, Buddha, is to be free of suffering and to remove suffering caused by your own mental functions so that you can live a more beautiful life in a better world. Through meditation and a Buddhist lifestyle, you can attract positive mental states and situations, bringing about a new reality filled with peace and love. In other words, this is nothing less than manifestation by the Buddhist method.

For example, the Theravada Buddhist tradition teaches a system in which the mind is divided into more than 50 clearly defined mental functions, which explain the correlation between an even greater number of types of consciousness. It is a system that offers a psychological concept of the human mind and explains the manifestation of both mental and physical states through mental activity.

The creation of reality is a central aspect of Buddhism. While there is often a focus on reality as defined as mental or internal states, the manifestation of physical reality is equally important. In fact, they are inseparable. Thoughts become things, influencing situations, success or failure, happiness or sadness, companionship or loneliness, and all the physical aspects that accompany them. And like yoga, Buddhism ascribes immense powers to the mind, namely the creation of reality. On Buddha's threefold path to spiritual awakening — the elevation of virtue, mind, and wisdom — it is the second path that is concerned with meditation and the power of the mind. Geshe Kelsang Gyatso, a respected Buddhist teacher and author, provides one of the best explanations of Buddhism's belief in the mind's ability to manifest.

> "Buddha taught that the mind has the power to create all pleasant and unpleasant objects. This is the view held in common by all four Buddhist schools. According to this view, the world is the result of the karma of actions, of the beings who inhabit it. A pure world is the result of pure actions and an impure world is the result of impure actions. Since all actions are created by the mind, ultimately everything, including the world itself, is created by the mind. There is no creator other than the mind. Buddhists believe this because they rely upon the explanations given by Buddha." – Geshe Kelsang Gyatso[19]

In the same book, he discusses a future where we control our mind instead of our mind controlling us like it does for most people today. "Since the beginning of time until now, we have been under the control of our mind, without any freedom; but if

---

19 Gyatso, *Understanding the Mind*, 4.

we now practice Dharma sincerely, we can reverse this situation and gain control over our mind. Gyatso,Only then shall we have real freedom."[20] And I would add: freedom by manifesting the conditions and environments that facilitate freedom.

Consider another tradition, Zen Buddhism, which elevates the role of the mind in your life experience by asserting that the mind is not merely a part of the universe but rather that the entire experienced universe is Mind. The capital M is no accident here, because it names this whole universe: Mind with a capital M, and the individual mind, the lowercase mind of a human being, for example, as the small mind. This is like the concept of the universal consciousness or universal mind versus the individual or unit mind in other yogic teachings. The small mind, or unit mind, is also the origin of the feeling of being separate or limited (ego), whereas the big mind, or Mind, is equal to a no-boundaries, everything-is-one experience. Zen Buddhists also call this latter state simply "no mind" for the absence of any sort of limitation. Other Buddhist schools, too, believe that everything is not just *of* the mind but actually is the mind.

If everything in the universe is made from the same stuff as the mind, if everything is "mind-stuff," and nothing exists outside of the mind, then everything in this realm is created, arranged, maintained, altered, transformed, and ultimately wiped out by the mind. In this sense, Buddhism affirms the notion that manifestation is an inherent power of every mind-possessing human being. But it's important to keep in mind that in this context, the mind is the consciousness that pervades absolutely everything. This relates to the concept of everything being consciousness, certainly another word for mind in this context, and we'll visit this concept again in later chapters, especially in the chapter on the mind.

So how is manifestation accomplished in the Buddhist view? Well, if everything is mind, then everything is yoked together. Manifestation in Buddhism, the creation of a peaceful, loving existence, begins with the clean slate of the mind as the goal of meditation and is primarily a sort of cleansing of the mind — not for relaxation but for insights into the mind, for better management of your mind, and for the creation of a specific projection or mind construct. To be clear, the pure mind is the mind in its fundamental state. Buddhism teaches that the mind is inherently pure, but it becomes cluttered with thoughts and distractions, like a blue sky can

20 Gyatso, *Understanding the Mind*, 5.

get covered by clouds and planes. For example, a mind filled with anger can be examined in meditation, understood, and then cleared and redirected. Breaking through the constant mental activity to the calm and clarity underneath is also what "spiritual realization" refers to as a goal of meditation. Generally, this can be achieved in three steps: mindfulness, concentration, and insight. Getting to your pure mind is like working with an absolutely clean hard drive on a computer. Nothing clogs it up; no old files or programming slow it down. It is ready to be applied for the optimum creation of the best life experience. This mind stage is described in one of the main Buddhist texts, called "The Peerless Continuum."

There is an entire book about manifestation by applying Buddhist teachings. It's called *The Diamond Cutter — The Buddha on Managing Your Business and Your Life*, by Geshe Michael Roach, the first American to earn the ancient degree of Geshe, or master of Buddhist learning. The book tells the story of how he used Buddhist principles to turn a small diamond division into a global operation making millions of dollars annually. He explains that every result in one's life is a manifestation of an imprint in one's mind that grows over time and that there are correlations between actions and imprints that lead to specific results in business and life. These correlations come from two Buddhist wisdom books, and here is a summary to inspire your own approach to manifestation:

Action	Result
Generous state of mind	Financial success in business
Ethical way of life	Happiness
Refusal to get angry	Physical health and attractiveness
Learn the principles of mental imprints	Things go your way
Compassion towards others	You and everyone get all they ever wished for[21]

MANIFESTATION IN THE BIBLE

It turns out the Bible is full of references to manifestations as a basic human capacity, but you will only see it if you read it from a certain perspective.

21 Michael Roach, *The Diamond Cutter: The Buddha on Managing Your Business and Your Life* (New York City: Doubleday, 2003), 323.

I received this perspective on the Bible text from reading the books of spiritual teacher Neville Goddard. He has written many books on manifestation and was a pioneer in introducing concepts like the law of assumption, similar to the law of attraction. Most of his teachings and books are based on the Bible text. His approach is to read the Bible not in the way the church teaches it — as a history book full of examples of people who lived a long time ago and whose stories and qualities we must revere — but as a psychological text in which the characters are representations of psychological states that are accessible to all of us now. Naturally, this interpretation will not be agreeable to some, but all scripture is open to interpretation. We are free to extract from it what helps us. So I invite you to read the following with an open mind and see what happens:

> "It cannot be stated too often that consciousness is the one and only reality, for this is the truth that sets man free. This is the foundation upon which the whole structure of biblical literature rests. The stories of the Bible are all mystical revelations written in an Eastern symbolism which reveals to the intuitive the secret of creation and the formula of escape. The Bible is man's attempt to express in words the cause and manner of creation. Man discovered that his consciousness was the cause or creator of his world, so he proceeded to tell the story of creation in a series of symbolic stories known to us today as the Bible. This understanding that consciousness is the one and only reality is the foundation of the Bible. To understand this greatest of books, you need a little intelligence and much intuition." – Neville Goddard[22]

This perspective was a revelation for me and healed certain aspects of my relationship with Christianity. I grew up Catholic and went to church for many years because my mother, out of a sense of obligation to the church, wanted her children to. But, just like much of the Catholic practice, Bible stories never touched me, mostly because they made little or no sense to me in my everyday life. When I rediscovered Christian teachings in Neville's books, they suddenly not only made sense, but they took on a vibrancy and aliveness. Discovering yogic teachings years ago made me feel the same — like I had found a valuable truth that could yield amazing results. So I tried it, and it worked. My ability to manifest has moved to another level since I started looking at the process from his perspective. Neville's viewpoint can be applied to the stories of Sikh gurus, Buddha's stories, and ancient sages in various religions. If scriptures and spiritual teachings can't be interpreted and adapted for contemporary life and personal situations, what value do they hold? A different approach would

22 Neville Goddard, "The Power of Awareness," in *The Collected Neville Library* (n.p.: Lulu Press, 2019), 160.

be fundamentalism, which involves interpreting stories and characters literally and advocating for fearful respect and subservience towards them.

Consider, for instance, Goddard's explanation of the immaculate conception, a widely debated event in the Bible where Mary became pregnant with Jesus without having intercourse. Neville suggests the story symbolizes humans' potential to create remarkable things beyond just having babies and construct entirely new realms. Other examples are the crucifixion and resurrection of Jesus — metaphors for requisites in the manifestation process, i.e., our need to die to our old self and step into a new state of being. These biblical examples serve as a reminder that every person possesses the ability to create miracles. Let's look at the first example in more detail with the actual Bible quotes in relation to manifestation techniques:

> "It is recorded that God sent an angel to Mary to announce the birth of His son. And the angel said unto her... thou shalt conceive in thy womb, and bring forth a son... Then said Mary unto the angel, How shall this be, seeing I know not a man? And the angel answered and said unto her, The Holy Ghost shall come upon thee, and the power of the highest shall overshadow thee; therefore also that holy thing which shall be born of thee shall be called the son of God. For with God nothing shall be impossible." – Luke 1:30-37

The characters in this story symbolize psychological states related to manifestation, as interpreted by Goddard in his book *Freedom for All*:

> "The Father symbolizes your consciousness. The Son symbolizes your desire. Mary symbolizes your receptive attitude of mind. The Angel symbolizes the method used to make the impregnation." – Neville Goddard[23]

He draws parallels between the story's elements and steps in the manifestation process, and I'll reword them accordingly in the book's language and manifestation techniques. You will see these steps repeated later in the book.

The Father gets a son without the involvement of anyone else. Manifestation technique (MT): Your desire appears without the help of others. You state your desire, clarify it, and you will receive it like the father received the son.

---

23 Neville Goddard, *Neville Goddard — The Complete Collection: The Reference Book by Neville Goddard with All Books, Radio Lectures and Lessons* (self-pub., Tolino Media, 2023), 101.

The Father chooses an angel to deliver this fantastical news to Mary. MT: This is equal to getting support from others for the fulfillment of your desire. Like the father, you choose a person, maybe a very good friend, who genuinely wants you to have your wish and who would enjoy witnessing its arrival. (Also see chapter on manifesting through the chakras.)

The angel tells Mary that she is already pregnant, even though she had no intercourse. MT: The feminine here represents a mental state of being receptive, regardless of gender, where you are open to what comes to you with no outside influence. You stay in a receptive state, in meditation, until the idea — the vision of the fulfilled desire within you — is fully formed and you accept it within yourself. Like a pregnancy, you have complete confidence in the idea's manifestation and protect it until it comes to fruition.

I hope this brief sample has piqued your interest. If you want more fresh manifestation-related interpretations from Bible stories, I recommend all of Neville's books. Most of them contain Bible stories, verses, and their hidden meanings. Just remember, reading scripture is a personal process, and what transpires from the written words to you is your personal transmission. I found this experience to be immensely enjoyable and liberating, and I hope you can too. The process perfectly reflects the quintessential yoga goal of expanding consciousness and making ancient teachings relevant to today's lives. To wake up to the true nature of everything.

MANIFESTATION BASICS IN KUNDALINI YOGA

There is a comment about one of the yoga sequences in Kundalini Yoga that crystallizes the manifestation process and the mind's role as per the teachings of Kundalini Yoga according to Yogi Bhajan.

> "The function of the mind is not to just spew out random thoughts. It is to fashion etheric elements into forms of energy that manifest through the earthly elements. A projected imagination that is guided is a fundamental power and gift of mankind." Yogi Bhajan[24]

Let's break this down: The mind does much more than produce thoughts. It interacts with the elements of the universe (all graduations of matter: earth, water,

---

24 Yogi Bhajan, "Meditation on the Self," in *KRIYA: Yoga Sets, Meditations & Classic Kriyas from the Early Teachings of Yogi Bhajan* (Espanola: Kundalini Research Institute, 2013), 110.

fire, air, and ether) and creates forms with them. Forms are anything made from matter: things, people, situations, events, thoughts (yes, thoughts comprise very subtle matter) — everything in the physical world, even the most subtle forms. The appearance of forms in the world is influenced by the mind's interaction with their ingredients, the elements from which all forms are created.

How the mind interacts with the elements depends on the projection of the individual's mind. Every human has a mind that interacts with the elements and creates forms. The composition and quality of the forms, however, depend on the skills and quality of the mind and how the human uses "projected imagination." Hence, knowledge of this power and refinement of the skills are essential for effective manifestation. What this also means in more technical terms is that the mind is not simply brain activity inside the skull.

> "You have come to live, not to act. You have come to be because you are. Everything comes from you. You think you can get something from the outside. It is not true. Nothing comes from the outside. It has been proven time and again. Getting everything from the inside is what Kundalini Yoga is all about. Uncoil yourself. Let the world know. That is the way to live." – Yogi Bhajan[25]

In this chapter, we have seen the roots of manifestation within ancient teachings and found a striking commonality across diverse spiritual paths through the discipline of the mind. Together, these teachings reveal that manifestation is not merely about obtaining wealth, mundane things, and fulfilling desires but a profound journey toward inner alignment and universal connection. Through this understanding, we step into a fuller, more empowered way of living, where ancient wisdom fuels our path to conscious creation. In the next chapter, we will explore the key elements of the manifestation process. We will also find a more detailed description of the mind's role in manifesting.

---

25 Yogi Bhajan, *Invincible Man*, (Los Angeles: Kundalini Research Institute, 1983), 11.

CHAPTER 2
MANIFESTING 101 — THE KEYS

In theory, manifestation is really simple. Its basic processes are likewise elementary; nonetheless, there are countless resources and materials available on the topic. There are thousands of pages and hours of related content, all built around the same truths you will see below. In this chapter we will address the basic steps towards consistent manifestations, their mechanics and key ingredients, as well as common downfalls you encounter along the way.

THE SIMPLE TRUTHS
There are only the following simple truths at the core of every manifestation technique, both ancient and modern:

- » Everything is consciousness. It is the one and only medium.
- » All that is, was, and will be is a manifestation of consciousness.
- » Your mind shapes consciousness into manifestations.
  The mind of every human being can do this.
- » It only needs these ingredients: desire, imagination, feeling, faith, and time.
- » It only takes these steps:
    - Determine your desired outcome and imagine it being fulfilled.
    - Live as if your desire has already been fulfilled.
      Have faith that it is. Know that it is.
    - Imagine your fulfilled desire by feeling it holistically through all your senses: see it, hear it, smell it, taste it, and touch it.
      Make it real. Have faith that it is. Know that it is.
    - Persist in doing this until your desire appears in the physical world. Have faith that it is. Know that it is.

This is all you really need to know to bring out the powerful creator and artist that you are. Now manifest! Saying is simple. If manifesting would indeed be that easy, why do we need so many resources and so much content? That's a fair question that deserves answers.

Because you'll forget to do it all the time. You can say breathing is simple. You don't need to teach a human to breathe. Yet there are countless books about breathing properly, for exactly the same reason: It's easy, but you'll forget the right way to do it a million times. You'll breathe deeply for a few minutes in class or with instructions, then you go back to shallow breathing for the rest of the day like most people. It's exactly the same with manifestation. You'll forget who you are and what you can do all the time as the world pulls you outward constantly. The key to success is maintenance, not initiation. The volumes that exist about manifestation aren't filled with basic techniques from cover to cover. They focus on keeping you motivated and providing countless reasons to keep going and ways to get back on track if you stumble. This book, too, is about making you a more confident and consistent manifestor through yoga. If you feel that yoga has taken you to another level of consciousness and effectiveness, it can do the same for manifestation.

Because you'll continue to doubt the process and yourself. It's easy to fall in love with your manifestation powers, but your love and enthusiasm are likely to wear off sometimes. Just like with your favorite people, there are times when you're unsure about trusting them and giving them space in your life. One way to overcome negative sentiments about your manifestation powers and your loved ones is to review your positive history and beautiful experiences with them: remember their genuine qualifications and the times when they really came through for you, plus deeply accept their integrity so that you can feel it even in those moments when it isn't totally obvious. That's why I filled this book with information that validates the rightful place of manifestation techniques in yogic philosophy and teachings, with tools and exercises that give a bona fide experience of your powers to help you get over any doubt and suspicion you might feel and to strengthen your faith in your innate ability to manifest.

Although something may seem simple, you can still become masterful at it. Learning about your manifestation powers is like being given the keys to a state-of-the-art sports car. Can you truly unleash the beauty of such a sophisticated machine? You may not know all the buttons and switches in the cockpit; you may go too fast or too slow; you may drive by something and miss it; or you may come to a screeching halt when there's a bump in the road. You may run out of gas, refuel, and then run out of gas again. You might even meet someone who stops you and claims it's their car and demands you get out of it, and you might even comply, as you have often given away your power. There's a lot that can keep you at an amateur level, and that's where yoga comes in. Its specific practices are tools to crystallize the mind's power, enabling you to master your manifestations at a level that no other school can provide. You will drive your own supercar, the creative mind that creates the universe, like a total pro.

For a solid frame of reference, it is also good to review the basics of manifestation from other perspectives and sources. I'll introduce several concepts in the following chapters. If any of these speak to you, learn more about them by studying the respective sources.

THE MECHANICS

Let's return to the basic manifestation technique. All that really needs to be done is contained in the following sentence: *Figure out what you want and what it's like, and from that moment on, live your life as though that desire is already fulfilled.*

That's how you manifest, and if you fully comprehend the power of this simple method and apply it, you can stop reading here. If you are like most people, you'll need more information, and this book gives it to you. However, we will always return to this simple process, but it certainly helps to look at the process from different perspectives and with different language, so I'll break the process down into three steps:

1. Label,
2. Activation,
3. Experience.

Or as verbs:

1. Decide,
2. Accept,
3. Integrate.

The three steps described here are similar to those you'll find in other manifestation teachings. You will also find instructions for a first trial at the end of this section. Let's elaborate on each step to help you understand:

1. **Decide your desire and give it expression with a concise label and specific feeling.**

   Timing: Any time.
   Duration: A few moments or minutes.
   Key Qualities: Clarity and focused imagination.

State your desire, but before you do, think of your desire as a clear message or a specific feeling that you want. If your desire is clear and strong, it's like a song that everyone understands and can easily sing along to. But if it's vague, it's like playing random chords that don't turn into a flowing melody. Imagine you are a skilled speaker whose words reach everyone easily. Use a short, clear label for what you want, and feel it deeply. For example, if you want a lake house, decide if you want to live in it, invest in it, or enjoy weekends there, and have a good idea of what it looks like. To make your desire real, don't say "I want" or "I would like," because these phrases imply that your desire is not truly here yet. Instead, use clear words that make you feel like it's already here. Pretend you're an actor, expressing all the feelings connected to your desire. When you say "lake house," feel the excitement. Notice the difference between simply saying "I want a lake house" and saying "lake house" while simultaneously feeling those qualities and features you desire most in that house. Practice until it feels right.26 You can state your desire out loud or silently.

This statement initiates the process of physical manifestation in the spiritual realm through sound and vibration. Your stated desire is a vibrational blueprint planted in silence, like a seed in plain dirt. This silence that takes place before your new vibration comes along is called *Anahata*. *Anahata* is the unstruck sound, the pure potential of consciousness in its most subtle form, a field in which anything is possible and ready for your vibration. Your mind, by stating the wish, strikes *Anahata* like the chords of a violin and sets the process of manifestation in motion. Your statement and its related mind activity are like a pebble thrown on the surface of a calm ocean, setting in motion ripples that are the beginning of the physical manifestation. *Anahata* can be struck by a thought, an idea, or any mind activity. That, by itself, is already a manifestation, but where it goes from there depends on the continued application of mind activity. For example, if you

---

26 See Kundalini Yoga Actor Meditation, on page 59.

want a lake house to live in as your permanent home, then your declaration of "lake house" carries in it the whole blueprint of your life inside and around this dream house. If you want it as a good investment, the blueprint carries the feeling of a substantial and easily gained profit. It is the particular, specific vibration that only you can create and that feels personal to you and the cosmic field in which you plant the seed. Sure, you could easily state, "I want a lake house to live in and entertain myself and my friends," but the real nucleus is the *feeling* of your fulfilled desire. And the closer you get to it from the start, the more successful the manifestation process. That's why I propose saying only the most concise description of your fulfilled desire so that you can fill the space with feelings and visions around it, not with more words. Now try saying "lake house," or the fulfilled desire you seek, with your eyes closed in a way that contains the full blueprint of exactly what you want it to look and feel like. Please know your statement can be longer than two words as long as it remains concise, and here are some examples of the most common desires stated clearly and concisely. Notice how easily you can feel them as you see a specific vision in your mind's eye.

> » the freedom and ease of financial independence from my investments.
> » the harmony and peace of a healthy relationship with my lover (known or unknown).
> » the satisfaction of a job in XYZ field that I enjoy doing regularly.

2. Accept the realness of your fulfilled desire without its physical manifestation.

Timing: Immediately after your decision and declaration of your desire.
Duration: For a few moments or minutes after the decision, fix the acceptance in the background of your mind as a permanent feature until physical manifestation occurs.
Key Qualities: Fulfillment, resoluteness, and trust.

This step is like placing an online order and then having peace of mind because you received a confirmation notification. You chose the item and checked it out of the shopping cart; now, you're certain that the item will arrive in its physical form and be in front of you soon. Similarly, when planting seeds in the cosmic field to manifest your desires spiritually, you confirm this from within yourself by being resolute and feeling closure in your mind. The seed holds the DNA of your order, containing all the necessary data for its processing. The bridge between the seed and its physical manifestation in your realm relies on your continued, unwavering attention, which is the next step. However, if your complete faith in the realization of your desire doesn't support this attention from the start, the delivery might stall or go unfulfilled. At this point, having doubt is equivalent to planting a seed in vinegar rather than fertile ground strengthened by your faith. In simple terms, choose to believe it's real and mean it.

Understanding and accepting that your fulfilled desire now exists in the ethers in its most subtle state is a concept that many struggle with because it requires the acceptance of something that really exists only in spiritual form. This is easier to do for a yogi because much of our experience in practice happens in the formless realm as insights, sensations, inspirations, visions, ideas, feelings, and emotions, and a big part of developing a yogic practice is learning to accept the formless as real as all forms.

Remember, your fulfilled desire is now a vibration that you have identified and initiated in the cosmos. It exists in an ethereal form, like a seed ready to grow. However, it's crucial to realize that it's not a separate entity; it is a part of yourself since your mind conceived it. To develop it effectively, step into the seed and immerse yourself in it. The seed contains the complete blueprint of your manifestation, requiring your full integration. This understanding, your complete acceptance of the seed's reality and its vibration, and your presence within it represent the second step.

Another important distinction is that this is no longer the statement of a desire. It's already the complete acceptance of the existence of your fulfilled desire. Neville Goddard says that at the end of desire is being and experience. In this second step, the being is accomplished, and your acceptance confirms this. The best perspective for this step, as Neville often mentions, is not to think about the fulfilled desire but to think from it. If you do this consciously, you can feel a shift in your visualization of the fulfilled desire, from something on the outside to something that radiates from your center, from a show that you are watching on a TV screen to being inside the play on the stage where it happens. Now accept the reality of it. You received the order confirmation. "Yes, my lake house exists in the ethers. That is where it is for me now — adding matter, getting fleshed out. Thank you. I got it now."

3. Live with and inside your fulfilled desire.

Timing: Start after (1) decision and (2) acceptance.
Duration: As long and often as possible until physical manifestation.
Qualities: ambition, courage, retention, resilient optimism, and steadiness.

You and the seed are in oneness now, and your consciousness continues to develop the ethereal blueprint into a physical manifestation with persistence. From there, this vibration, the seed consciousness, collects elements to become denser and denser and eventually emerges in the physical world as a visible, audible, feelable, or tangible manifestation. It does this with your conscious mind activity until it manifests on the earth plane. Just like you can only grow a sprouted seed into a full-grown plant if you give it ongoing nourishment and care, a new vibration needs the same to grow into a full physical manifestation. Here the water is the consciousness, and ongoing care is the constantly applied mind activity. Faith is fertilizer, and doubt is poison. Conscious manifestation is the proper application of consciousness and mind activity to the seed vibration for the purpose of growing the full desired manifestation. In other words, maintain the feeling and vision of your fulfilled desire as long and as frequently as you can until it manifests. This step is the constant remembrance, integration, and reintegration of the fulfilled desire into your everyday life. It's akin to basic meditation instructions where you keep bringing your mind to the breath or the object of the focus. The time from now on until the physical manifestation is like a long meditation in which you keep bringing your mind to the object of your desire, specifically the feeling and the reality of the fulfilled desire. As you do this, whether it takes days, months, or years, you live in your world with your fulfilled desire held and kept active in your mind as often as possible and with as much detail as you can bring to it. Your imagination, clarity and focus, perseverance and discipline, plus your faith, optimism, and love are all needed in this process, and a strong yoga practice will make all of these required traits much easier.

That is all in terms of the basic process. If this is still a bit abstract, you might get a better idea when you see, later in this book, variations of it from other spiritual teachings. They are variations of the same concepts, and it always helps to look at the same thing from different perspectives to understand it better — so we will. Like I said earlier, the reason there are volumes and volumes of books, recordings, and media is to help you remember, refine, and optimize the process as much as you can. The yoga and yoga-related information in this book are all about optimizing the process for greater success through the elevated consciousness of your yoga practice. But here are a few clarifications to help you understand the technique better before we dive deeper.

CLARIFICATIONS

The quality of the mind activity is essential. So is the level of focus and concentration. Make no mistake: if your tendency is to jump from sensation to sensation, like constant scrolling and clicking on your smartphone, your attention is too weak for optimal manifestation. Strong focus and consistency in feeling and integration are key, and a good yogi will have a much easier time with this. Just like the careless treatment of a seedling might yield a weak and fruitless plant or an uncontrollable weed, the sloppy application of your mind activity may cause a manifestation that you do not desire or no manifestation at all. I learned this the hard way and watched manifestations wither and die before they could blossom because I shut off the steady stream of high-quality attention, as anything in your life will die if you don't give it the proper attention.

If you want to grow a full tree, it can take many forms as it grows. While you can't control everything, with proper care, the tree will grow as you intended. For example, a maple seed will only become a maple tree because the seed only carries the blueprint for that specific tree. The more attention and care you give it, the healthier and more beautiful it becomes. Neglect, on the other hand, can lead to undesirable growth or no growth at all. This principle applies to conscious manifestation as well. The quality of your thoughts and the clarity of your consciousness determine the outcome. That's why a developed consciousness, a focused mind, and clear thinking can create manifestations as impressive as the most magnificent tree you've ever seen. Yoga helps develop consciousness and improves focus, clarity, and consistency of mind, making it an ideal support for your conscious manifestations.

Ether is not equal to the sky or a place above the clouds. Although people often use ether synonymously with heaven, please let go of the idea that it is a specific location or some distant force up in the sky. If a seed is planted in the ethers, it just means it exists in the most subtle of elemental forms, and you are connected to it.

It's better to think of your growing seedling as connected to you rather than being in some far-off celestial place beyond your control. Remember, the mind is vast and can be anywhere, and as long as you control your mind activity, the mind takes care of the rest. While location will play a role at a later stage in the manifestation, you do not need to be concerned with the longitude and latitude of the seedling, just like you don't need to be concerned with all the details of the manifestation process. Faith will help this (and we'll see more about it in a later chapter).

Seed is another term that's easy to misunderstand or underestimate. A seed, any seed, is not just a component but always the full object. A tree seed truly carries the entire full-grown tree in its shell, not just one twig or piece of a root. It is important to view your desire as the full manifestation in its most subtle state and let that be your definition of seed. If you don't see it complete from the start, fleshing it out will not work well. And while we use the analogy of a seed, remember that every seed only carries the potential for one specific creature. For example, a sunflower seed can only turn into a sunflower, not a rose or an apple tree. Hence, it must be clear to you and the universe what potential your seed contains. If it carries a wishy-washy idea, it can only grow into a wishy-washy thing.

Your attitude towards the process. Do you believe things only come to you through hard work? The idea that you'll have to roll up your sleeves and break a sweat to get the best results in life is one of the most stubbornly held beliefs in the world. In manifestation, it's a fallacy, so I invite you to relax that belief during the manifestation process. Still, when you read about the steps and ingredients, you will probably think of it as hard work because we have been conditioned to view every process as something that results in more work when chosen. That's not necessarily true.

For example, when you read the basic manifestation instructions and learn that you have to maintain a vision and a feeling of the fulfilled desire, it sounds like effort. But it's less a comparison between effort and non-effort, than between choosing to exist in a positive state of mind versus a negative state. And it's less about spending extra energy on something and more about allocating existing energy for a better purpose.

Here's what I mean: Think about the day-to-day reality of living in absolute certainty that something good is arriving for you (and isn't it always something good we desire?). As a conscious manifestor, you see it in your mind's eye all the time and keep up the good feeling of having it in your life. Now think about what your day would be like if you didn't do that. You'd be more likely to see a lack all the time and feel the absence of what you want. You are more likely to be in a negative state without engaging in the manifestation process. Engaging in the manifestation process doesn't require extra energy. It just requires you to redirect the energy you lost from living with lack to a life of abundance. Just because that which you desire is not there in physical form does not change the fact that you can feel good with the energy that is available to you. You simply use your energy for better results across all steps, all the time. This is the difference between conscious versus unconscious living, and yoga is the science of living consciously.

Mind activity. Imagination, feeling, focus, and repetition are all examples of mind activity that add substance to the process of manifestation. I will explain all relevant mind activities in detail in the following section, but before we end this section, let's revisit a quote from Yogi Bhajan mentioned in the earlier chapter, and this time we'll look at the entire quote. Knowing what you know now, it might make more sense:

> "The mind is given to you to use in self-expansion. But you do not channel it or capture it. It runs wild on old thought patterns and habits. If you cannot have the mind when you need it, it is useless. The function of the mind is not just to spew out random thoughts. It is to fashion etheric elements into forms of energy that manifest through the early elements. A projected imagination that is guided is a fundamental power and a gift to mankind." – Yogi Bhajan[27]

THE MIND'S INGREDIENTS EXPLAINED

The previous sections discussed various mental activities related to the manifestation process. Below, you'll find examples of these activities, all of which are valuable and powerful. When you start considering or practicing these methods, you might feel skeptical about their effectiveness or your own abilities. I'll address these challenges and offer solutions and exercises. In fact, I dedicated a significant portion of the book to overcoming these mental hurdles so you can enhance your manifestation skills.

---

27 Yogi Bhajan, "Meditation on the Self," in *KRIYA: Yoga Sets, Meditations & Classic Kriyas from the Early Teachings of Yogi Bhajan* (Espanola: Kundalini Research Institute, 2013), 110.

Imagination

"Imagination is more important than knowledge." – Albert Einstein[28]

Imagination is a tremendous asset and an essential ingredient in creating your world, but how often have you heard someone say, "I'm really proud of my imagination?" Our relationship with imagination is a strange one, which might be another indicator of how little we know about our own creative powers. We often underestimate the power of imagination, viewing it as something cute but not particularly impactful, like a colorful feather on a bird. It's time to move this basic human faculty from the back burner to the center as the power generator of manifestation that it is.

Your imagination is the starting point of anything, the source of blueprints for anything you want to manifest, for anything in the world. The biblical phrase "In the beginning was the word" not only refers to actual words but also symbolizes the emergence of new thoughts, ideas, and concepts within your own consciousness. You'll need imagination for all the manifestation steps described here and all the techniques in the book. Imagination is the fuel and the glue that enables you to visualize your desire manifested, to conjure the associated emotions, and to hold your fulfilled desire as a reality in your mind during the manifestation's trajectory. Imagination works on the level of all senses, not just your vision. You can imagine touch, smell, sound, and taste in your imagination. Moreover, you can imagine entire symphonies of sensations, and for successful manifestation, you should.

For the sake of successful manifestation efforts, from now on, consider your acts of imagination, like daydreaming, an utterly serious, honorable, and worthwhile pursuit that deserves your full attention. Take a moment, sit down, and say to yourself unequivocally: "My imagination is my biggest gift. It is infinite, like my true self, and when I use it, I can manifest anything I want." Now let this truth sink to the depths of your being and make it part of your belief system, which is the operating software of your life.

---

28 Walter Isaacson, *Einstein: His Life and Universe* (London: Simon & Schuster UK, 2008), 287.

FEELINGS

Feelings, not just emotions, are the key, and you must "proact" them before your manifestation can arrive. Feelings are so crucial for successful manifestation that they must come before the actual manifestation. It is a prerequisite, not the result of a manifestation. This may be one of the most important sections and also one of the most confusing concepts. First, we must acknowledge that all feelings and emotions are mind activities. Emotions are defined as automatic and universal responses to stimuli, and feelings are the subjective experiences of emotions based on personal interpretations. For instance, you might be triggered by something threatening to have the emotion of repulsion. The emotion can turn into a feeling of repulsion after you interpret your reaction and process it with your individual sensory systems, thoughts, and cultural influences. Many feelings begin as emotions when they turn from automatic to consciously experienced. I'll use both terms in the following text, as both apply to manifestation.

"Emotions are where the mind meets the body" is a common definition in yogic and therapeutic language, and that phrase is commonly understood as mind activity that you feel in the body, like fear in the mind, for example, that translates in the body as sweaty palms or increased heart rate. In this model, emotions are consequences and have a reactive quality. They are merely the byproduct of some preceding event, like the sighting of an escaped lion, which can give you fear. Even in therapy, this order of events is mostly reinforced, as emotions are usually considered a result of something external, often a negative event like a conflict, an injury, or poor treatment by others. It's fair to say that most of us consider emotions something inevitable, like weather, that can only be managed but not created out of nothing. Yet, the latter is exactly what we need to do for successful manifestation. We have to create feelings around the manifestation without the actual manifestation. As yogis, we are accustomed to reversing typical sequences, such as starting with inner spiritual growth instead of trying to manipulate the external world. The following yoga sutra illustrates the concept of initiating an emotion when faced with a negative mental "disturbance," like anxiety, anger, or insecurity: "When disturbed by negative thoughts, opposite (positive) ones should be thought of."[29]

---

29 *The Yoga Sutras of Patanjali, Sutra* 2.33, Integral Yoga Publications, 2002.

In manifestation — and I cannot overstate the importance of this — an emotion or feeling must come first. That is, the act of feeling or the emotion must come before the mind activity and before the manifestation. Here feelings thus take on an active and leading role, not a passive or subordinate one. When you want a particular manifestation that doesn't exist yet, you begin with the feeling of it and add that feeling to your projection, the spiritual blueprint of the manifestation, and this specific mind-stuff consciousness cocktail then somehow becomes the physical manifestation. In many recipes, the order of mixing ingredients is crucial, and this manifestation recipe calls for feeling first.

The realization that I can feel about something in a particular way — in other words, that I can *create* a particular emotion and feeling about something before it is part of my life — has been an epiphany for me. Specifically, what was most astonishing to me is how helpful it is to feel something before it manifests, because a) it gives me the power to decide how I want to feel about anything instead of reacting to it, and b) it accelerates my manifestations. I admit, it's not like I've never heard an invitation to create a new feeling before. "Relax, pull yourself together, and see it in a different light" are all examples of this kind of invitation, but I just didn't understand the atomic power of creating emotions for manifestation until I studied and practiced manifestation methods. Most of all, I feel better most of the time because I choose to and because manifestation is an excellent motivator for that choice. Deciding how you feel may be one of the most underestimated and underappreciated superpowers in a world where nobody seems to feel good for extended periods, although everyone wants to. Millions of solutions are presented, but hardly ever this one: decide to feel good. You, too, may not fully understand the power of this technique until you use it in manifestation and get the results.

Here's one yogic reference to this phenomenon, which I already mentioned in an earlier section. Swami Anandakapila Saraswati states in his book *A Chakra and Kundalini Workbook*: "Few realize that the base upon which Hatha Yoga rests is an implicit axiom stating that if the mind can influence the body (psychosomatics), then the converse is equally true. The body influences the mind (somatopsychics)."[30] It's certainly a challenge and an advanced practice for most of us to conjure emotions without the conditions that otherwise might

---

30 Jonn Mumford, *A Chakra & Kundalini Workbook: Psycho-spiritual Techniques for Health, Rejuvenation, Psychic Powers, and Spiritual Realization* (Woodbury: Llewellyn Publications, 1994), 3.

evoke the emotions, but yogic teachings are filled with tools for this kind of upside-down approach. Here is a way to build your emotion-summoning muscle: **Put the cart (emotions & feelings) before the horse (desired outcomes) for successful manifestation.**

A great way for yogis to learn to conjure emotions is by starting with the emotion of gratitude, because there are many techniques for conjuring gratitude, not just in yoga but in religions as well. For example, there are Hindu gratitude meditations where you give gratitude to the divine for what you have in your life. Muslims incorporate gratitude expressions in their daily prayers after every prostration, and one example of a Jewish gratitude meditation is to recite the Shehecheyanu blessing as a thank you to God or the Modeh Ani prayer when you wake up to express gratitude for a new day. The main point is that gratitude, like any emotion, can be created inside of you without receiving anything else. And to conjure gratitude, you'll need nothing more than your own heart, which, of course, is a self-generating love machine by nature if you allow it. Once you are a practiced gratitude feeler and giver, transitioning from here to other emotions and feelings, such as the feeling of being healed, wealthy, cozy with your lover, and surrounded by the people and circumstances that are the object of your stated desires, becomes easy.

Sit comfortably in Easy Pose or any seated position with a straight spine. Still your mind, then bring to it one thing you are grateful for. Feel the gratitude rising in your heart, expand it, and let it permeate your whole body.

Take another thing for which you feel grateful and hold it in your mind while you let the gratitude flow through you. Do this for several minutes with the same object or various objects until you feel you can hold gratitude easily.

Now bring to mind the thing or situation that you want to manifest and feel gratitude for it as if the object is already in your life. Get specific about the details you are grateful for. For instance, if you want to manifest a house, be thankful for its ideal layout and easy navigation, appreciate the windows and natural light, and be grateful for the garden, architecture, neighbors, and furniture you'll bring in. Visualize all these details with ongoing gratitude.

> "The difference between feeling yourself in action here and now and visualizing yourself in action, as though you were a motion-picture screen, is the difference between success and failure." – Neville Goddard[31]

31 Neville Goddard, *Neville Goddard - The Complete Collection: The Reference Book by Neville Goddard with All Books, Radio Lectures and Lessons* (self-pub., Tolino Media, 2023), 179.

◇

Repetition

Much of your spiritual practice involves repetition, such as regular sequences of asanas, daily breathing exercises, and chanting mantras, all aimed at managing vibrations for a better life experience. Similarly, for successful manifestation, you repeat essential mental activities for days, weeks, and even years until your desires come to fruition. As meditation teacher Sharon Salzberg aptly puts it, "If you have to let go of distractions and begin again thousands of times, fine. That's not a roadblock to the practice — that IS the practice. That's life: starting over, one breath at a time."[32]

Sounds like a lot of work? Maybe, but consider that you're already engaging in repetitive mind activities all the time, maybe even for most of your days, just mostly unconscious to you. These automatic, ongoing mental patterns tend to be negative in nature: your fears, beliefs, and the attention you give to things and people because they annoy you or you blame them for the miseries in your life. The repetition required for successful conscious manifestation not only gets you what you want but also provides an opportunity to replace negative patterns with productive and uplifting thoughts, making you feel good along the way. Repetition of affirming mind activities fosters a persistent sense of positivity in you.

> "Yoga comprises numerous practices — both physical and mental. These can be reduced to two major categories: *abhyasa* and *vairagya*. *Abhyasa* is the repeated performance of exercises or techniques that are intended to produce a positive state of mind in us. *Vairagya* is the complementary practice of letting go of old behavior patterns or attachments. *Abhyasa* gradually reveals to us the deeper, hidden aspects of the mind, while *vairagya* moves us step by step beyond appearances toward reality." – Georg Feuerstein[33]

Faith

Faith is believing that something can be that isn't yet, that something can happen that hasn't happened yet. It is the acceptance that your fulfilled desire already exists as a blueprint in the ethers, and your faith summons it into physical existence. Faith

---

32 Sharon Salzberg, *Real Happiness, 10th Anniversary Edition: A 28-Day Program to Realize the Power of Meditation* (New York City: Workman Publishing Company, 2019), 52.

33 Georg Feuerstein, *The Deeper Dimension of Yoga: Theory and Practice* (Boston: Shambhala, 2003), 232.

is an all-important ingredient, and there's a lot to say about it, especially for yogis. That's why I've added a whole chapter on faith later in the book. (See chapter 7.)

THOUGHTS

Manifestation teachings emphasize that the manifestations in our lives reflect the thoughts in our minds, both positive and negative. Therefore, managing our thoughts is crucial for successful conscious manifestation. Yoga and meditation share this aim on a technical level, focusing on greater control of your mental processes as the foundation for all the practice's benefits, physical, mental, and spiritual. As mentioned in chapter 1, Patanjali's yoga sutras state this clearly in Book 1, defining yoga as the control of the twists and tumbles of the mind. The combination of yoga and manifestation helps a yogi easily qualify their thoughts and become skilled in manifestation. Yogi Bhajan said: "You automatically start meditating when you qualify your thoughts."[34]

It's important to manage your thoughts with a neutral view of how they arrived in your mind in the first place. Often, there is a tendency for self-criticism, but in yoga and meditation, practitioners often address emerging negativity by harnessing mental functions and developing mental consciousness to become free from the confines of their own thoughts. One way to manage your thoughts is by consciously replacing a negative or unhelpful thought with a positive or more productive one. You can accomplish this in meditation, by using a specific technique, or by reading spiritual writing. Alternatively, you can redirect your attention continuously and consistently to one thought, like a mantra, or practice following your breath. This way, the other thoughts lose power, recede into the background, and disappear along with their influence.

> "Fill your mind with stuff that you can use, that will make your perceptual universe different. Fill your mind with other thoughts. Pick a thought, which is called a primary object of meditation, and let all the rest of them come and go. In Buddhism it's called right thought and right understanding, part of the eightfold path." – Ram Dass[35]

---

34 Yogi Bhajan (lecture, Los Angeles, April 20, 1996).

35 Ram Dass, "Motives for Spiritual Practice," 1976, lecture, https://www.youtube.com/watch?v=Xln32jtVpyw&t=2739s.

In Buddhism, for example, mental consciousness is considered one of the six major types of consciousness (the others are auditory, gustatory, olfactory, tactile, and visual). And mental consciousness, in the Buddhist sense, is not just mental activity but also includes emotions and feelings. In the Bhagavad Gita, Lord Krishna teaches Arjuna the technique of *sthitaprajna*, or "steady wisdom," which involves focusing on positive thoughts to achieve a peaceful mind. When you're feeling stuck in a negative mental state, like frustration or judgment, meditation techniques can provide relaxation and a way out. Similarly, the development of concentration or focus can aid your manifestation powers. Ultimately, qualifying your thoughts can lead to genuine happiness by freeing yourself from false identifications, and you'll also achieve successful manifestation as a bonus.

The Dalai Lama encourages employing meditation techniques, including those from Tibetan Buddhism, to transform your perspective and attain genuine happiness. "Achieving genuine happiness may require bringing about a transformation in your outlook, your way of thinking, and this is not a simple matter. It requires the application of so many different directions, so many insights, so much knowledge."[36]

If this sounds like a lot of work, look at it energetically, because the energy you spend on managing your life with the manifestation of unconscious thinking — the kind of life that most people experience, a reactive, ongoing process of problem-solving — is at least equal in quantity to the energy you might spend on managing your thoughts. Eventually, the new and positive results will liberate you and free up energy to elevate yourself and your occupations. For example, I've been wanting to write for many years. The idea for this book only came recently, but I've been wanting to write for a very long time and simply couldn't. I was very frustrated with the fact that the wish didn't come true, and it stopped me from achieving anything. Once the idea for this book came to me, I understood that making it a reality would also require applying the techniques of manifestation. Rather than being frustrated about my inability to write, I harnessed my energy towards the flow of my thoughts and visualized myself finishing the book. Ram Dass describes the results of such a strategy beautifully in his lecture "Embracing the Mystery," in the context of activism: "When you march for peace, you do it

---

36 Dalai Lama, *The Art of Happiness: A Handbook for Living* (New York City: Penguin Publishing Group, 2020), 32.

with peace in your heart. Not saying: 'until I have peace, I can't be peaceful.' You say I am peaceful; now let there be peace."[37]

> "Yoga is a gradual process of replacing our unconscious patterns of thought and behavior with new, more benign patterns that are expressive of the higher powers and virtues of enlightenment." – Georg Feuerstein[38]

The Buddhist discourse on loving-kindness, particularly the Metta Sutta and related meditations, offers a tremendous inspiration for qualifying thoughts and leveraging them for positive outcomes. What makes Metta Meditations ideal for our purposes is that they can be adapted to different goals and people. Following it below, you can find another meditation that builds in you a foundation for the ability to shift your thoughts, feelings, and emotions towards those that you choose. Regarding the name of the meditation you will see below, Kundalini Yoga has such a vast repertoire of yogic tools for every life situation that it even includes meditation to become a better actor. Isn't acting exactly what we've been talking about, filling yourself with the words and feelings that enable you to step into a different identity and reality? For that, I don't think it's wrong to call the application of qualified and chosen thoughts and feelings acting. Find it below and use it to improve the kind of acting skills that accelerate your manifestations.

37 Ram Dass, "Embracing the Mystery," 1993, lecture, https://www.youtube.com/watch?v=V4Zw06xwk1s&t=1872s.

38 Georg Feuerstein, *The Deeper Dimension of Yoga: Theory and Practice* (Boston: Shambhala, 2003), 24.

Sit in a meditative pose. Repeat the following phrase to yourself out loud or silently in your mind: "May I be filled with loving-kindness. May I be well. May I be peaceful and at ease. May I be happy."

◇

Sit in Easy Pose with a straight spine and a light Neck Lock.

Mudra: Make fists with the Jupiter (index) and Saturn (middle) fingers extended and the other fingers held down with the thumbs. Raise the arms with the elbows stretched to the side, the forearms parallel to the ground and hands in front of the throat. Touch the tips of Jupiter and Saturn fingers to the fingertips of the opposite hand.

Eye Focus: 1/10th open.

Breath: Inhale for **2-3 seconds**, suspend the breath for **5 seconds**, exhale for **10-15 seconds**.

Time: 11-31 minutes.

To End: Inhale deeply and relax.

Comments: This kriya will help the aspirant find the source of creativity that is in the heart. It solves the problem of finding how to make a lucrative livelihood and satisfy the soul at the same time.

◊

FIRST ROUND OF CONSCIOUS MANIFESTATION

Now it's time to apply what you've learned so far. Take about 3–5 minutes for this. Please sit down and take the following steps.

1. **Decide: find the seed. Crystallize your desire and declare it.**
   State your wish in the clearest, most concise way possible and inject it with the felt experience of what you associate with it. You are plucking the seed from your consciousness that carries your desire and its full realization. The term "kernel of truth" is useful here. Say or write clearly what you want. State it without insecurity or ambiguity. This step can be a sort of admission to yourself. For example, some of you might have a hard time admitting that you want a relationship, a lot of money, and/or a new car. You might consider these desires shallow, as your priority should be wishing for world peace and happiness for everyone. Don't forget, this is about what *you want* — a declaration from you to the universe. It's not a script for an audience with particular expectations. If you are embarrassed about your wish, that constitutes a distortion and will impede your manifestation. If you want a lover, state it. If you want a million dollars, state that. If you want to heal from a disease, state that. And if you want to reconnect with an estranged loved one, say that. The list is endless, but you have to be clear. If there is any ambiguity in your statement, ask yourself: Why do I want that? Other underlying desires might come from that. For example, if you want to be a doctor but have doubts, ask yourself why you want it. You might realize it's because your father wanted you to be one. This exercise is not about fulfilling someone else's wish. State what you want.

2. **Accept: Live inside the seed. Understand and feel all aspects of your fulfilled desire.**
   The seed carries the complete blueprint of your manifestation. This step's primary quality is closure, completion, and acceptance. Use the knowledge you've gained from the following chapters about the mind and the universe. Acknowledge that your wish is now in seed form in the field of energy we call the universe, where it has sprouted and will grow into its full manifestation according to your care. Accept the manifestation, the object, or the situation you want as complete. Remember, acceptance is no longer wanting; it's an acknowledgment of existence, no longer a longing for it. Switch on your powers of imagination as much as possible. Do a good yoga set to refine your ability to

visualize, or do any other mental and physical preparation you find in this book (find more practices in Chapter 12). Own the idea and the image, and accept the reality of them. If there is any doubt or ambiguity, clear it up, then repeat until your vision and acceptance are whole.

3. **Integrate: You and the seed are one. Develop the ethereal blueprint into a physical manifestation.**

    Nurture the seed with your conscious mind activity until it manifests on the earth plane. This is equivalent to caring for a plant in your garden, but here you carry it with you all the time, like a Tamagotchi pet[39] you have to attend to it or it will die. Care equals conscious mind activity here. Let the knowledge and practices carry you through the ups and downs, every day, week, and month, until the manifestation is complete. Listen to your needs and give yourself what you need to keep nurturing the seedling through every phase of its growth. To improve your focus, practice tratakum on some days. On other days, you might have to fine-tune your beliefs or the imaginary details of the desired manifestation.

    For now, just hold yourself as the vessel of positivity and the center of the environment in which your manifestation will grow. Feel, rather than think about, what that is like. You taste the first sip of the manifestation cocktail. The flavor of the situation will change over time, but not your continuity in holding the space. Accept what it feels like while staying open to movements along the way.

How was the first session? Were you able to make a clear statement and then accept that the fulfilled wish is now an ethereal entity in the field of the universe? Were you able to feel the related feelings you came up with? And were you able to maintain them? If the answer is yes to all questions, congratulations. Most likely it won't be, but you start where you start and move forward from there. Just like you have the innate ability to create, you also have the innate ability to sharpen that skill, and most of this book helps you exactly with that. So let's move to the next chapter to refine your engine towards conscious and empowered manifestations.

---

39 A Tamagotchi pet is a toy that became popular in the late 1990s. It was a handheld digital device, often egg-shaped and with an LCD screen, that required the user to attend to its needs to keep it "alive."

CHAPTER 3
MEET THE ENGINE OF MANIFESTATION

THE MIND. A NEW VISUAL AND DEFINITION FOR YOGIS

Can you say on the spot what the mind is? I've injected this question into conversations over the years, and it stumps people almost every time. Most people associate the mind with brain activity, something that is active inside your skull but not beyond it. Spiritual teachings paint a different picture. Unlike the soft tissue of the brain, the mind is more like a gaseous entity that is active beyond the brain, and it can travel instantly to the farthest corner of the universe while shaping your reality through engagement with the elements.

Daniel J. Siegel, a Clinical Professor of Psychiatry at UCLA, in an interview with Psychiatric Times about his best-selling book *The Mind*, defines one aspect of the mind as "an embodied and relational, self-organizing emergent process that regulates the flow of energy and information both within and between." He continues: "Where is this occurring? Within you and between you."[40] If the mind can really be between two people and between people and their environment, it makes sense to think of it as an entity that exists beyond the body to interact with the elements of the universe. Imagine a cloud-like form that extends from you into your environment while it is still bound to you and continues to compute for you. For example, if you think about the moon, your mind goes from you to the moon instantly and generates the picture that you see in your mind's eye. This concept makes the mind a moving, fluid, computing mist. More and more people are saying it is so.

A similar reconceptualizing is happening in computer technology as well, which is an apt comparison as the mind is very much like a computing device. For example, the concept of a computer as an interconnected object freed from classic memory devices and similar computer components is one way that the rapidly developing field of quantum science is looking at building new computers. Quantum

---

40 Daniel J. Siegel, *Mind: A Journey to the Heart of Being Human (Norton Series on Interpersonal Neurobiology)* (New York City: W. W. Norton, 2016), 252.

computers today can already store information in the atoms of natural substances like calcium. These atoms, as memory storage devices, can even exist and function in various states, just like matter can exist in various states — think of water as ice, liquid, or gas. This makes the idea of a cloud-like, highly adaptable, and shape-shifting computing device more realistic, and it also gives us a helpful image for our new concept of the mind.

> "I am not referring to 'mind' merely as one's cognitive ability or intellect. Rather, I'm using the term in the sense of the Tibetan word 'Sem,' which has a much broader meaning; closer to 'psyche' or 'spirit,' it includes intellect and feeling, heart and mind." – Dalai Lama[41]

The mind is your bridge to everything. It's just not shaped like a bridge at all. Just like yoga is the technology to make your connection to the entire universe conscious, the mind is the bridge to your expanded, infinite self. The mind as a bridge is not just a metaphor here; the mind is the actual device that builds the connection to all places in infinity by actually going there. Quantum science confirms that particles can occupy multiple positions simultaneously. Therefore, we can define mind activity as particles of consciousness that exist, interact, and compute in more than one place at the same time. It gives new meaning to the question: Where is your mind?

In the teachings of some Buddhist traditions, the mind is synonymous with the entire experienced universe, the same as universal consciousness. Some Buddhist masters take the concept of the infinitely mobile and expandable mind to another level by declaring that the mind is not just capable of reaching and permeating any part of the universe instantly, but that absolutely everything is the mind. This view ties in easily with our discussion of consciousness in this book. Think about it: if the basic building material of everything in the universe is consciousness, and the mind is consciousness, then it seems logical that everything is the mind. The mind, in that case, is simply another term for the infinite field of activity in which everything is connected. It's mind-boggling and simple at the same time.

As we've seen in Chapter 1, there is a term in Zen Buddhism called the Big Mind, which describes the totality of consciousness. That concept shares similarities

---

41 Dalai Lama, *The Art of Happiness: A Handbook for Living* (New York City: Penguin Publishing Group, 2020), 4.

with the universal or higher self, a consciousness that transcends the limitations of the ego and its narrow mindset. In this context, the Big Mind not only means a state of consciousness that transcends an individual identity or ego but also defines the totality of all existence as non-dual awareness, including all experiences, emotions, and manifestations. More and more, it becomes clear that both ancient yogic sciences and Buddhist philosophies are all saying the same thing: everything is connected, everything is the same, and everything is one. The mind is simply another word for the totality of the experienced universe. Any of the images we talked about can greatly assist you with your conscious manifestation, so select the one that is simplest for you or think about all three. Here are examples of how you can use them:

✤ **Your mind as a cloud.** The mind-mist emanates from you and envelopes all ingredients that go into your manifestation. See the mist surrounding the places, people, and things that are needed, and see it creating the atmosphere in which all of it somehow becomes what you want, like a cocoon in which transformation happens. And while you don't see and know every detail of the transformation — just like you don't need to see the inside of a cocoon to know that one entity turns into another — you know exactly what will eventually come out of the cocoon — your fulfilled desire.

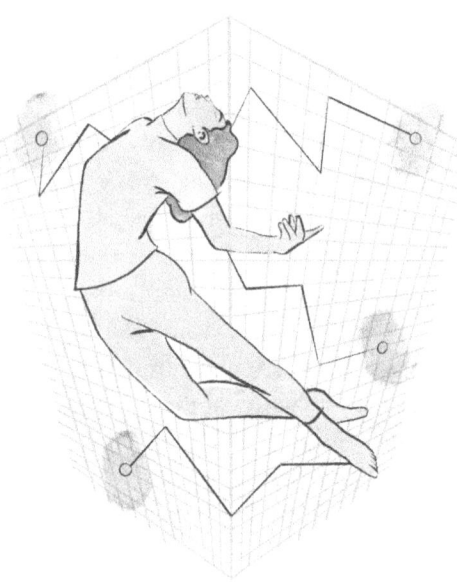

✤ **Your mind as an instant time and space traveler.** See your mind zigzagging through the universe, sourcing each ingredient of your manifestation and tying them together. The lines connecting the ingredients form a subtle structure that gets fleshed out into the desired manifestation.

✤ **The mind as the totality.** See yourself beyond any physical boundaries and expand into the universe, simply melting into everything. Then see lights going on in key positions, like bulbs connected to one electrical grid, and one by one they illuminate the shape or the situation that you want to manifest, like a scene appearing on a dark stage.

Feel free to explore and improve these ideas or come up with your own way of thinking. You have the power to create anything with your mind at the center.

"The mind is a structure, a process, and an energy that lets your awareness operate and manifest in this creation. You can observe it, and you can change it. You can affect it with gross things like food, powerful things like breath, and subtle things like thought. It has its own flow, structure, and metabolism." – Yogi Bhajan[42]

HOW DOES THE MIND CREATE MATTER?

The mind creates matter and everything comes out of nothing. How? Let's address a significant obstacle to believing in manifestation. When we talk about humans manifesting, we mean they create something that didn't exist before. When you embrace the idea that everything comes from nothing, manifesting becomes more accessible. It's easy to imagine moving something from one place to another, like from an Amazon warehouse to your doorstep, but in manifestation, you bring something out of nothing. Yogic science has given us an explanation for this. Here we go back to the concept that everything is consciousness. "Nothing" here then is just consciousness that is not matter yet, the invisible stuff in the empty space between sense-able objects. We have already established that consciousness is vibration, and "nothing" is consciousness that is not yet vibrating at the level of matter but has a lighter vibration. "Nothing" represents pure consciousness, holding the potential to manifest into something yet unknown. In yogic science, this is called *Anahata*, which means unstruck, unbeaten, as in the unstruck sound, the dormant vibration. We already discussed *Anahata* in the section on manifestation mechanics, but it's such an important concept that we'll elaborate more here. Think of *Anahata* as absolute stillness, the ultimate peace. What can strike this dormant vibration to make it vibrate? Your consciousness touches it, your mind and its activity, like a bow put to a violin. By the way, *Anahata* is also the Sanskrit term for heart chakra, representing a state of purity and balance at the core. If you consider that no life exists without a beating heart, it makes perfect sense that manifestation — a bringing forth into existence — begins with the activation of sound at the core. Isn't that beautiful?

When your mind meets *Anahata*, consciousness begins to vibrate. And from here, the transformation of pure consciousness into matter begins. The process

---

42 Yogi Bhajan and Gurucharan Singh Khalsa, *The Mind: Its Projections and Multiple Facets* (Espanola: Kundalini Research Institute, 1998), 121.

moves in stages, and the level of density of the matter defines these stages. The most subtle, the least dense level of matter, is called ether. Now your mind has moved from pure consciousness to vibrating on the level of ether. This could be the vibration of your idea or any thought. It lives in the ethers now. What happens next? Remember the quote from Yogi Bhajan: "The mind is to fashion etheric elements into forms of energy that manifest through the earthly elements." The earthly elements are, from lighter to heavier: ether, air, fire, water, and earth. Now the mind is interacting with the elements to bring something into manifestation and give something greater density. This is a gradual change, like dawn making the world visible in shapes and colors as daylight gets stronger.

With more density comes more separation from the oneness, the big soup of unstruck sound. This isolation into units, from oneness into separate forms and entities, is also called *maya*, a well-known concept from ancient Indian philosophy. The yogis call each stage of separateness a *tattva* and ascribe each *tattva* its own qualities. Yogis say there are many stages, many *tattvas*, from absolute ones to pure individual atom separateness. In Kundalini Yoga, for example, there are 31 *tattvas*, and only the final five (ether, air, fire, water, and earth) provide the sensory input that most people experience as physical reality. This is not to say that humans cannot sense vibrations on other *tattva* levels. However, it would require enormous sensitivity. Just think about the increasing levels of subtlety as you move up from the fifth *tattva* to the 31st and how high in frequency the mind could go.

The mind combines various elements uniquely, leading to infinite physical manifestations on Earth. That's one explanation for the immense diversity of life forms on Earth. Comparisons to sculptors or architects fall short in capturing the true essence of this process, as they imply external creation. Instead, consider starting from the inside with consciousness as the initial blueprint. The development of the human fetus inside a mother's body is a better example than the creation of sculpture outside of an artist's body. Over the course of approximately nine months, a body develops without external direction, and even the mother does not micromanage the composition of all the parts and pieces that form the little human. How then do cells know which organ or body part to construct at the right time? Is it really just DNA — the mechanic unfolding of a body from a static map? I imagine that consciousness serves as the initial blueprint within the mother's womb and possibly beyond, gathering elements throughout pregnancy to form the physical body. Although there is no scientific evidence yet to support the idea that matter doesn't arise solely from cell multiplication but instead originates from and within consciousness, it provides a more suitable analogy for comprehending manifestation. I think it also helps to have different perspectives on the same process of manifestation through the mind. For that, I want to share a description by Ram Dass:

> "When you have broken your connection to a specific time-space locus, when you have pulled your awareness back from an identification with your body and your thought, so that your awareness becomes one with all awareness, then you start to have the powers to manifest that awareness and to reconstitute things, move them around with your mind. These are powers that are available, you'd say to God. When your faith is complete, meaning you no longer doubt you are one with the one. When he (the person in the example) says, I am in the father and the father is in me. And I am in you as you are in me, etc. That's the same one. When your faith is complete, the merging between the separate entity and the one occurs, and at that point you could think the universe any way you want to, in the same way that God does, and it would be created in that way, so that you could manifest any form you wanted at any time." – Ram Dass[43]

What we are discussing in this section is, of course, an immensely complex process, and we can't help asking: how exactly does the mind do all this? How does it fetch the elements? How does it keep track of all the steps? There is no obvious answer yet, certainly not through any empiric approach. The most truthful answer is still that we don't know, but it's safe to say we are looking at incredible project management. What we can do, however, is to remove the word "incredible" and stop seeking explanations or proof for every step of manifestation for now. Science might catch up one day, but we don't have to wait until then to use the process. More important is accepting that it's possible. That's what faith is. Faith is knowing that something that hasn't happened yet can happen without knowing how it can happen.

> "The universe is full of magical things, patiently waiting for our wits to grow sharper." – Eden Phillpotts[44]

---

43 Ram Dass, "Innocence, Lightness," 1989, lecture, https://www.youtube.com/watch?v=4CTsWdjT5sc.

44 Eden Phillpotts, *A Shadow Passes* (London: Cecil Palmer & Hayward, 1918), 19.

A NEW SPOTLIGHT ON THE UNCONSCIOUS

We've explored the idea of the mind as a vast, ethereal computer connected to universal consciousness before. This computer software architecture includes an operating system that represents your entire cognitive experience, including beliefs, thoughts, opinions, ideas, images, and filters. As you become more self-aware, you can identify these elements, much like an experienced cook discerns the ingredients in a dish.

Your mind is made up of a distinct combination of these cognitive elements, like a personalized "processing style" or cognitive cocktail. Your life in this universe, where everything is shaped by creative consciousness and resonates with your specific vibrational essence, is as if you're swimming in an ocean of your own "self-cocktail." However, you may not realize that its flavor is an unmarked category until you attain the consciousness to label and understand it. This realization is gaining a meta-awareness of your world, like the fish does in the classic trope when someone asks, "How is the water today?" and the fish replies with a question: "What water?" Just like the fish in that story, you have a fixed perspective and understanding of your surroundings and experiences until a new opportunity presents itself. Now, think about living in and around consciousness, just like the fish in the story now thinks about living in water. Another point I want to make is that your life experiences, your cognitive cocktail, involve two types of ingredients: the ones you're aware of and the ones you're not. For the fish, it was the underwater world in which it saw everything around itself, but not the actual water that holds everything. For humans, I assume, it's a bit more than just the external physical world, as we are also aware of our inner landscape with thoughts and feelings. However, it's fair to say that most of us rarely consider an underlying field that holds our entire world together and us in it. This field, roughly, is the unconscious, a substantial part of our software architecture and influence of its output. Please hold on to this neutral definition of the unconscious for a moment, as we will expand on it to create a more positive definition that will enhance your acceptance of hidden aspects of yourself, just as it did for me.

Please note that you will see references to both the unconscious and the subconscious in this chapter, as both terms appear in the relevant teachings and sources I use here. The subconscious usually refers to those contents and activities of the mind that are just below the level of consciousness but can be accessed, whereas the content of the unconscious mind resides at deeper levels and usually cannot be accessed. For the sake of this discussion, all layers and levels of mind activity that are below the level of consciousness are involved in the process of manifestation, and the lines between them may vary for everyone as they tend to shift with new consciousness gained through yoga and meditation, which is why it makes sense to include both, the subconscious and the unconscious.

In the Western world, people typically interpret the unconscious using concepts from Sigmund Freud, who portrayed it as a repository for dark mental activity, lower-level impulses, desires, and processes often related to something sexual or utterly inexpressible and shameful — and lots of it. He used the analogy of "an iceberg floating in the ocean with one-eighth visible above water (the conscious) and seven-eighths below (the unconscious)."[45] I used to see my own unconscious in a similar light, a vast container filled with darkness. Most Westerners, I think, have quietly embraced and internalized Freud's notion of the unconscious, perceiving it as a negative and troublesome aspect of the mind, much like the Christian belief of people being born sinners. Interestingly, this concept is unique to Christianity and not present in other religious traditions like Islam, Judaism, Hinduism, and Buddhism, all of which regard humans as inherently good. This presents a strong case for drawing inspiration from Eastern philosophies, in my opinion. If Eastern philosophies, like yoga, provide an alternative to the belief that we are inherently rotten and driven by a dark and inevitable repository of ugly and disgraceful attributes of our minds, then it makes them particularly worth exploring.

In our quest for a positive concept of the subconscious, Neville Goddard offers a very plausible one, and it's totally yogic. He, like Freud, says that the subconscious operates below the level of conscious awareness, but not because it fears the light like some demon, but simply because it works behind the scenes, like an army of invisible helpers or etheric elves, and we just can't see all of its activity, nor do we have to. If the mind is everything and works with the universe, and everything is mind and consciousness, then the subconscious mind is everything that the mind does without us being aware of it while still being connected to it.

45 Carl Gustav Jung, *Psychology of the Unconscious: A Study of the Transformations and Symbolisms of the Libido* (London: Paul, 1922), 22.

This same idea is reflected in the teachings of the pioneers of modern psychology, including C. G. Carus (1789–1869) and Carl Jung (1875–1961). In his *Handbook of Jungian Psychology*, author Christopher Hauke writes about the interpretations of the unconscious by both Carus and Jung: "the unconscious, unlike the strenuous efforts of the conscious mind, uses little energy and thus does not 'need rest' like consciousness does. It is the source of healing for the mind and body, and it is through the unconscious that we remain in connection with the rest of the world and other individuals."[46]

So there's the conscious mind and everything else, and it's all connected as a whole. Now the yogic concept of each self containing and reflecting the whole universe finally makes perfect sense! What we all are is that which you are conscious of being plus everything you are not conscious of being. But the twist is that all of it is rooting and pining for you, and nothing is working against you. Isn't this a refreshingly positive take on the totality of the mind?

Here's another yogic way of looking at the qualities and collaboration of the two minds: by relating them to the essential substances of the creative universe, the male and female energies. The emphasis here is on energy, not form, and it has nothing to do with societal gender roles or identities. The sun and the moon are symbols for these energies that are commonly used in yogic traditions to better understand the complementary energies. The essential male energy is projection, and the essential female energy is reception. The sun projects its light onto the world, and the moon receives the light and reflects it back. This is a basic relationship that balances life on Earth, just like the balance of the two essential energies maintains the entire universe beyond the sun and the moon. Other adjectives to describe male energy are active and protective, and female energy are passive and nurturing. It's very important for our understanding of the universe and our own nature, including our minds, to know that male and female energies are present in everything and everyone. Just like there is no hard line between day and night but a smooth transition through dusk and dawn, and just like the moon is only visible through the sun and the moon is present during the day, we all carry male and female energy in us. If we apply the essential energies here, the conscious mind represents male energy as it projects and protects with

46 Christopher Hauke, "The unconscious: personal and collective," in Handbook of Jungian Psychology, ed. Renos K. Papadopoulos (New York: Routledge, 2006), 57.

its thoughts and ideas, like how sun rays bring light and warmth to the world. The unconscious and subconscious represent female energy, as it receives the ideas from the conscious mind and creates reality accordingly, like seeds growing into a plant or a fertilized egg into a grown being.

Let's look at an expanded version of this idea, which is also perfect for manifestation: If you are everything, and everything is consciousness, then your unconscious is literally the entire universe, the fertile ground in which your seeds are planted and grow into the manifestations of your reality. Regardless of your gender, you can both produce seeds and develop what grows out of them. The more consciously the conscious mind is involved, the more it can project and protect its input into the unconscious mind, and the more beautiful your manifestations become. Yet here is another argument for conscious living (and manifestation) through yoga. The power of your entire mind, with its complementary energies and functions, can create entire worlds for you and others. May this yogic definition of your mind guide you to accept yourself wholly without condemning any part to obscurity.

> "The mechanism of creation is hidden in the very depth of the subconscious, the female aspect or womb of creation." – Neville Goddard[47]

The following yoga set helps you to understand the elements better, the five components out of which absolutely everything in the universe is made, including you and your manifestation. The elements are the materials that your mind engages with to flesh out your desires in physical form. Doing this set makes it easier to identify the elements within yourself as feelings and then use these feelings for more specificity in your imaginations for the manifestation process.

---

47 Neville Goddard and Fabio Mantegna, *Neville Goddard — Feeling is the Secret: Use the Power of Your Subconscious Mind to Manifest Anything You Want* (self-pub., Tolino Media, 2023), 15.

November 9, 1989

1) **Arm Waves.** Sit in Easy Pose with a straight spine and a light Neck Lock. Extend the arms straight forward parallel to the ground, hands facing down, fingers together relaxed, with the elbows gently bent. Dive the hands down and then extend the wrists up in a wave-like motion, and then repeat, like waves of the ocean. Use the entire arm to create the wave: shoulder, elbow, and wrist. **Continue for 8 minutes.**

TO END: Inhale deeply, suspend the breath for 20 seconds, exhale, and relax.

You are directly dealing with your toxins and your poisons in the body.

2) **Five Tattvas Play.** Bring the hands in front of the chest. Touch the tips of the fingers of one hand to the corresponding fingers on the opposite hand, with space between them. The palms face each other and are separated, creating a tent shape. Separate the hands and then tap the fingers together all at once in rhythm with the music. You are playing with the five *tattvas*. (The recording of Punjabi Drums was played in the original class.**)** Continue for **4 minutes**.

TO END: Inhale deeply, suspend the breath for 30 seconds, meditate at the Heart Center, and exhale.

3) **Shoulder Dance.** Remain in Easy Pose. Bring the fingertips to the shoulders and raise the elbows out to the sides. Dance the shoulders like wings, any way you like, to the rhythm of the recording Punjabi Drums. After **2 minutes**, extend the tongue and begin heavy, long, deep breathing through the mouth, using the power of the navel, as in Lion's Breath. Continue for **5 more minutes**. Total time: **7 minutes.**

TO END: Inhale deeply, suspend the breath for 15 seconds, and exhale. Repeat 2 more times, suspending the breath for 10 seconds. *Your spine will start adjusting, and your lower back will hurt if it is out. Using the Navel for the Lion's Breath engages the fire element.*

4) **Arms to 45 degrees**. Remain in Easy Pose. Extend your arms out to the sides and up to the heavens as in a wide V, 45 degrees above parallel, with the palms facing each other. Drop your head back and bring your gaze up to the sky. Listen to beautiful, inspiring music. (Nirinjan Kaur's "Peace and Tranquility" was played in class.) Continue for **5 minutes**. *Pray as your original self.*

5) **Hands on the Heart**. Remain in Easy Pose. Place your hands on your heart, one hand resting on the other. Concentrate on the fontanel (the soft spot in the skull) in the crown of the head. Close your eyes. Try to become a little sparrow of time and space and project out. Leave the body and let it heal. (Gong was played in the original class). Continue for **9 ½ minutes**.

6) **Hands on the Heart with Breath of Fire.** Hands still on the heart, inhale deeply and do Breath of Fire for **3 minutes**. (Nirinjan Kaur's version of "Mera Man Lochai" was played in class.)

TO END: Inhale deeply, suspend the breath for 20 seconds, circulate the breath and focus on the area you want to heal, and quickly exhale. Repeat 2 more times, suspending the breath for 15 seconds.

Comments: "The entire destructive behavior [and] improper human dialogue is because we want attention — and we get it by either behaving good or bad. It is stressful... We have to become a stress-free zone. We have to deeply understand that [being free of stress] is the source or key to happiness." – Yogi Bhajan

---

CHAPTER 4

Quantum Physics Support

Manifestation Concepts

When we need scientific explanations for our discussions of manifestation phenomena, quantum physics is a wonderful source. Quantum physics has been around for more than a hundred years and presents a departure from classical physics as a branch that feels more analogous to Eastern philosophies.

Classical physics describes matter and its behavior at a macro level, while quantum physics describes it at a micro level. Quantum means "the smallest amount of a physical quantity that can exist independently." Classical physics studies objects with many particles, while quantum physics focuses on the smallest particles and their laws in the unseen realms. It turns out that these laws are very different from our reality of everyday things and objects. Everything in the universe, including matter and energy, is composed of atoms, which consist of three primary particles: protons, neutrons, and electrons. In a nutshell, quantum physics explains the characteristics of the elementary components of the universe.

Energy does not occupy space in the same way as matter does, but energy can be stored in physical systems such as magnetic and electric fields that emanate into space. These fields consist of photons, particles of light that possess energy. Energy, broadly defined, is the potential to become something, the potential for transformation into physical manifestations such as matter. This idea resonates with ancient spiritual teachings linking energy fields to light particles. In Buddhist teachings, for example, the concept of *dharmakaya* refers to the ultimate nature of things (consciousness) and is described as a luminous, vast emptiness that underlies all phenomena. In Taoism, the ancient Chinese philosophical and religious tradition, *Qi* is analogous to the energy that permeates all things and is also known as "the mysterious power called the Light" in the Tao Te Ching.

The birth of quantum physics in the early 1900s clarified that light consists of tiny, indivisible units of energy, known as photons. More subatomic particles have been discovered, which tells us that there are probably many more to discover. However, to keep things simple, let's just say that protons and neutrons also consist of smaller particles, called quarks. Now, we can connect Eastern philosophy's view of light and consciousness with the Western scientific understanding of subatomic particles, examining quantum physics phenomena. These phenomena in quantum physics are often labeled as weird, yet they bridge the gap between modern science and yogic philosophy and help us shed new light on manifestation.

EVERYTHING IS ENTANGLED

The Theory of Quantum Entanglement says that particles interact with and influence each other at a rate that is faster than the speed of light, regardless of how far apart they are. This means we cannot classify them as independent and that they are somehow connected with each other, although it's not clear how they connect, whether they communicate somehow, or if they are simply the same particle in different places at the same time. Albert Einstein called this phenomenon "spooky action at a distance." Similar to yoga, this idea highlights direct and immediate connections between particles or bodies and takes the concept of interconnectedness to a higher level. In practical terms, the theory suggests that your thoughts about someone can immediately affect them in some way. Along the same lines, if you are thinking of the moon, a particle of your mind might communicate with a particle on the moon, or it might even be on the moon at just the same time (as we've seen on the topic about the mind). Consider all the yogic abilities and ideas that are clearer from this perspective: remote viewing, telepathy, and most importantly, the impact of your thoughts and emotions on the manifestation process, regardless of location.

Another scientific model that relates to the interconnectedness of everything is the Big Bang Theory, which suggests that the universe began with a fiery explosion from which the universe has been expanding and cooling ever since. In other words, everything came out of something that was one at a time and remains connected.

According to the Big Bang Theory, everything in the world is forever connected through quantum entanglement. This includes objects and people, all living beings, and even thoughts; it also includes subatomic particles inside every living organism. This implies that your connections extend to everything and everyone you have ever encountered or thought of. Don't forget to consider the reverse perspective: that there is no true separation and that a connection remains with everything and everyone. This might even provide an explanation for our longing for people and places we don't know yet, as well as our longing for unity and belonging that lives in everyone, even if we often struggle to comprehend it within ourselves. There is a poetic interpretation of this connection as it relates to planets. According to this, planets are comparable to former lovers who are currently rotating around one another in an eternal dance of longing.

Atoms, similar to snowflakes on a smaller scale, are both composed of the same particles and distinct from one another. Like any form of energy, we cannot destroy atoms, but they keep showing up in various forms as both animate and inanimate objects that rearrange each other. They connect, yoke, at the most fundamental level of electrons into an infinite number of new forms all the time. Furthermore, electrons possess wave-like properties and can be molded into an infinite number of outcomes. But what decides what they become and which forms they take? Consciousness does — at least that is one theory on which both ancient and modern science are agreeing without yet fully understanding the actual process.

Quantum science also supports the notion that consciousness plays a role in the reorganization of matter, as observation and attention have been demonstrated to alter wave functions and quantum entanglement. If you consider that thoughts and feelings are also energy, also made of neurons, and that they can connect with other neurons on the levels of both matter and energy, it makes sense that our thoughts create reality by rearranging subatomic particles into brand new forms and waves of energy that make up everything from small objects to individual realities and whole worlds, even when we don't understand every detail of this process.

EMPTY SPACE IS NOT EMPTY

Another way of looking at the contribution of quantum physics to manifestation understanding is thinking of empty space, or even what exists in what appears to be nothing or empty. If you were to magnify anything with a giant microscope or deconstruct it into its smallest parts, you would eventually reach the limit of what could be observed or distinguished. Empty space would be all that remains. However, what looks like a void or absence between you and another person or between any two objects is a field of activity, full of energy and teeming with particles that come in and out, connect, and disappear. Even when we see nothing in space, it is filled with constantly moving particles in one endless three-dimensional web of interconnected particles. That's why they are called virtual particles, and the search for the existence of something in that empty space is called "virtual particle theory."

The empty space can also be described as vibration. The yogis say everything is consciousness and that consciousness is vibration. Sound is also another way of describing vibration. Thus, if sound is at the core of absolutely everything, then changing the sound means changing something at the core. By changing the waves, we change the nature of the object that carries the waves. This is basic manifestation, and it's an idea that is found in ancient teachings as well. That is certainly where mantras fit in. Mantras are sound currents, encoded spiritual experiences, and we use mantras to bring about some kind of change, like healing, different emotional states, and even prosperity and wealth. What all mantras have in common is the application of consciousness and sound. We usually chant with a particular mindset and intention (consciousness), expressed in the sound of a mantra, which means we exert influence at the most fundamental level of waves of particles. For example, the Hindu scripture Mandukya Upanishad describes mantra as the manifestation of the Supreme Being, the universal consciousness, as sound (*Nada Brahma*). Not only is the entire universe maintained by the vibration of this sound, but the active production of sound, as with chanting mantras, brings about new manifestations. This includes the realization — i.e., the manifestation of an understanding — of the true nature of reality by aligning our own subatomic particles to the wavelength of the universe.

Here is more evidence from quantum science that matter really behaves more like waves and sound and therefore can be affected on the level of waves and sound. The double-slit experiment shows this. In the experiment, scientists shoot tiny particles like electrons through a barrier with two narrow slits in it and a detector screen behind the barrier. If the particles really behaved like particles, then the detector screen should show two bands shaped like the slit through which the particles transferred. However, what shows up on the detector screen are new patterns of bands that suggest that the particles behave more like waves, or rather that the particles are waves. This adds to the strangeness of the quantum world because it means that particles can be both waves and particles, depending on how we look at them. It certainly means that they can arrange in an infinite number of patterns influenced by consciousness. This also means, in theory, that consciousness can manifest anything.

In Kundalini Yoga, there is a sutra that illustrates how we can actively influence our reality at the subatomic level. It says, "Vibrate the cosmos, and the cosmos shall clear the path." We can find a path — a way out of anything and an entrance into everything — by approaching the situation on the level of vibration. This can be a mantra, a shift in attitude or perspective, or a different belief. Any of these can change the wavelength we project and lead to different vibrations and manifestations. By changing the vibration, the sound of the cosmos, the cosmos brings about manifestations that are aligned with our intentions and desires.

PART 2 **MERGING YOGA AND MANIFESTATION**

CHAPTER 5
YOUR DEFINITION OF YOGA MATTERS

You are a yoga teacher or therapist, or you've been practicing for a while — but can you explain yoga easily and concisely so that anyone can understand? I found that many yoga teachers and practitioners have a difficult time articulating the meaning of yoga and its impact on people's lives. Let's make sure we're on the same page before we dive into the technicalities of reconciling yoga and manifestation. If we don't have a proper understanding of yoga, our practice won't be as effective.

The word yoga comes from the Sanskrit word "yuj" and has the same meaning as the English word "yoke": to unite or tie together. But with what exactly do we unite? Our higher self? The universe? When I ask this to a group of students, I usually just blurt out: with everything!

Yoga is a spiritual practice. We practice as spirits, develop our spirits, and work with spiritual energy all the time. Yoga is a technology to feel connected to everything instead of feeling isolated and limited. While some people mistake a spiritual practice for having a religion, it's worth exploring their similarities, as the word religion comes from the Latin word "religare," which means to bind, to tie, to connect — almost identical to yoke in yoga. Make no mistake: every religion at its core has the same purpose as yoga, leading a person to oneness with all (God, universe, all of creation, all these terms apply), which is why I also draw on religions to highlight the manifestation techniques in ancient teachings. However, religion (excluding Buddhism and Sikhism) usually guards the channels towards oneness and relies on the church and its doctrines as intermediaries, while yoga doesn't have true guardians at the gates. Although teachers and professional organizations monitor procedures and advancements, there is no hierarchical structure in yoga traditions. In the West, practicing yoga does not require initiation, membership, or any kind of justification. You can usually walk into any yoga class or event and join.

Yoga wants us to experience a union with everything, and it provides techniques to experience this and lifestyle options to make a unified world your full-time reality. It provides an alternative perspective to our daily lives, when we often feel isolated, small, and at the mercy of external forces. What we can feel instead, yoga says, is a sense of belonging, support, and love, as well as agency, possibility, expansion, and an ongoing invitation to participate in life.

When we grasp the concept of being connected to everything and the universe's makeup of consciousness, we understand the essence of connection. Everything is connected because everything is one and the same. By understanding our essence, we understand our true selves: pure consciousness. And when we identify as consciousness, we know we can do what all consciousness does: create. Alan Watts said it beautifully, and please note that, in this context, God and consciousness are interchangeable terms:

> "To know that you are God is another way of saying that you feel complete with this universe. You feel profoundly rooted in it and connected with it. You feel, in other words, that the whole energy, which expresses itself in the galaxies, is intimate. It is not something to which you are a stranger, but it is that with which you — whatever that is — are intimately bound up. That in your seeing, your hearing, your talking, your thinking, your moving, you express that which it is, which moves the sun and other stars." – Alan Watts[48]

When we try to better understand the meaning of something, it's always a good idea to look at its opposites as well. What is the opposite of something yoked? Something separate, isolated, and alone. Alan Watts talks about it in the same lecture and uses one of the best words to describe a state opposite to what yoga can give you: alienation.

> "And if you don't know that (you are God), if you don't feel that, well, naturally, you feel alien; you feel a stranger in the world. And if you feel a stranger, you feel hostile. And therefore you start to bulldoze things about, to bite it up, and to try and make the world submit to your will, and you become a real troublemaker." – Alan Watts[49]

Yoga, then, is a way to get to the other end, from alienation to feeling united. Away from loneliness to feeling connected. Our powers of manifestation are inextricably

---

48 Akṣapāda, *Tao of Alan Watts: 444 Expressions of Zen* (n.p.: self-published), 34.

49 Alan Watts, "On Being God," Being in the Way, episode 6, Be Here Now Network, recorded at First Unitarian Church, San Francisco, CA, YouTube video, 36:37, posted March 11, 2022, https://www.youtube.com/watch?v=sZ4lzgWHs_I&t=2711s.

connected to our powers of belonging and feeling connected. If we know we are everything — we are creation and creator at the same time — we have found our power. More than anything, yoga is a restoration of our own powers.

I have always trusted the basic yogic teachings because they always supported self-reliance. All true yogic teachings point to one simple truth: The power is within ourselves. They equate this creative consciousness that we are with God itself. In other words, our consciousness is God, and that puts God inside of us. Most major religious voices today disagree with this and put God on the outside, a force separate from us to be feared. In yoga, we are always addressed directly; the self is always the subject spoken to, never some outside entity. The communication is through the body (asanas), the breath, and the mind, but it is always at our core. Make no mistake: the power does not come from mudras, mantras, masters, or other entities, but begins and ends, like everything, with our consciousness. Yogic techniques can only do one thing: support us in activating our own power.

> "At the heart of all forms of Yoga is the assumption that we have not yet tapped into our full potential as human beings. In particular, Yoga seeks to put us in touch with our spiritual core — our innermost nature — that which or who we truly are." – Georg Feuerstein[50]

All the benefits of yoga can come in our lifetime, of course, and are in direct relation to our practice and level of consciousness. It's the reward of oneness given to us now, not in some afterlife. And this is another additional way in which most major religions obstruct our path to oneness even further: by promising the delivery of the reward after a life lived in adherence to the particular religious practices and teachings. In Judaism, salvation is tied to the idea of the Messiah, who will bring redemption, peace, and prosperity to the Jewish people. According to Islam, salvation is obtained by submitting to the will of Allah, the teachings of the Quran, and the prophet Muhammed. In Christianity, the reward is a life in heaven, also described as returning to the kingdom of God, which simply means reuniting and no longer being separate from God or universal consciousness. And finally, in Buddhism, we have the concept of Nirvana, the ultimate goal of spiritual practice, which is also a merger into pure consciousness. Despite the difference in the timing of the reward, you might also agree that the similarities between yoga and religion are glaring, as re-li-gion, like yoga, is like re-turn-ing home to pure consciousness.

50 Georg Feuerstein, *The Deeper Dimension of Yoga: Theory and Practice* (Boston: Shambhala, 2003), 25.

MANIFESTATION AS AN INCENTIVE FOR YOGA PRACTICE

Now that we are on the same page regarding our understanding of what yoga is, let's analyze what people generally consider to be the ultimate reward for practicing yoga. Based on my conversations with non-yogis, I've noticed two common stereotypes. First, people often associate yoga with physical flexibility, believing that a skilled yogi must be extremely flexible. Second, there is the mystical component, a vague notion of attaining enlightenment. Even though most people aren't sure what enlightenment means, there's this image of sitting cross-legged and super Zen for a long time every day.

Simple generalizations like this are very common and emerge every time people assess a lifestyle and its rewards. Here are some examples that I'm sure you've heard before: Pursue a career with hard work, and status and financial blessings will be yours. Eat well and exercise, and you'll be healthier and more attractive. No pain, no gain. And even in religions, there is a carrot in front of the nose of the faithful: Eternal life for Christians and Muslims; liberation from the cycle of death and rebirth for Hindus; and for Buddhists, it's life in Nirvana, or enlightenment.

To many, the idea of being in a permanent elevated state of *samadhi* or some form of enlightenment is strange at best and might even be a turn-off. And what if you really achieved enlightenment? What kind of life is that? This is a legitimate question for any person leading a regular life in our society. Ok, so I meditate for hours and days, eat really well, and sit in absolute stillness, and, then, what's my reward? I'm not belittling the idea of enlightenment; rather, my point is this: if we aim to encourage people to embrace a yogic lifestyle, we need to consider if the goals we present are both realistic and appealing for everyday life, and enlightenment might not be the best incentive for beginners.

To make yoga truly appealing, we can focus on obvious outcomes that people genuinely desire. Achieving a joyful, abundant, and blessed life through my own efforts is a meaningful goal to my mind, and I believe many others can relate to it easily. Beginners may find more motivation in pursuing a fulfilling and prosperous life rather than aiming for abstract goals like connecting to a higher consciousness. Let enlightenment be a secondary incentive until it naturally becomes a top priority. For now and throughout our lives, aspiring to create a beautiful life using our own abilities is a worthy and realistic goal. Even the Dalai Lama talks about this kind of priority setting and balance in his book, *The Art of*

Happiness. He says that Buddhism divides happiness into four pieces, and they include wealth, worldly satisfaction, spirituality, and enlightenment. All four of them are important and contribute to happiness. Bringing any and all of these into your life is a successful conscious manifestation.

Manifestations include not only objects but also people, situations, circumstances, thoughts, and feelings. In other words, every experience is a manifestation. This is an important distinction. Manifestation is the experience of the fruits of your interaction with the universe, conscious or unconscious. They are the results of your mental activity — thoughts, beliefs, imagination, and what you think about yourself and the world you live in. Your consciousness shapes your manifestations and every experience in your life can be understood through it. Most people consider the things that show up in their lives to be things that happen to them, like two paths that happen to cross. The proverb "being in the right place at the right time" is rooted in this worldview, as are the common ideas that life is a gamble and you never know where you will find yourself from one day to the next. It's a worldview that reflects the subjective perception of the level of control you have over your life and equates it to the control a person in a small boat has over the wide ocean — the view that human life is mostly trying not to tip over and drown. This perspective changes with the concept of conscious manifestation.

BEING A MANIFESTOR

Conscious manifestation is participation in the process of creation from beginning to end. Every reflection from the universe back to you is a manifestation, as much as it reflects your own consciousness. What you see at any moment is the current scene in a sequence of things you have manifested through the engagement of your mind activity with the universe. Even if you don't know the process, you can still know what you manifested in your life by observing what is right in front of you, because everything that appears in your field of perception also exists in your inner world. That's why so many things feel familiar when they show up. If something looks and feels new to you, it may just be the unexpected expression that the inner representation took on the outside. For example, if you wanted to have more time to relax in your life, it might arrive not simply as an addition, like more vacation days at a new job, but as a subtraction, like the reassignment of a time-consuming project to a colleague or the departure of a high-maintenance friend. When the manifestation arrives, it might stun you for a moment, but when you investigate your own wishes and projections, you can always find a cause for the change in your inner life.

If it's not clear at first, try to get to the bottom of the manifestation by analyzing it with the help of a friend or someone who can understand the process — or conversely encourage your students or patients to find the connection between their thoughts and the manifestation. With time, you can identify cause and effect easily, and your sense of living in a universe of your own making grows stronger. It becomes increasingly enjoyable to walk around with an open awareness and look for the beautiful shapes and forms in which the universe delivers your manifestations. It gives new meaning to the yogic concept that reality is *maya*, a game, or a show, but you are no longer a passive spectator. Once you fully understand your role in manifestation, any strategy for shaping your life no longer needs to be existential but can focus on greater quality and value.

Then, it's time for you to accept a new title, that of a manifestor. The word makes sense instantly, yet it's not a word that's officially in any dictionary, and I've heard not a single use of it. This is a linguistic gap, like the lack of a word for a parent who has lost a child, the equivalent of becoming an orphan or widow(er). You might have heard of the latter example of a linguistic gap before; it's always mentioned in the context of giving words to pain, and usually in a tone of awe: the pain of losing a child is so indescribable and unimaginable, there isn't even a word for it, people say. If it's true that we avoid naming things or experiences because no word would make them comprehensible, then we might have found the reason we don't use the word "manifestor" yet.

We have words that come close to manifestor, for example, the word "creator" for a person or entity that makes something. But notice the limited use of this word, usually in art — a content creator, a piece of art, and of course "God the Creator." Beyond that, we have a hodgepodge of words to describe the creative powers of people in certain situations: builder (anything physical, a business, an empire, a bridge, a fire), architect (buildings and structures), producer (visual, performance art, media), composer (music), curator (collections), and so forth. But have you noticed that the only word that encompasses all creative activities is "creator"? However, "creator" is not ideal in our quest to name a manifestor because it is already charged with religious meaning, and calling most people "creators" outside a small domain carries a vainglorious note.

Hence, I am proposing the inclusion of "manifestor" in our vocabulary. Yes, it includes all the ethereal aspects we are discussing in this book, but it's important to use the right language to include everything that something entails. And manifestor is that word. If the word *unbelievable* still lingers in the realm of this discussion like a magnetic adjective that wants to attach itself, remember that nothing is unbelievable once it has been experienced. What part can possibly be unbelievable about any experience after you've had it? Maybe awesome, but not unbelievable. If you practice manifestation even for a short while, you know it's believable and awesome, and I suggest dropping the word unbelievable if you've experienced conscious manifestation on any level. You and everyone, by nature, are manifestors and awesome!

THE CASE FOR CALLING MANIFESTATION THE MYSTICISM OF YOGA

Is manifestation a mystical aspect of yoga? This is an interesting question on our mission to yoke both, because yoga is already considered the mystical aspect of Hinduism and Buddhism. But what is mysticism exactly? Here's a definition from the Encyclopedia Britannica: "The practice of religious ecstasies (religious experiences during alternate states of consciousness), together with whatever ideologies, ethics, rites, myths, legends, and magic may be related to them."

Mysticism is inherently linked to the religious framework in which it arises, whether it is Islamic, Hindu, Jewish, Christian, or Buddhist. You will usually find genuine opposition in most major religions towards their mystical parts. For example, in Islam, it's Sufism, and many Muslims reject it. In Judaism, it's Kabbalah, and many Jews do not incorporate it into their faith practice. And in Christianity, mysticism can hardly be found in most church communities and services.

In all these examples, there is a split between the mainstream religion and its mystical part, although both are invariably connected. This parallel is remarkable, and we might ask what might be the reason. The answers could certainly fill another book, but one clear similarity among all religions and their mystical counterparts is that the non-mystical part of the religion strongly emphasizes the organization and its hierarchy, the exoteric practice, and the rituals. In this aspect, the agency typically rests with the leaders and the institutions, while the members play the role of obedient participants who are expected to accept the hierarchies and greater power of others. In mysticism, the power is personalized, and the spiritual tools are typically sought after by individuals. The similarity, then, is the distribution of power, or rather, the refusal to assign power to a few individuals. In other words, access to the mystical power tools is not encouraged in a group or in regular practice (no mysticism is ever offered in mass, for example). Instead, access is wanted and practiced alone or in small circles as more of an esoteric or inner spiritual practice. What I am describing is also a conflict between the traditional and the esoteric, like the classic example where the orthodox religious element rejects the yogi or yoga, labeling them rebels, heretics, or deviants, which is not uncommon at all.

Is the split between manifestation and yoga of the same kind? Yoga is certainly not an organized religion to begin with, but I think a separation between yoga and manifestation is a more organic process because most people simply do not believe in their own powers to the degree that yogic teachings imply them. I think the basis of the separation is an insecurity in individuals and groups about their own powers when they think along the lines of, "I might be able to do this and that, but I certainly don't have the godlike power of creating worlds." When you have such a belief at your core, it's easy to reject anything that suggests higher powers and not notice the growing separation, like a branch growing away from the trunk.

However, manifestation is not totally severed from yoga; quite the opposite. As mentioned in the first chapter, the Yoga Sutras devote an entire book to the powers that yoga practitioners can acquire, and they include manifestation. My conclusion is that, if manifestation is a subset of a yoga practice according to the sutras, and yoga is definitely the mysticism of both Hinduism and Buddhism, we can make a strong case to call manifestation mystical and the mysticism of yoga.

WHY YOGIS MAKE BETTER MANIFESTORS

Yogis make better manifestors because the focus of the entire practice is oneness with everything — yoking with the universe for merger into one. Understanding that you are one with everything doesn't just help you relax more; it becomes the key to the power of manifestation. Simply put, if you are one with the universe, you are also one with the power that creates it. This makes you not just a participant in creation but also the creator.

The skills yogis learn are dynamite for manifestation. Remember that we can optimize manifestation with clear intention and consistent laser-sharp focus, with which we hold the fulfilled wish in our minds. A good yogi will simply be much better at this because a yogic lifestyle that includes regular meditation, stillness, holding poses, and focused thought is a perfect preparation for the spiritual work of manifestation. Add to this the fact that many yogis already practice a personal sadhana, that is, a daily spiritual practice. Manifestation is then just a natural expansion and expression of these skills and habits. In fact, my own sadhana is now built around manifestation and it lacks no yogic quality. In the following sections, I'll explore more ways in which the positive relationship between yoga and manifestation expresses itself.

Yogic Reverse-Engineering for Better Manifestation

Yoga is the science of reverse engineering for results. So is manifestation. I think a yogic worldview can roughly be described as everything turned upside down or inside out. Your inner world will reflect your outer world. Turmoil in your mental landscape sooner or later becomes turmoil in the physical world. In yoga, this is not a tragedy but an opportunity because you can quiet the turmoil in your outer world by quieting your inner world. This approach works from the opposite end (the inner self) of how most of the world identifies a path to change (starting with the outside conditions). Yogic practice is training to manage reality from the inside out, not from the outside in. This works on all levels — physical, mental, and spiritual.

One way to demonstrate how a yogic technique can bring about external changes by starting internally is through the act of uplifting oneself emotionally using asana. Consider a scenario where someone cuts in front of you at the bank, and after you politely ask them to wait, they respond by telling you to go to hell. Being treated like that can weigh you down, causing you to walk with your head down and your heart closed. Now you could try to change the situation from the outside, go back and give that person a piece of your mind, for example, get an apology, complain to the store staff for not interfering, post about the event on social media, and so on. Or you can do the yogic work to get out of your predicament, and it would start with asana, maybe a mountain pose: lift your chin up, roll the shoulders up and back, lift your chest, and deepen your breath.

Voila, you feel better already. After the outer circumstances (the rude person in line) have put you into a vehicle for a deflated state (slouched body), your inner work (a change of attitude) turns your body into a vehicle for a stronger, more confident state (you stand upright with your head high). More inner work can include detaching yourself from the story of the rude customer through focused meditation or breath.

The process I just described is synonymous with manifestation, where you want to create a new state (an uplifted person), you visualize the end result (walking in confidence and joy), and you get there by creating the emotion, both through your body posture and your imagination. From here, the positive consequences ripple through the world because now a joyful person walks the world instead of a sad one. We'll have plenty of specific practices later in the book, as the yogic tool chest is filled to the brim. There are mantras to stop or reverse a current flow of negative thoughts and negative thought patterns in general. There are tons of ways to elevate your thinking, from loving-kindness practices to meditations for activating the positive mind or subduing the negative one. We usually apply these to uplift a person in the short and long term. But why stop there? Consistent positive thinking and imagination are essential for manifestation, and all these tools are applications for that purpose.

Also, we should acknowledge the spiritual shifts that can occur through practicing yoga, including a shift in self-identification from being a body with a story to recognizing oneself as consciousness, as well as experiencing a profound connection with the world. These perspectives don't just happen to be beneficial for manifestation; they are ideal. If you understand yourself as the center of your own universe and connected to everything, manifestation looks easy from there.

Another way of looking at it is the yogic understanding that everything is inside of you and specifically that everything on the outside of you is also inside of you. When you work with that concept for a while, a new belief system can develop. The non-religious idea of God being you becomes a reality, and once you understand that, manifesting is just an easy, natural consequence. As we've seen in a previous chapter, manifestation requires you to enter a state of being before the physical senses can confirm it. You imagine what you want to manifest (inside) and then live in this made-up reality as if it is already there (outside), and by doing so, the inner vision becomes the outer reality.

Yogis Manage Their Attention

"As a person thinks, feels, and believes, so will the person become."
Bhagavad Gita, Chapter 6, verse 5

In a different chapter, I used the analogy of a garden for the unified field in which we manifest by caring for the vibrational seeds we planted there. A simple way of calling this care we give is attention, and it's a truism in manifestation that everything you give your attention to will grow. Hence, consciously managed and directed attention will make you a better manifestor. The idea that anything you give your attention to will grow includes negative things, and the implication is that negative experiences that are currently present in your life are there only because you have been giving them attention. The solution for everything boils down to this: give or withdraw your attention for the desired results. Giving your attention in the form of all the techniques described in this book will help you manifest. If you withdraw attention from things you don't want, they won't grow or manifest, and eventually, they will cease to exist in your life. Plug this little truth into your basic understanding of the universe and especially into your belief system for massively different results. If you look closely, you'll see another opportunity to apply the upside-down approach of yoga once more here, because giving attention to that which hasn't manifested yet is exactly what most people don't do and the reason they don't manifest what they want. Instead, they pay attention to what they don't want.

Yogis Look at the World as One Universe Made of Consciousness

Yogis identify themselves as consciousness. In manifestation, everything is vibration. Consciousness and vibration are the same. We've discussed in the fourth chapter that modern science is realizing that everything in the universe is vibration. Put anything under a giant microscope, and eventually what you see is a field of vibrating energy. Yogis call this field, which underlies absolutely everything, consciousness. Moreover, they *identify themselves* as consciousness. Most people identify through their egos. Ego in this context is everything you think you are — the things you would list if someone at a cocktail party asked you to tell them about yourself: profession, education, where you grew up and where you are now, background, age, body, people you know, titles, accomplishments, preferences, and so on.

Now notice that all these items on such a who-am-I list can disappear in a moment: your possessions, your friends, a bus might run over your body, your skills become obsolete, and even your style outdated. Simply speaking, everything ego-made is highly vulnerable and impermanent. From a certain age and level of consciousness, every human understands this and never forgets it, which creates a constant current of fear, both conscious and unconscious. Eastern philosophies say this is the root of all pain — an identification of the self with impermanent things. The yogic solution is to extract your identity from this pile of nouns and adjectives and place it in your spirit. In other words, identify yourself as a spirit and tell yourself you are first and foremost a spirit. The old famous saying by Jesuit priest Pierre de Chardin, which we often heard repeated by Yogi Bhajan, nails this sentiment when he reminds us that "I am not a human having a spiritual experience, but a spirit having a human experience." If you truly identify with spirit and something happens in your life — you lose your job or a loved one leaves you — you can sincerely say that "this does not devastate me; it does not end my life, because I am spirit, eternal substance." In manifestation, too, everything in the universe is vibration, including your own self. American author and inspirational speaker Esther Hicks asks the question all the time: "Do you believe you are a vibrational being?" If you can answer this question with a yes, you have added a major piece to the foundation for successful manifestation and greater contentment in your life. One way to get to this identity, besides just accepting it, is to have spiritual experiences, which help you realize that the person having the spiritual experience and the spiritual experience are one and the same thing. Many of the practices in this book can help you have a direct experience of your spiritual nature.

BECAUSE YOGIS DO THE PHYSICAL WORK

All contemporary manifestation teachers and methods agree that a clear and steady mental focus is essential for manifestation and that you can develop it by practicing meditation, but they include almost no instructions for preparing the body effectively. For example, Esther Hicks, author of *The Law of Attraction*, only gives basic meditation techniques for quieting the mind, such as listening to the sound of the air conditioner in the room. Even Neville Goddard, who's written many books about manifestation techniques, only recommends the most rudimentary physical component in all of his instructions, a reclined or horizontal position.

There is no better preparation for the spiritual work that is manifestation than the physical practice of yoga beforehand. If you know the difference between meditating after a good physical yoga set and meditating with no physical preparation, you know what I mean. In fact, much physical yoga is designed as exactly that: preparation for deep absorption. It's a fact that is often forgotten, even in yoga class. I've taken many Hatha and Vinyasa classes where meditation after the physical set was totally absent or too short to matter, and the potential for a wonderful meditative experience was not harnessed. It's like walking up the stairs of the Empire State Building and then going right back down instead of staying to enjoy the view. Here's what yogic scholar Georg Feuerstein says about the marriage of physical yoga and meditation:

> "Yoga is a continuum of theory and practice. That is to say, Yoga is not mere armchair philosophy, nor is it merely a battery of practices. In order to engage Yoga properly and successfully, one must pay due attention to the ideas behind its practical disciplines and, vice versa, to the exercises and techniques embodying its theories. This calls for thoughtful and mindful practice. For instance, regular and correct practice of the yogic postures will undoubtedly help us maintain good physical health. Yet, to tap into their deeper potential, we must understand them as being merely one small aspect of Yoga's integrated approach toward spiritual liberation. Similarly, meditation definitely balances the nervous system and calms the mind. However, only when we understand the nature of the mind — thanks to the yogic theories — can we hope to overcome the inherent limitations of our mental make-up and discover transcendental Consciousness." – Georg Feuerstein[51]

YOGIS CAN MOVE BETWEEN STATES OF ENERGY AND REALITY MORE EASILY

A big part of a yogic practice is working with energy — understanding what energy is, how and when it moves, and how you can manage it to your benefit. If you go through several rounds of sun salutations, you get a good sense of energy moving through your whole body, and often that becomes the primary focus. Over time, a new perspective often develops — a way to see and experience the world more energetically and less intellectually. This has certainly been true for me. I can now walk into any room or situation and almost immediately get a sense of what the dominant vibration is and what people are up to. Before I had a yogic

---

51 Georg Feuerstein, *The Deeper Dimension of Yoga: Theory and Practice* (Boston: Shambhala, 2003), 22.

practice, I mostly just collected facts before and during the event and processed them intellectually, but rarely felt very sure or comfortable with the results. With my new navigation skills in a world that is all energy, I do much better, and I manifest more easily because knowing energy means having an easier time working with it.

THE REASON FOR PRACTICING YOGA IS THE SAME AS FOR MANIFESTATION

Last but not least, there is only one reason anyone does yoga or wants to manifest something in life: they want to be better off than before. You commit to a yoga practice because you believe you'll feel better with it, and the same belief is usually behind anything you want to bring into your life consciously. In the book *Ask and It Is Given*, Esther and Jerry Hicks discuss the concept that people desire things because they believe having those things will make them feel better. It's easy to look at manifestation as a separate vehicle for material improvement and yoga as a tool for physical and mental health, while they share the same root desire for greater overall well-being.

In Buddhism, the eightfold path, which is a guide toward enlightenment and happiness, emphasizes the importance of compassion and mindfulness. One specific practice that combines both is a meditation on the true motivations behind people's actions. The underlying insight is that every action, even those that cause pain, is driven by the fundamental desire for happiness. When we understand that all anyone really wants is to feel better, it's easier to find common ground for acceptance and forgiveness. Ultimately, this Buddhist practice wants to unite people by showing them that they all share the same root desire, and it certainly helps us to unite the concepts of yoga and manifestation on the same basis.

MANIFESTATION & EVOLUTION

As we've seen the interconnectedness of manifestation and the desire to feel better and be better, it's natural to wonder about the relationship between manifestation and evolution. Manifestation and evolution both describe a part of a process or development, but each describes a different point in the process. While we often understand manifestation as the reaching of a destination, the end of a journey, we think of evolution as an ongoing process toward ever higher and newer heights. Are they really completely separate, or do they overlap? Could manifestation be involved in any step of evolution, and is there evolution in manifestation? Depending on the answers, our definition of evolution can either strengthen or weaken the effectiveness of our manifestation efforts.

Our idea of evolution is still very much shaped by the teachings of Charles Darwin, who says that species develop into different versions of themselves solely because of genetic mutations, accidents of nature, or changes in environments — a sort of genetic gamble that either results in an upgrade or a downgrade of the previous version of the species. An upgrade is a version better adapted to the environment than before, and a downgrade means the species is falling behind in the world, procreating with less success, and might disappear altogether. For example, a lizard might have, through a genetic accident, developed feathers on its limbs that enabled it to fly. Suddenly, the lizard-bird could fly to places that it couldn't reach before, like trees and high rocks, and now it prospers because there's more food and safety in these places. Other lizards might not have adapted to changing environments and become extinct like dinosaurs.

These theories always include eating and mating as major variables, but never consciousness. In that view, evolution is usually something that happens to the creature, something done by a literal force of nature. For example, wings showed up on a lizard out of nowhere but somehow had the right shape and stability to support flying, which led to better food and more productive sex. An ancestor of a giraffe grew a long neck, and suddenly the animal could reach higher-growing leaves, which became an advantage for the species and helped it survive. The conventional evolution story never goes like this: the giraffe's ancestor wanted to reach the higher leaves, so it decided to grow a longer neck. We are left to believe that each creature in its current form is just a sum of accidents of growth, advantageous mutations, and winners of genetic lotteries with combinations of traits that somehow worked out. What about consciousness and desire as factors?

Darwin's interpretations of evolution lack consciousness and desire, so let's incorporate these elements going forward. Let's look at our lizard friends some more and speculate that all the lizards in that place had been seeing the same fruits in the same tall trees for generations, and for as long as they lived there, all of them had been wanting and dreaming about somehow getting up there.

They also saw other creatures buzzing through the air, maybe butterflies and other insects, and that *inspired* our lizards. Not only did they want the fruits, they also wanted what made other creatures fly to get to the fruit, and they started seeing themselves do what the flying creatures did, and little by little they started growing wings. First, single feathers, and with that encouragement, more grew over the next generations as the lizards carried and fed the dream. Who can say that this is not how it happened? Anyone who owns a pet knows that animals have desires. Why would their desires and minds not interact with the universe and make their wishes come true?

Spiritual teacher Ram Dass must have considered the process of evolution in species similarly imbued with desire when he experienced the following mental episode, which he describes in his lecture "Fear and Journey of Awakening." The story is about an LSD high he had while sitting in the audience of a ballet performance with Rudolf Nureyev as part of an opening ceremony for the Lincoln Center in New York City in 1974. He says this: "When Yurief was dancing and we sat in the loges looking down and I took some LSD, and what it all turned into was this species of bird that kept leaping up and falling and leaping up and falling, and I thought, Just a few more evolutionary rounds and it'll make it."[52] What he saw in the dancing was the staged story of human evolution, an expression of animism, spirit driving organic development: here, pretending to be something that you want to be, in this case a bird that can fly, with desire as the fuel that keeps the momentum going. This example is wonderful on many levels, certainly as an odd and refreshing interpretation of ballet, but also because Ram Dass saw in the dance a representation of an incident of evolution that included desire and will.

I cannot prove that conscious manifestation has ever been part of evolution for non-human species, and as far as I know, no related studies exist, but the element of consciousness is considered more and more in Western science, especially quantum science, and I think there is a good chance that it will be integrated in future studies of evolution. Until then, I certainly know that my own inspirations — like a lizard seeing a bird fly — fuel my desires and speed up my manifestations. With that, I can take the liberty of believing that conscious manifestation can very well be an integral part of species' evolution, just like Darwin took the liberty

52 Ram Dass, "Fear and Journey of Awakening," 1991, lecture, https://www.ramdass.org/ram-dass-now-ep-123-fear-journey-awakening/#more-18850.

to explain evolution without the element of consciousness. At the same time, I argue that manifestation is not necessarily a linear process, like the evolution of a species, but has a very different trajectory. This, too, requires a different belief, which I offer you in the following paragraphs.

If you think of manifestation as a process that needs time, the results will match your beliefs and take longer. For the feeling that what you wish is already here, you don't need time in the mix. When you imagine that the desired reality is already here, no time needs to pass. On the other hand, traveling to your new reality is, therefore, a misleading metaphor. It implies that, on the way, you don't have the wish fulfilled yet.

Instead, think of a manifestation as the varying degrees of solidity in reality — the process of materializing something, like an image on a Polaroid becoming clearer as the shapes and colors become more opaque. A great metaphor can be found in science fiction: the beaming of people or objects to other places, like when a character in Star Trek is beaming from the deck to another planet or back. Before the person is completely there, we see varying degrees of the person's physical solidity. First, we see them as a shape of mist, then thicker mist, and eventually the person in their full form and opacity. So, for clearer and faster results, think of your manifestation as beaming your imagined reality into the present reality, and your job is to pull the switch so steadily and thoroughly that the new reality takes on its solid shapes and colors in mere moments.

CHAPTER 6
MATCH YOGA AND MANIFESTATION TERMS

A TRANSLATION MANUAL

Earlier in the book, we delved into Patanjali Sutras on manifestation. You might be familiar with the eight limbs of yoga outlined in Patanjali's writings. These guidelines serve as the foundation for yogic consciousness, and practitioners work to incorporate them into their daily lives. In this chapter, I aim to show that these principles can also serve as guidelines for successful conscious manifestation. The following is a list of the eight limbs, along with brief descriptions and translations for manifestation. If you didn't know the eight limbs before, you'll learn the basics here. The goal is not just to translate yogic concepts into the language of manifestation but to illustrate that each essential yogic concept finds its suitable counterpart and application in manifestation practices. It answers the question: What are the specific benefits of the yoga limbs when I participate in the creation of reality for myself and beyond? Later chapters address some of these limbs with specific practices.

THE EIGHT LIMBS OF YOGA SPEAK MANIFESTATION

SAMADHI

Definition: Awakening and absorption in the spirit are the ultimate goals of yoga, and *samadhi* describes the stage where a person's sense of self merges with the universal consciousness. It is a sense of being formless, boundless, and part of the entire universe. It can also be called the dissolution of the ego and is often accompanied by feelings of joy and tranquility.

Applied to Manifestation: The absorption in spirit and the absolute identification with infinite creative consciousness imply not only the being but also the doing. If you are it, you can act like it, and that means taking part in the creation of absolutely everything in the universe. It's the realization of your powers that comes from being fully integrated into the creative mechanics of the universe.

DHYANA

Definition: A state of deep meditative concentration with a mind still and focused on an object such as your breath, a thought, or a visual image, without engaging in distractions like unrelated thoughts and sensations. *Dhyana* can lead to a deeper understanding of the object of focus, your own connection with it, and your own nature as consciousness. According to the Yoga Sutras of Patanjali, "*Dhyana* is the continuous flow of cognition toward that object."[53]

Applied to Manifestation: a deep, skillful focus of your mind on the object of concentration, with the imagined fulfilled desire as the object of your focus. When you're free from distractions, you can clearly envision and grasp the nature of your desired outcome. With full engagement of your mind's creative energy in conjuring the desired state or object, it moves into physical reality faster and with more precision. Concentration is equally useful in keeping the mind both in the present and engaged in overlaying the present moment with the reality of the desired object. Many exercises exist to develop your concentration (see chapter 12 with related practices).

PRATYAHARA

Definition: A redirection of your mental energy and focus inward. You cut off stimuli so that your mind, emotions, and physical body can become present for greater inner stillness, clarity, and self-awareness. The Yoga Sutras of Patanjali offer this definition: "When the senses withdraw themselves from the objects and imitate, as it were, the nature of the mind stuff, this is *pratyahara*."[54]

Applied to Manifestation: Another way to isolate your focus on the desired

---

53 *The Yoga Sutras of Patanjali*, sutra 1.2 (Ashland: Integral Yoga Publications, 2002).

54 *The Yoga Sutras of Patanjali*, sutra 2.54.

state and to crystalize its qualities and attributes. Without distractions and interruptions, the fulfilled desire remains completely steeped in your imagination and receives greater doses of mind energy to manifest faster on the physical plane.

PRANAYAMA

Definition: Control of the life force *praana* through breath control techniques. Patanjali says: "That [firm posture] being acquired, the movements of inhalation and exhalation should be controlled. This is *pranayama*."[55] Effects include greater physical health, greater calmness, reduced anxiety and stress, stronger focus, and mental clarity. In yogic science, *praana* is the force that animates everything, the energetic fuel not only in motor functions but in all movements in the universe. *Praana* is also behind the concept of breath of life.

Applied to Manifestation: By integrating controlled breath into manifestation techniques, you direct the breath of life to the fulfillment of your desire. For example, you visualize a situation that you want to manifest and add the detail of breath in all creatures involved, then let them breathe and be animated with *praana* in your mind's eye. The following passage from the Bible describes not only an action by God but the everyday activity of animating your own life: "God created Adam from the dust of the earth and breathed into his nostrils the breath of life, and man became a living being."56 This passage makes sense for your own life only if you see yourself as the creator of life situations who directs the life-giving force in manifestation projects for yourself and others, not like a Dr. Frankenstein character who animates a monster.

ASANA

Definition: The practice of physical postures for the cultivation of greater well-being in the body, mind, and spirit. Certain physical postures also direct *praana* in different ways. It's important to note that asana not only refers to the physical

---

55 *The Yoga Sutras of Patanjali*, Sutra 2.49.

56 Genesis 2:7

aspects but also to the concept of a container for a more conscious inner life. For example, when you put yourself in a new position, a specific yoga asana, your focus on the sensations in your body, the changes in the flow of energy, and the way you feel can bring greater self-awareness, understanding, and comfort with your own body and all related systems. Patanjali describes it as "a steady, comfortable posture."[57]

Ultimately, asana in traditional yoga is the physical preparation for a liberated state for thoughts and actions aligned with universal consciousness. This is often overlooked in the West, where much of the physical practice labeled yoga still focuses mostly on becoming fit and flexible.

Applied to Manifestation: The effects of asana can greatly enhance manifestation by improving mental and spiritual activities. This statement will be understandable to anyone who has entered a deep and satisfying meditation after a good physical yoga set. Asana is an excellent preparation for conscious manifestation, and the difference in mental clarity and focus is like day and night. This book contains several examples of great physical preparations for better manifestation.

The final two limbs of yoga, *Yamas* and *Niyamas*, are divided into five sub-aspects.

Yamas

Yamas is one of the last two limbs of yoga and along with *Niyamas*, it comprises five sub-aspects. *Yamas* refers to five restraints — that is, what not to do to obstruct your path to yogic union and effective manifestation. They are the following:

· AHIMSA
   Definition: Do not hurt others; use no violence or harmfulness in your actions, words, or thoughts out of respect for all living beings and to avoid suffering and harm. Instead, cultivate kindness and compassion in all interactions with all living beings.

---

57 *The Yoga Sutras of Patanjali*, sutra 2.46 (Ashland: Integral Yoga Publications, 2002).

Applied to Manifestation: Do not use your universal connection and powers of manifestation to create negative situations for others, including harm, disadvantages, or losses. Let the basis of your desire not be envy, competition, or ill will. And for your relationship with yourself, keep your inner space free of conflict and resistance so that manifestation can arrive. Any form of self-criticism, doubt, and negative thinking about yourself and your manifestation goals will slow down or prevent their arrival.

- SATYA
  Definition: The practice of aligning yourself and all your processes with honesty and truthfulness. Be authentic and truthful in your actions, thoughts, and words, and do not lie or deceive yourself or others.

  Applied to Manifestation: State your desire unequivocally, especially to yourself. Investigate the origin of the desire and its consequences before you manifest towards its fulfillment. Are you sure that you aligned your intentions with who you are and with all other ethical guidelines in your yogic practice? Also, be aware and reject desires that are not genuinely yours or influenced by others who want you to deliver something for their own benefit.

- ASTEYA
  Definition: Don't steal or cheat and don't take advantage of others. This includes keeping healthy boundaries. Instead, cultivate a sense of contentment and gratitude for what you already have.

  Applied to Manifestation: Create your own reality as opposed to desiring what belongs to others. Be inspired by others, but don't try to recreate their lives and possessions.

- BRAHMACHARYA
  Definition: The practice of moderation and self-restraint in all aspects of life to maintain space and alignment with your spiritual goals and ethics.

  Applied to Manifestation: This call to moderation is an invitation to check your greed and capacity for ownership. Are you desiring something because you genuinely want it or because you have the common habit of always wanting more? Make sure you really have space in your life for what you want to manifest. Can you maintain a sense of grace and spaciousness when the desired manifestation arrives, or will it clutter up your life and overwhelm you?

· APARIGRAHA
Definition: The yogic concept of letting go of attachment to material possessions for the benefit of contentment and simplicity in your life. By not overloading any process and avoiding excess and greed, you can stay pure, clear, and focused.

Applied to Manifestation: Greed and excess dilute the grace of your manifesting powers. Do you really need what you want to manifest? Is there a competitive element in your desire to have something? When you manifest from a heart free of one-upmanship, entitlement, or ego needs, the process and manifestation remain pure and graceful.

Niyamas

Niyamas is the last limb of yoga, and, along with *Yamas*, it comprises five sub-aspects. It refers to five spiritual to-dos for success and advancement on your path. They are the following:

· SHAUCHA
Definition: The practice of good hygiene and cleanliness in all aspects of your life. This includes an evenness of mind, thought, speech, and the purity of your body.

Applied to Manifestation: A clean and uncluttered mental space is as good for your manifestation as it is for your mental health, and both go together. Also, your manifestation powers will grow the greater the level of purity in your thoughts, beliefs, and projection of your fulfilled desire. Moreover, a clean diet will purify your mind and all its functions for manifestation.

· SANTHOSHA
Definition: Gratitude, acceptance, and calmness with success or failure.

Applied to Manifestation: The key to good manifestation is the projection of circumstances equal to those of the wish fulfilled. Gratitude for and acceptance of the realness of the manifestation even in its physical absence and before its arrival are great ingredients for both faster manifestation and for feeling good throughout the entire process.

- JAPA
  Definition: Purification, zeal, determination, and willingness for practices.

  Applied to Manifestation: A general sense of enthusiasm paves the way for positive emotions, which then allow manifestations to flow in. A willingness to practice also gives you the endurance and grit to perpetuate your vision and hold your projection until it becomes physical reality.

- SVADHYAYA
  Definition: Study yogic teachings, reflection, meditation, and the expansion of your knowledge.

  Applied to Manifestation: The study and understanding of both yoga and manifestation teachings and processes will give you a stronger mental foundation through positive thoughts, beliefs, and attitudes. This makes it easier for you to expand your visions in your imagination and to elaborate on details, effects, and benefits, which will speed up the manifestation process.

- ISHVARA PRANIDHANA
  Definition: Faith, dedication, devotion, surrender to infinity, and trust in the universe.

  Applied to Manifestation: Your faith in the arrival of the manifestation is unshakeable, as is your faith in your own manifesting powers, even when you don't know every detail of the process, as the infinite universe puts it all together for you. Trust, instead of doubt and impatience, will speed up manifestations and make you feel good from beginning to end.

KARMA EXPLAINED THROUGH THE LENS OF MANIFESTATION

Understanding karma can be challenging, but seeing it through the lens of manifestation can make more sense. Karma is often portrayed as a cosmic system in which our actions set off a series of consequences, but the system is obscure, and the consequences are usually a mystery and not subject to simple logic. For example, if I steal something and create karma, what will it look like when it comes back to me? Will it be in the form of someone stealing from me in the future? Or maybe I'll lose a hand in an accident or will never again be successful in business. Not just the how but the when is a mystery as well. Will I have to deal with the consequences of my actions in this lifetime or in another? It seems that the karmic model is full of surprises from an unpredictable universe that operates on its own schedule. Some believe there is a logical system and highly evolved individuals can decipher these connections between cause and effect, but for most of us, the reasons behind life events and their karmic origins remain unclear.

Manifestation suggests that our thoughts shape our reality, and this, too, can create a loop similar to a cycle of karma. For instance, if someone holds the belief that every person in their life will leave them eventually, the universe might reflect this belief by bringing about situations where relationships end and the person feels abandoned. This reinforces the belief and creates a cycle, leading to more similar manifestations.

In the manifestation example, the correlation is much easier to decipher. Someone who feels abandoned all the time could get clarity and break the negative patterns by deeply meditating on their own behavior, getting an analysis in a good therapy session, or talking with a friend. If the same person wanted to explain a string of abandonments with karma, there could never be complete clarity. Who can say with certainty that an event in someone's life is the karmic result of a specific action in this or a past lifetime? Looking for truly helpful answers in the karmic systems can be a fool's errand. On the other hand, if everything in your life can be explained with related mind activity in your current lifetime, an analysis of life events through the lens of manifestation mechanics can provide much more helpful and plausible answers. This can be better explained through the beliefs we hold and the effects they have in our lives, as in the example about abandonment I just gave above. In the next chapter, we will explore this theme and align our beliefs with what we want to manifest in our lives.

TABLE OF PITFALLS & HOW YOGA HELPS

Now that we've come this far in our understanding of the different aspects of manifestation, it's important to know what hinders manifestation. They are mostly internal processes that are in opposition to the mind activities we've discussed before. I list most of them here, and seeing so many might be daunting to you, as though the path to manifestation is filled with countless obstacles. But no worries; most of these are related and fall under the general category "resistance to your own power," and we address everything in this book well beyond this section. Think of this section as your download center for upgrades on your old and slow mental concepts.

As always, consciousness is your friend, and the more conscious you become about the pitfalls, the less likely you'll include any of these ingredients in your manifestation recipes. Much of the book, especially the specific yogic techniques, is all about removing resistance to optimize your manifestation powers. To make this more obvious, all pitfalls are listed with possible solutions and corresponding techniques.

When you study these, I want you to do the following: Notice how the pitfalls in manifestation are often pitfalls for many other endeavors in life that might not bring you the success you had hoped for, and notice how the solutions might be solutions for these other situations as well. So for a moment here, I would like to remind you how beneficial yoga can be for anything in your life that you want to bring success to.

PITFALLS	HOW YOGA HELPS
Doubts from lack of faith and gaps in understanding	**New consciousness about duality, oneness, the experience of creativity and connection**
Not believing that your imagination and feelings are enough for the entire process; thinking that something else needs to happen.	Beliefs that are rooted in a worldview of hierarchy and power based on status. Yoga focuses on your own agency and the completeness of your own powers.
The belief that that which you imagine is not already existing but needs to be built over time.	More ease with living in the spiritual realm, the fourth dimension — study and practice.
The belief that the past matters, that you first have to clean up what came before, and that you have to earn the manifestation.	Living in the present moment and the practice of disconnecting from the past and future.
Holding on to the belief that hard work must be involved.	Acceptance of blessings, feeling of worthiness, self-acceptance, self-love, and sense of being complete as you are — and all related practices.
Dealing with contradictions and unresolved gaps in intellect. Internalizing polarity and contradictions. Example: Wanting to be rich but being triggered when you see something you assume a wealthy person does. Or wanting to be more conscious but being triggered by a spiritual person who describes something to you as "hippyish."	Yogic teachings about polarity and oneness. See Meditation Eliminating Inner Conflict (page 116).
Not truly accepting infinity; not surrendering to infinity.	Experiencing infinity — all related yoga.
Believing in good and bad as opposed to a neutral universe.	Cultivating the neutral mind; developing the ability to see things neutrally, just like the universe does.
Not taking the imagination seriously. Maintaining a space between yourself and your imagination.	Experience of meditations based on visualization gives you an understanding of the power of imagination.

Not recognizing that thoughts with emotions create, including joy but also anger and hatred. Hence, another pitfall is not keeping your mind clear from those thoughts that create negativity.	New consciousness about the consequences of your thoughts and emotions.
Creating beliefs from what you observe on the outside, instead of creating beliefs that serve you (you must ignore conditions you see on the outside).	A worldview shaped mostly from experience.
The belief that desire is a problem.	Happiness is your birthright. Desire is the fuel, a gift, as is your imagination.

PITFALLS RELATED TO TECHNIQUE	IMPROVED SKILLS THROUGH YOGA TECHNIQUES
Lack of endurance.	Endurance through regular yoga, including the practice of asanas and kriyas.
Not observing your thoughts.	Qualifying your thoughts.
Lack of focus.	Meditation, Tratakum.
Not actually doing the visualization (e.g., teaching or talking about it, but not practicing oneself). Not repeating the visions. Not doing daily practice.	Become familiar with the concept of sadhana. Make manifestation part of your daily practice.
Lack of imagination; flat imagination.	Specific yoga practice to bring out creativity and intuition and strengthen the third eye.
Weak projection.	Navel work, sixth chakra.
Little experience with neutrality and calmness.	All related yoga practices.
Lack of repetition.	Repetition is key in mantras, meditation, and pranayama.

October 24, 2000

Sit in Easy Pose with a straight spine and a light Neck Lock.

Mudra: Interlace the fingers in Venus lock and place the hands in front of the Solar Plexus with the palms facing the body.

Eye Focus: Closed.

Breath: Not specified.

Mantra: Chant HUMEE HUM BRAHM HUM (The recording by Nirinjan Kaur was played in the original class.)

To End: Inhale deeply, suspend the breath for 15 seconds, and exhale. Repeat 2 more times.

Comments: Listen to the mantra and meditate on the meaning of the words: "We are We, We are God." When you understand this mantra, inner conflict is eliminated.

You are directly dealing with your toxins and your poisons in the body.

◊

PART 3 **YOGIC ENHANCEMENTS TO UNLOCK YOUR MANIFESTATION POWERS**

CHAPTER 7

Yogic Enhancement #1:

Aligning Your Beliefs

We've established that in the yogic worldview, everything is consciousness, and manifestations are what we humans, with our innate ability to create, have made out of consciousness. We turn consciousness into matter through our mind activity and the manipulation of the formless into form. Then, these manifestations will exist as long as we supply them with power. The particular forms in your life and the particular forms of your own being match your beliefs about them. When you change a belief, a change in manifestation follows. A belief is the concentrated power of attention that gives fuel so that forms remain in existence, which is why it is crucial to examine what you believe and to change beliefs accordingly if what they produce is not what you desire.

In this chapter, we'll take the recurring theme of "what you believe makes your reality" and take a logical step forward towards better manifestation by being selective about our beliefs. More specifically, I invite you to make the decision to believe in essential yogic teachings. For successful manifestation, as for a successful yoga practice that gets you to your desired state, a certain set of beliefs brings better results. Additionally, you'll feel better overall with optimistic and realistic beliefs standing brightly and humming cheerfully in the background of your mental landscape. Here are the fundamental beliefs I want you to accept. I will introduce more later, but let's start with these:

- » You are the creator.
- » Everything is consciousness.
- » Your true nature is consciousness.
- » You are one with everything.
- » Working long and hard is not the only path to your goals.
- » Joy is your natural state.

You might say, "Let me protest before you go on about these statements, because accepting beliefs from others is exactly the thing I want to get away from. One reason I chose yoga as a spiritual practice is because I don't feel a constricting doctrine like I do with religion, and I don't want to swap one for another. Moreover, I can't just change my beliefs. They define who I am." To that, I say: "You are confusing dogma with a freely chosen belief and a habitual concept of yourself with a consciously chosen identity. I am asking you to choose new beliefs about who you are and what you can do in order to liberate yourself from a mental prison and get the results you want. You don't have much to lose, and when the desired results start coming, or not, you can qualify your beliefs with your experience. You then get to choose again whether you keep the beliefs or adjust them to get different results. It really is that simple and unshackled."

IS FAITH TEACHABLE? OR: HOW TO BELIEVE

If you had asked this question to my younger self, who spent years going to church feeling no affirmation of its teaching and finding no way to validate what I was hearing, I would have said no. Moreover, when my own spiritual awakening happened — when I moved from not believing in a higher power to clearly feeling it — I felt it was a gift, an act of grace that had nothing to do with learning or intellect; it just happened. My conclusion from that experience was that a belief in a higher power is a gift that you either receive or don't receive in your lifetime. However, that belief has changed as I learned more about our natural ability to manifest. Consciousness becomes and is what you believe it to be, and this process begins and continues with your belief.

> "Stop looking for signs. Signs follow; they do not precede. Begin to reverse the statement 'Seeing is believing' to 'Believing is seeing.' Start now to believe, not with the wavering confidence based on deceptive external evidence but with an undaunted confidence based on the immutable law that you can be that which you desire to be. You will find that you are not a victim of fate but a victim of faith (your own). " – Neville Goddard[58]

What I am suggesting to you is the concept of Deliberate Personalized Faith (DPF) for empowered manifestation. This means flexibility at the level of belief, willful believing, and a chosen certitude for practical reasons. It requires a flexible mind, and this is again something that often comes easier to yogis. Ask

---

58 Neville Goddard, *Your Faith Is Your Fortune* (self-pub., Lulu Press, Inc., 2012), 14.

anyone who has practiced physical yoga and gained muscular flexibility. There's a good chance that they also experience greater flexibility of the mind — wider perspectives, new tolerance, more patience, and refreshing changes of the mind. That, of course, is one reason why we find yoga relaxing and why you'll find it easy to let go of everything at the end of a yoga session after you have stretched your body and softened your mind.

But when it comes to changing your beliefs, I totally get that you have reservations. Believing something is serious business in our society, especially in the context of religious faith. So let's look under the hood of the mechanisms of belief, and hopefully you'll get a new perspective. Ultimately, I want you to feel more relaxed about taking on a new set of beliefs.

> "Western psychology is based upon theory proved empirically by tests which have provided statistical data. Eastern psychology has as its fundamental basis personal, subjective experience. The Eastern student does not rationalize truth – he or she experiences it. It is an Eastern maxim that the student accepts nothing as true until he or she validates it by personal experience." – Swami Anandakapila Saraswati[59]

Belief entails accepting something as true, usually something that can be easily proven. Faith is similar to belief, but it goes beyond accepting something as true and often requires trust in something that cannot be easily proven. In manifestation, for example, you'll need faith that something will come into existence for which you have no physical proof yet other than your own feelings. Let's be clear: faith is not a recruitment in yoga and manifestation. Faith is a tool for entering a new state of being. The problem with faith is that the concept itself has become too charged because it is associated with religion, as faith is often synonymous with a set of beliefs specific to a religion, and accepting a particular ideology or creed can easily put you in a particular camp of the population. Identification with a group or becoming a card-carrying member of any group these days can lead to profound consequences. It is, in a nutshell, the foundation for the polarization in society that has been rampant these days.

---

59 Jonn Mumford, *A Chakra & Kundalini Workbook: Psycho-spiritual Techniques for Health, Rejuvenation, Psychic Powers, and Spiritual Realization* (Woodbury: Llewellyn Publications, 1994), 50.

Talk to someone about a belief that you have but they don't share yet, and they are likely to recoil. It is clear why they would: talking about a belief or faith in something carries the implication that the next step is acceptance of that concept. You can already hear the crusaders approaching on horses, ready to capture you and drag you into a new belief system. Moreover, embracing a new belief system would mean a load of new responsibilities: showing up regularly at a new gathering place (church, community), learning the body of teachings (literature, scriptures, lectures), dressing differently, no longer doing things you used to, and telling all your family and friends about it. It's no wonder you'll see arms crossed on people's chests when you open the subject. Additionally, asking "do you believe in manifestation?" is probably not a successful icebreaker in most encounters with strangers. You could have endless discussions about faith, but it's most likely a waste of time if you want someone to change their mind. Instead, deescalate faith. Take off its heavy religious coat and strip it down to the mundane everyday activity that it is and should be. Everyone is already using faith anyway, as they go through their day.

"A belief is a thought you keep thinking." – Esther Hicks[60]

FAITH + EXPERIENCE = MEASURE OF YOUR BELIEFS

There is a teaching in Kundalini Yoga that goes: "Is yoga a religion? It is and is not. In religion, you have to believe something, and in yoga, you have to experience what you want to believe."[61] It's certainly one to chew on, and please read the quote more than once if it feels wobbly. At least try to remember it or go back to it as we continue this discussion. I've always loved this quote because it shows the contrast between yoga and religion and relates to our discussion on fixed and fluid beliefs. Both yoga and religion offer beliefs.

In today's major religions, if you want to be part of one, it's sufficient to accept the beliefs given by that religion's clergy. As long as you don't question their rules, follow their procedures, and participate in the exoteric practice, if you will, you get to stay in the church and the community. If you rebel or break the rules, there

60 Esther Hicks and Jerry Hicks, *The Amazing Power of Deliberate Intent: Living the Art of Allowing* (Carlsbad: Hay House, 2007), 52.

61 Yogi Bhajan, "Kriya for Self-Renewal," in *Physical Wisdom* (Espanola: Kundalini Research Institute, 1994), 2.

will be consequences. However, the funny thing is that religions don't necessarily expect you to have a spiritual experience or feel better just by following their rules or practicing rituals. This is certainly true for Christianity, and in my years of participating in the Catholic Church, I have heard no authority say that it's unacceptable not to have a spiritual experience. Total flatness in your religious interior landscape is perfectly fine, it seems, and I agree with American author and scholar Tom Strelow, who writes, based on observations by Carl Jung, in his book on ancient psychology, Serpent in the Cellar, that "one of the main functions of organized religion is to protect people against a direct experience of the numen or god."62 My take is that this explains why you have millions of people sitting in church service bored and disconnected — the same regular experience I had in church as a child and teenager. Not once did I feel anything profound, but my experience was of no interest to anyone; it was no qualifier for my membership. Only my outward participation mattered, which consisted almost exclusively of sitting in church services in utter boredom. Membership in most main religions usually requires little more than showing up regularly and playing by the rules. As the quote says, "You have to believe something." Period.

Is yoga like that?, the quote asks. And answers: "It is, and it is not." It is like religion in the sense that it gives you a set of beliefs and rules. But then it inserts a qualifier right after, and that is your experience. Yoga wants to know: Now that you've tried believing our beliefs and practicing our rules, do you have an experience of spirit? And specifically, do you have the experience of what we presented to you as a possibility, an experience that confirms the belief we offered? The implication here is: If your experience doesn't match the blueprint of what we presented to you, you have every right to question our teachings, stop practicing, and leave our community honorably.

> "Over the millennia, Yoga has become associated with various philosophical and theological systems — none of which can be said to define Yoga itself. For Yoga is first and foremost a practical spiritual discipline that emphasizes personal experimentation and verification. In other words, direct personal experience or spiritual realization is considered senior to any theory or conceptual system. For this reason, Yoga can and, in fact, has been practiced by people with widely differing philosophies and beliefs." – Georg Feuerstein[63]

---

62 Tom Strelow, *Serpent in the Cellar: Love and Death in Life and Myth.* (N.p., Chrysalis Media, 2022), 79.

63 Georg Feuerstein, *The Deeper Dimension of Yoga: Theory and Practice* (Boston: Shambhala, 2003), 26.

What in yoga is an example of "an experience you want to believe?" Let's look at a practice for calmness or inner peace. This is a good example because many yoga traditions offer some form of meditation or pranayama for becoming calm and peaceful on the inside. Let's say you've never done this kind of meditation before, but you are curious, and your first step is your conscious choice to believe that it is possible to feel calmer by doing a specific meditation. That is the process of "wanting to believe." If you didn't trust that the meditation could deliver you calmness, there would be no point in sitting down and trying it.

So let's say you believe in the advertised outcome of the meditation. By the way, that's faith at the most basic level, believing that something will happen that hasn't happened yet. Now, with faith in the meditation and in what you've been told about it, you go ahead and do the meditation. And since it's your first time, you might feel something or not. Let's say you didn't. Then, depending on your level of faith, you might do the meditation a second time and a third, or maybe even for a period of 40 days, because you also believe that some tools just take longer to work. Eventually, however, you'll seriously have to ask yourself: Am I getting the return that I envisioned? The experience that justifies my energy investment in the meditation? Depending on your answer, you decide what to do next — either continue, stop, or try something different.

Eckhart Tolle says that "Even belief in God is only a poor substitute for the living reality of God manifesting every moment of your life."64 Think about it. The main point is that the decision is yours. You decide what you want to believe, and then you qualify it with your experience. You can have great guides and teachers, but ultimately, all that matters is your experience. If you ever encounter a yoga teacher who says you must do yoga and meditation under any circumstances, walk away.

Now, let's say you practice the meditation for calmness, you enter a state of calmness, and it's clear that the meditation works. That means you have qualified the practice for yourself. Your faith has led you to the desired result, and now you understand: faith can fuel a yoga practice, which in turn can fuel faith. And along the same lines, faith aids manifestation, and manifestation aids faith. The calmness at the end of the meditation is a result, which is another way of calling it

---

64 Eckhart Tolle, *A New Earth: Awakening to Your Life's Purpose* (New York: Penguin Publishing Group, 2008), 267.

a manifestation. And if you have faith in manifestation techniques and you get the results, your faith in the practice will grow. It's the same for yoga or manifestation, because the two are the same. That is what I mean by assumed belief for practical purposes. Or in other words, calculated faith.

> "Faith is feeling or living in the consciousness of being the thing desired; faith is the secret of creation" – Neville Goddard[65]

RELAX ABOUT FAITH – IT'S LIKE BUYING MILK

Faith is so adaptable that you can even use it for shopping. Let me explain: Until I became more conscious of the concept of faith and my relationship with it, I used to think of faith as something heavy-footed and always tied to religion. Faith meant believing in God as the church presents it, fixed and protected, like a madonna under glass in a museum. Yoga and manifestation taught me that faith is fluid, voluntary, and ever-changing. We change beliefs all the time. Almost every day you start believing something and stop believing something else, but it's often so subtle that we barely register a shift. A TV commercial can start a new belief, and a negative review that you read somewhere can kill another. It's as simple as that, and my feelings about faith changed over time, mostly gradually. However, there was one incident that caused a significant shift.

It must have been around 2005, shortly after what I can pinpoint as the start of my spiritual awakening. I was shopping around for spiritual places and communities and attended a lecture at a Buddhist center in New York City one night. I don't remember the speaker's name, but he was very articulate, and I enjoyed his clear teaching very much. At one point, he talked about the illusion of reality (*maya*) and that nothing is real but a sort of drama put on by the universe. This idea roiled one man in the audience, and he spoke up with an irritated tone. He said, "How can you expect me to put my faith in a teaching like that when I can touch and feel everything around me? I am obviously not having an illusion!"

The teacher reacted brilliantly by not trying to explain the nature of *maya* further but by addressing the man's inability to believe a new concept. He said to the man, "You

---

65 Neville Goddard, *Neville Goddard – The Complete Collection: The Reference Book by Neville Goddard with All Books, Radio Lectures and Lessons* (Germany: via tolino media, 2023), 99.

take faith too seriously. Faith is not such a serious thing." He continued: "You put faith in new things all the time without knowing it. When you go to the supermarket to buy milk, you have faith that milk will be on the shelf. When you go to work every day, you have faith that your employer will pay you at the end of the week."

His main point, of course, was that faith is a straightforward choice that can be deliberate and adjusted according to the circumstances and needs. Faith is something you can relax about; there is nothing ironclad that needs to be defended by an army. In the same way, you can adapt your beliefs around manifestation and all spiritual matters — as long as you qualify them with your experience eventually. It all starts with you: an intention, a plan in which you put faith. And it ends with you: the qualification by your experience and the subsequent acceptance or rejection of the premise. Neville Goddard said: "All longing should end with being." The reward of your faith should be your desired state of being, or else your liberation from an inept belief.

Are you still hesitant about empowering yourself and managing your beliefs independently? Maybe you can relax more when you learn that even the Dalai Lama adjusts his faith for better outcomes. Here's a story that illustrates it: Several years ago, the journalist and author Jonathan Landaw had the opportunity to meet privately with the Dalai Lama, and one topic of their discussion was a Tibetan master by the name of Tsongkhapa, who was also the teacher of the first Dalai Lama about 600 years ago and who has been revered by the entire line of Dalai Lamas since then, including the current. Landaw writes: "In general, Tibetans have great reverence for Tsongkhapa and think of him as a human manifestation of Manjushri, the bodhisattva of wisdom. But on this occasion, the Dalai Lama said, 'I prefer to think of Tsongkhapa as a regular human being who, through great effort, was able to complete the spiritual path in his lifetime. I find this way of thinking about him more inspiring than thinking that he was born already enlightened.'"[66]

You see, you are in good company when you allow yourself to use deliberate, personalized faith for more effective management of the world. Holding on to old and static beliefs is like turning your world into a museum and blocking the flow of creativity and life. If everything is subject to change, so are beliefs.

---

66 Jonathan Landaw and Stephan Bodian, Buddhism For Dummies (Hoboken: Wiley, 2011), 179.

APPLYING DELIBERATE BELIEFS TO SCRIPTURES

I want to add an example of choosing beliefs deliberately. This example refers to scripture and the idea that you can choose an interpretation of scripture. It includes two possible interpretations of a biblical text, so that you can try the before-and-after out for yourself. When working with scripture, let's not forget that most stories in it were written with the intention of making you think, with settings and characters as stand-ins for illustrating concepts. Not everyone agrees, and, of course, there are literalists in all religions and spiritual traditions who will tell you that everything in scripture actually happened and must be understood as exact historic events. But that's fine, and we'll actually use a juxtaposition here for more clarity. At the end, I will ask you to choose the interpretation that feels true in the purest sense of religion and that brings you closer to who you are.

The story is the well-known Bible story of Noah's Ark, and we'll start with the classic interpretation. The second, augmented interpretation comes from Neville Goddard. He takes the biblical event that many believe to be literal history (for instance, there have been countless efforts to locate the ark as an archaeological finding) and interprets it as a metaphor for manifestation, for the creative ability that lives in all of us. Please read the following lines and observe how you feel about the different interpretations of Noah's Ark.

Interpretation 1: Noah's Ark really happened. Noah built a ship because God told him to, because God planned to send a flood. God was disappointed in humankind, and the flood was God's attempt to wipe the slate clean and start the world over with a set of chosen creatures, a few humans and many animals, all sets of male and female, who could multiply once the flood was over and the Ark found new land. So He made Noah build the ark and fill it with a few pairs of humans as well as many species of animals. All other humans and creatures on Earth at that time drowned in the rising waters. The boat floated on an endless ocean for a long time, until one day they reached land after a dove from the boat had flown there and brought back a twig as confirmation. This interpretation implies that, technically, every human being alive now is a descendant of Noah's group of chosen ones.

Interpretation 2: In this version, Goddard makes the ark story a psychological one in which all characters and events become metaphors. The long trip on the ark and the search for land are really a journey of the imagination (water) with the purpose of manifesting a new life (reaching land) and arriving at an existence that is improved and graceful. The pairs of creatures are really ideas inside the human mind (boat) with the potential to grow out of their own accord (procreate like pairs of male and female) into new beings in a new reality (land). Neville lays it out:

> "The story of the flood is really being enacted today. Man is the ark containing within himself the male-female principles of every living thing. The dove or idea which is sent out to find dry land is man's attempt to embody his ideas. Man's ideas resemble birds in flight — like the dove in the story, returning to man without finding a place to rest."[67]

You see that everything in the story is symbolic of the psychological process of manifesting through desire from within the human consciousness. Now ask yourself: Which interpretation is more useful for your own well-being? The one that treats Noah's story as a historic event that leaves everything unprovable in a very distant past, or the version that resonates with processes in the minds of every human being? If you agree with the latter, why not believe that version? You will then have the support of scripture for your faith in your own manifestation power. I'd say that's an excellent influence for a better life. What can you do with the first version? Well, you can think of God as a vengeful ruler who wipes out all of humanity if it doesn't please him. That would certainly add more fear to your life, and you can think of yourself as a descendant of a chosen few, which is great fodder for your ego. You don't get confirmation of your own agency from the first version, but certainly from the second version. As always, the choice is yours

OLD BELIEFS VERSUS NEW BELIEFS

The discussion in this chapter so far and the struggle that many have with manifestation today reflect, like so much today, the battle between new and old beliefs, especially in science. The old and new beliefs currently battling with each other are beautifully summarized in Lynne McTaggart's book The Field, a book dedicated to modern science that shows the ancient belief that humans are not separate but connected to their environment through constant engagement and communication:

---

67 Neville Goddard, *Neville Goddard - The Complete Collection: The Reference Book by Neville Goddard with All Books, Radio Lectures and Lessons* (self-pub., Tolino Media, 2023), 63.

Old beliefs:

» The human being is a survival machine largely powered by chemicals and genetic coding.
» The brain is a discrete organ and the home of consciousness, which is also largely driven by chemistry, the communication of cells, and the coding of DNA.
» Man is essentially isolated from his world, and his mind is isolated from his body.
» Time and space are finite, universal orders.
» Nothing travels faster than the speed of light.

New beliefs:

» The communication of the world did not occur in the visible realm of Newton but in the subatomic world of Werner Heisenberg.
» Cells and DNA communicate through frequencies.
» The brain perceives and makes its own record of the world in pulsating waves.
» A substructure underpins the universe, which is essentially a recording medium of everything, providing a means for everything to communicate with everything else.
» People are indivisible from their own environment. Living consciousness is not an isolated entity. It increases order in the rest of the world. The consciousness of human beings has incredible powers to heal ourselves, to heal the world, in a sense, to make it as we wish it to be.[68]

There is a scientific equivalent for virtually every concept we are working with in the context of manifestation. Yet, the mere existence of these facts does little if they don't reach humans on the level of belief. We often think that presenting facts makes people change their minds and puts them on a new track, but internalizing a new belief takes more than a verbal transmission. We'll talk more about techniques to help people develop new and more beneficial beliefs for everything, including manifestation, but a good start is to relax about your beliefs and not take yourself so seriously. Here's one more quote by a true yoga scholar and expert:

---

68 Lynne McTaggart, *The Field: The Quest for the Secret Force of the Universe* (New York City: HarperCollins, 2009), 215.

"At the heart of all forms of Yoga is the assumption that we have not yet tapped into our full potential as human beings. [...] Rather than being expected to believe in any of the traditional explanations, we are free to allow our personal experience and realization to shape our understanding." – Georg Feuerstein[69]

69 Georg Feuerstein, *The Deeper Dimension of Yoga: Theory and Practice* (Boston: Shambhala, 2003), 25.

KRI KUNDALINI RESEARCH INSTITUTE

CHAPTER 8

YOGIC ENHANCEMENT #2:

TARGETED BELIEFS FOR BETTER RESULTS

HOW TO BELIEVE YOU ARE THE CREATOR

According to yoga philosophy, you are the Creator, the same as the power that creates the universe. There's a logic to it if you see it from a yogic perspective: You are connected to everything; everything is creative consciousness; hence, you must be the same consciousness and have the same powers. It's an identity that's offered to you as an explanation of your true nature, and yoga wants you to experience it and accept it because it's a true game changer for your consciousness and life experience. But can you? Many people feel resistance to declaring to themselves and others that they are godlike in their powers. That's understandable, and we'll look at some reasons in this chapter and try to translate the idea that a person is equal to God into words that sound plausible and not deluded and off-putting.

This idea can work if you think of God as everything equal to the universe, its own all-encompassing field. If Gaia is the Earth defined as one interconnected organism, then God is the Gaia version of the entire universe — all just one cohesive organism that has another organism living inside of it. This is not far-fetched. Just look at the emerging science of microbiology, or specifically Human Microbiome Science, which explores the composition of the human body as not just one closed system of human parts but as a complex system of microorganisms, thousands and thousands of them.

Every element in this God-field, including you, the Earth, and all seemingly separate entities, plays a similar essential role. They all generate energy into form, organize forms into infinite permutations, and destroy forms back into energy. This is certainly what all humans do all the time: generate, organize, and destroy (now shorten this into G.O.D., a clever acronym from Kundalini Yoga teachings). Our human actions reflect those of the universe. Why? Because we're one. Can you feel yourself getting closer to the idea that God and you are one? Even modern science is moving more and more toward the acceptance of an all-connected, one-field concept of the world.

Again, you are the creator. We'll repeat this statement often during our yoga practice, and that's fine, because repetition is the foundation of any good practice for the growth of our consciousness. Context also matters. If you said "I am the creator" in reference to the production of a TV show, designer clothing line, or any other highly visible commercial endeavor, most people could accept this easily. However, if you say it in any spiritual or religious context, the flavor of grandeur comes into the mix.

Still, you are God is a true statement in yoga. Not just in yoga. It is exactly what all religions tell you again and again through the examples of their main representatives. All of the figures in the world's major religions — Buddha in Buddhism, Muhammad in Islam, Moses in Judaism, and Jesus in Christianity — were real people, not gods, and the main reason for the existence of each religion is that these regular people have found a way to oneness and codified the way towards it into their teachings to help others get there as well. Each religion is basically a message to every regular person like you and me: You possess the same creative potential as the revered characters in scriptures. You, too, can accomplish extraordinary feats and embody godlike qualities. Even Shiva in Hinduism appears frequently as a human being in these stories to drive that message home to other humans. And in Buddhism, the concept known as Buddha Nature says that every sentient being has qualities similar to those of the Buddha and the potential to become enlightened.

For effective manifestation, it is essential that you understand and believe in your fundamental creative powers, which are exactly like those of the universe or God, and by the end of this chapter, I want you to believe it with your whole being. I know it's hard to accept and internalize, but nothing is more hindering to manifestation than doubt, so let's look at the reasons for doubt a bit more, and hopefully we can annihilate it. Alan Watts gives us a great explanation for the prevalent doubt in us about our true nature as creators and why, in this culture and history, "I am God" is something you don't say.

> "Saying anything along the lines of "I am God" has become blasphemy in the Western world influenced by Christianity and Judaism (although it is the opposite for Eastern religions like Hinduism and Buddhism), even though Jesus himself said, "I am a Son of God," when he spoke for all humans on earth. What he meant was that everyone is, but that his original words have

been edited, first into "I am the Son of God," changing the meaning completely by conferring the status upon him only and taking it away from the rest of humanity." – Alan Watts[70]

Western society places God outside of the human being, and there is a clear line between God and the human. Jesus himself was crucified for saying that he was the son of God, and the crucifixion is certainly one religious event that sits deeply inside the fabric of Western culture and collective thinking. There's a good chance that you know exactly what it feels like — this collective resistance against saying that you are God. Try it and say, "I am God." Or this version, sometimes used in meditations: "God and me, me and God are one" (see meditation at the end of this chapter). If it's your first time, it surely feels weird. And if you, who I assume to be aware enough of your spiritual nature to read these lines, feel resistance, then just imagine the rest of the western world and beyond. Even yogis, consciously or not, might move away from anything that feels like heresy on the deepest level, and sometimes that includes manifestation.

One of the most popular pop culture teachings about manifestation is those by Abraham, said to be several conscious entities channeled by Esther Hicks. There are many books and hundreds of videos featuring Ms. Hicks, and their message can be boiled down to this sentence: "You are the creator of your own reality, and this is how." It comes out of Ms. Hicks' mouth again and again, and she has made it an art form to repeat the same thing a million different ways. Why is there a market for the exact same message packaged in countless ways? Because the eradication of this belief in ourselves has been so thorough and so radical that it takes endless repetitions of the message to reach the heart of a person who has lived without this truth for all their life and generations before that. Do you know the fable of the ugly duckling? He's really a baby swan that hatches in a nest of ducklings and grows up believing he's just an ugly, oversized yet inferior version of a duck until he grows up and finally accepts his true identity as that of a beautiful swan when he catches a reflection of his adult self. Spiritual teachings telling us we are God are like yelling at the baby bird: "You are a swan! You are a swan!" He sees us yelling, then looks at his reflection in the water, hangs his head, and waddles away in sadness. All of us are like that; we refuse to accept the glorious truth about ourselves.

---

70 Alan Watts, "On Being God," 2022, lecture, https://www.youtube.com/watch?v=sZ4lzgWHs_I.

Nevertheless, every teaching on manifestation underscores the veracity of this statement. Like all genuine spiritual teachings, they are diamonds strewn upon a beach, easily ignored by those of us who do not yet have the self-trust and assurance necessary to know their own essence and the liberation that comes from that knowledge.

"To know that you are God is another way of saying that you feel complete with this universe. You feel profoundly rooted in it and connected with it. You feel, in other words, that the whole energy, which expresses itself in the galaxies, is intimate. It is not something to which you are a stranger but it is that with which you — whatever that is — are intimately bound up. That in your seeing, your hearing, your talking, your thinking, your moving, you express that which it is, which moves the sun and other stars. And if you don't know that (you are God), if you don't feel that, well, naturally you feel alien; you feel a stranger in the world. And if you feel like a stranger, you feel hostile. And therefore you start to bulldoze things about, to bite it up, and to try and make the world submit to your will and you become a real troublemaker."
– Alan Watts[71]

Here's one way to help you accept the truth about you and God being one — by simply stating it as a fact. For that, I invite you to do the following meditation.

71 Akṣapāda, *Tao of Alan Watts: 444 Expressions of Zen* (n.p.: self-published), 34.

Sit in Easy Pose with a straight spine and apply a light Neck Lock.

Mudra: Place your hands in Gyan Mudra by touching the thumb tips and the tips of index fingers and keeping the other fingers straight. With the hands in this position, cross the right hand over the left at the Heart Center, but do not touch the chest. The right palm is against the back of the left hand.

Eye Focus: Closed.

Mantra: God and Me, Me and God, Are One

Time: 11-31 minutes.

To End: Inhale, suspend the breath, exhale, release the mudra, and relax.

◇

HOW TO BELIEVE YOU ARE CONSCIOUSNESS

If everything is consciousness, so are you. The yogic notion that your true nature is consciousness is captured in a phrase that is often heard in yogic circles and can blow people's minds when they hear it for the first time: "I am not a human having a spiritual experience; I am a spirit having a human experience." I've often shared this expression in class, and it evokes a playful sense of intrigue among students, like trying on a wild new outfit and enjoying how well it fits.

Still, grasping this idea or accepting it as truth is not easy for most people. Most of us grew up building an identity that is entirely based on forms such as the physical body, our family and lineage, our background and social status, our education, our work, our stories, our hardships and successes, our friends and possessions, and so on. This is called an ego-based identity, with our ego being our self-image and the things we tell ourselves about ourselves. Defining our full identity as a physical being and its stories alone is a deeply rooted approach in the Western psyche, which makes changing it a formidable task. But here we are, telling ourselves and others basically this: "Stop thinking you are just made of flesh and bones and brain matter, and start thinking you are made of a substance called consciousness, which is the invisible essence of everything in the universe, and even scientists don't fully understand yet what it is."

Accepting that our true nature is a formless spirit is a stretch for anyone, but it's much more than just a way to become a better manifestor. Identifying as consciousness is the essence of yoga and one of the best things we can do for ourselves and others because it is a key to true happiness, as in living without fear. How does identifying as consciousness get rid of fear, you ask? Let's do a quick review of the origin of fear.

The root of all fear is the fear of death, and as long as you identify as a body and its stories, you know deep inside that all these parts are impermanent and will eventually die. You know your body will deteriorate and die; the same will happen to everyone you love; your job and career are only temporary; your money and possessions can disappear; and even your own feelings about anything can easily change. This knowledge may not always be on the surface, but it's active in the background because once we know that death can strike any of our perceived identities at any time, we can never really forget it. However, if you identify as consciousness or spirit, or, in other words, divine energy that, like all energy, cannot be destroyed but only changes form or vibration, the concept of death no longer applies. You know that your essence is timeless and deathless. I can say from my own experience that accepting this identity is a true game changer and helps me live a more fearless life. I still experience fear, but usually it happens when I forget who I really am. At the same time, I don't dismiss any part of my physical existence, because everything I experience still goes through my body, but I live in it with the awareness that there's another dimension to my being. By being in the body, I know that I am not just a body. Thich Nhat Hanh explains beautifully the relationship between consciousness and absence of fear when he says that "enlightenment for a wave is the moment the wave realizes it is water. At that moment, all fear of death disappears."[72]

---

72 Sreechinth C, *Thich Nhat Hanh Quotes* (n.p.: UB Tech, 2018), 121.

When you accept your own true nature as consciousness and also the nature of everything in the universe as consciousness, you realize that anything you create must also be a reflection of your essence, an extension of yourself. Now think of those aspects of your life that you already consider an extension of yourself: your favorite accomplishments, your children, your passions and greatest interests, and many more (often things we are proud of). Just as you effortlessly connect with these aspects of your life because they feel like integral parts of yourself, viewing absolutely everything as an extension of yourself makes the process of manifestation logical. When your sense of connection expands to encompass all things, you can also understand them as products of your own manifesting mind powers. Everything that shows up in your field of perception is connected to your mind and senses, and the way everything appears to you depend entirely on your mind and senses. If you can accept this truth, manifesting becomes natural and effortless.

HOW TO TALK TO SOMEONE ABOUT YOUR TRUE NATURE AS CONSCIOUSNESS

This section presents a framework for a dialogue aimed at awakening a person to their true nature as consciousness. It uses a concept that Neville Goddard discusses in his book *The Power of Awareness*: the "I AM" written in uppercase. In this context, "I Am" stands not merely as a phrase but as a substantial entity, a complete identity, the personification of consciousness that is both form and formless, tangible and intangible at the same time. This approach places the essence of "I AM" at the forefront and highlights its completeness rather than focusing on any words that follow.

Let's begin small by talking about how we usually identify ourselves. We usually identify ourselves by using labels related to the history and accomplishments that we think define us — labels that always come after an I AM. The list of labels often begins with gender, then origin, then our education, then our profession, and then we might move to adjectives (I am excited to be here, I am interested, hopeful, disappointed, a bit overwhelmed, in or out). Notice that most of these statements follow an "I am," and each statement creates an identity, a separate I AM. When you keep talking to a person about who they think they are, you end up with a collection of I-AMs. For two individuals, their collections might look something like this:

KRI KUNDALINI RESEARCH INSTITUTE

Carmen: I AM a mother, the daughter of Xavi, sister of Tatum, employed by XYZ, living in Melbourne. I AM an avid cook, an artist on the side, and a member of a volleyball team.

ZASHA: I AM a mechanical engineer, a yogi, 64 years old, from Zimbabwe, I AM a reader; I AM inquisitive, I AM not easily convinced.

Look at the first drawing. We have the identities for both persons in our example above. We see both are collections of identities, but they all live in the same I AM for each person, in the same circle. This is easy to understand. At this stage, the word after I AM is still the main identity for both people.

It is also easy to understand that each person, at the center of all their collections, feels I AM, no matter what comes after. There is an awareness of being something, an underlying consciousness of being that is the same for any word or identity that comes after. Just like every human, these two, regardless of what names or labels they put after their I AM, feel this I AMness every time and all the time. The point here is to focus on the experience of "amming" something as the foundation for absolutely anything they decide to call themselves. We now shift from the right side of the statement (the noun or adjective) to the I AM. This becomes obvious when we remove from the circle every word that comes after I AM. All that remains is I AM as in image 2.

With this foundation of the understanding we have built so far — that everything is made and comes out of consciousness — it is easier to accept that consciousness, the formless, can take absolutely any form. Can you accept it?

We are reaching a threshold now because we are assigning agency to the individual, which is still difficult to accept for many, but it's really not hard to see if you relax a bit. What you think about yourself creates the shape and experience of each and all of your identities. In other words, your identities emerge out of one substance and are made of one substance, consciousness.

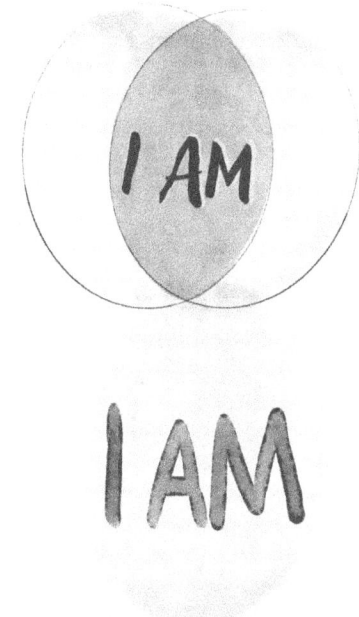

Each form that it takes is simply another arrangement of the same stuff. This form is determined by your mind activities, your thoughts, attitudes, beliefs, etc. Once you have arranged this stuff with your mind activities and it has taken shape according to your workings, these arrangements affirm themselves by creating the particular reality that you experience. According to Neville Goddard, the I AM attitude toward itself determines the form and environment of its existence. He says, "Your concept of yourself, such as "I am strong," "I am secure," or "I am loved," determines the world in which you live. I AM is rearranged and must, therefore, manifest that which its rearrangement affirms. This principle governs every aspect of your life, be it social, financial, intellectual, or spiritual."[73]

Below is a meditation that uses I AM as a mantra and pathway to pure consciousness, in which you can plant the seeds for manifestation. The purpose of this meditation as a manifestation tool is to release you from all identifications with present forms and situations so that you can withdraw from your present manifestation the energy that fuels them and bring yourself into a state of formless emptiness, from which you can easily imagine yourself in the forms and situations that you desire.

73 Robert C. Worstell, *The Collected Neville Library* (Raleigh, NC: Lulu Press, Incorporated, 2019), 285.

This meditation technique helps you create a clean slate, a blank canvas, on which you can mold consciousness without dilutions and distractions into what you want. A variation of the following meditation also appears in Neville Goddard's book, *Your Faith is Your Fortune*[74].

1. Sit in a meditative pose.

2. Know your desire.

3. Repeat "I AM," in a soft whisper or silently for several minutes, intending to shed any structure of your being and your thoughts. Let I AM become your entire identity. Become formless. Be nothing but awareness of being, pure unmanifested consciousness.

Now mold the consciousness that you are into the form that you want. Experience yourself as your fulfilled desire. Fill this new form and situation out fully with your presence, be it completely. Remain in this state for several minutes or as long as you like.

---

74 Neville Goddard, *Neville Goddard – The Complete Collection: The Reference Book by Neville Goddard with All Books, Radio Lectures and Lessons*, (self-pub., Tolino Media, 2023), 67.

"Just declare yourself to be, and continue to do so, until you are lost in the feeling of just being — faceless and formless. When this expansion of consciousness is attained, then, within this formless depth of yourself, give form to the new conception by FEELING yourself to be THAT which you desire to be." – Neville Goddard[75]

Comments: Previously, we have looked at the concept of emptiness as the natural, pure state of the mind. It is the mind as pure consciousness, like a still lake of crystal-clear water without movement or objects in it. Pure consciousness, as we discussed in previous chapters, is also the identity attributed to the whole being in spiritual teachings, often symbolized by the phrase I AM. For example, the Sanskrit phrase "Aham Brahmasmi" can be translated as "I am Brahman" or "cosmic spirit" and is used in Hinduism to confirm an individual's spiritual identity. In the Jewish mysticism of Kabbalah, the similar concept of "I AM that I AM" is contained in the phrase "Ehyeh Asher Ehyeh" and is used to connect with God, which is simply another interpretation of universal consciousness. More specific to manifestation, the Hebrew phrase is also often translated as "I will be what I will be."

---

75 Neville Goddard, *Neville Goddard — The Complete Collection: The Reference Book by Neville Goddard with All Books, Radio Lectures and Lessons* (self-pub., Tolino Media, 2023), 12.

HOW TO SHIFT YOUR IDENTITY FROM FORM TO FORMLESS

After studying the previous section, are you already able to say the following words and mean them: "I am made of the same stuff as the universe, pure consciousness. If the universe can create anything, so can I, because I am the same cosmic magic"? I know that believing that you are everything is challenging. While you read the previous sections, you might have felt a shift inside, but not complete satisfaction or self-realization. Even if you've already had some success manifesting your thoughts in the past, you may still not be fully identified with the energy field in which these manifestations occur.

True realization can begin with intellect but cannot be complete without experience. There is nothing better than yoga and meditation to facilitate a deep experience of yourself as formless in oneness. In fact, most yoga is designed to give you exactly that experience. Here are two related techniques that can create a shortcut to this realization. It's a meditation found in the Kundalini Yoga set Kriya for nerves and lower spine strength.

The official name of this set is "For Nerve, Navel, and Lower Spine Strength," but I also call it "The Kriya for False Identifications" based on its notes, which say that this set is an "excellent preparatory kriya for meditation that releases you from false identifications of the body or mind." The false identification, in the yogic sense, is what we've talked about so far: your identity as a physical body in time and space, plus your stories. If you believe everything is solidified consciousness and that your essence is consciousness, you will have an easy time believing that you can lead consciousness into a physical being. This set reveals your true identity by engaging the body in much spinal and navel work so that the mind can relax about old rigid identities and access the new identity of the formless spirit more easily. I find this kriya to be one of the fastest ways to internalize this belief. It begins with the physical preparation through the nine asanas, and it ends with one of the most powerful meditations I've seen to give you an experience of who you really are.

Before we get into the practice, let's look at the meditation first. While this meditation is typically part of the kriya that follows, you can also practice it separately. It bears a striking resemblance to the ancient Neti Neti meditation, a technique rooted in Hindu philosophy for experiencing non-duality. It's possible that the Kundalini Yoga version of this meditation evolved from the principles of Neti Neti.

146

(Variation of Neti Neti Meditation)

Sit in a comfortable meditation posture. Pull in the Navel Point and apply Root Lock. Mentally view the entire body. Then negate each identity that comes to mind: "I am not a man, not a woman, not a student, not a teacher, not sitting, etc." You are not the body, mind, or spirit, but the consciousness that gives rise to and integrates them all. Continue for at least **3 minutes.**

My personal comments on this meditation: We can elaborate on this meditation without altering it to make its effects for manifestation evident. Try the following with your student, clients, or yourself: Take your time identifying your identities and negating them to make sure everyone gets a genuine sense of liberation from the prison of their particular identities. After starting off with "I am not a man, not a woman, not a student, not a teacher," etc., continue and make the negations specific and personal:

"I am not [insert your name]."
"I am not the child of..."
"I am not the parent of..."
"I am not the sibling of..."
"I am not [insert your profession if you have one]."
"I am not the employee of..."
"I am not the boss of..."

→

Give yourself and others permission to negotiate these roles, because there's a good chance you've never said these things to yourself before in your life, and saying them can feel like betrayal. For example, a mother needs to be able to say here, "I am not the mother of..." for the sake of building consciousness. Foster a level of comfort with this exercise. Continue with all the labels you have given yourself, and you can use adjectives as well as nouns. Include these two deeply ingrained identities: "I am not a consumer" and "I am not a human being." From here, take a step into the actual identity of consciousness. Just sit, or instruct others to sit, with all identities stripped away. Now ask, "What is left?" Your true self. Pure consciousness.

For many, this might be the clearest experience of identity in consciousness, which makes this meditation especially useful, not just for manifestation but for any bona fide yoga lesson.

I find it helpful to give more guidance during or after the meditation, maybe a small discussion, to understand what happened. For a few moments, you existed without labels and forms because you chose to drop them, but we all know that life can take them away just as easily. Your children and parents might die, your job and possessions might disappear, and your physical form might be destroyed. But what is underneath all that cannot be destroyed, and it continues to exist just like you exist despite taking off all your worldly identities.

If you can truly identify with consciousness, then you identify with that which is eternal and all-powerful. And knowing this, you never have to be afraid again, because nothing that happens can change your true nature, and your nature includes access to all the creative powers in the universe.

◊
_____

Originally published in Sadhana Guidelines

1) Right Leg Forward Stretch. Sit with the left heel at the rectum and the right leg extended. Bend forward and grasp the toes with both hands. Straighten the spine and focus your eyes on the toes. Stay perfectly still with normal breathing and a light Root Lock applied. Continue for **3 minutes.**

TO END: Inhale deeply and pull back on the toes, completely exhale, pull back more, and apply a strong Root Lock. Repeat 2 more times. Relax.

2) Kundalini Lotus: Balance on the sacrum, grasp the toes of both feet, and extend the legs up and wide at 60°. Keeping the spine straight, apply a constant Root Lock. Breathe naturally. Continue for **3 minutes.**

TO END: Inhale deeply, exhale, and apply a strong Root Lock. Repeat 2 more times and relax.

→

3) Life Nerve Stretch. Sit with a straight spine and extend both legs straight. Reach forward and grasp the toes. Pull the spine straight up by pulling back on the toes. Apply a strong Neck Lock. Do Long Deep Breathing and continue for 3 minutes.

TO END: Inhale, exhale, and apply a strong Root Lock. Repeat 2 more times.

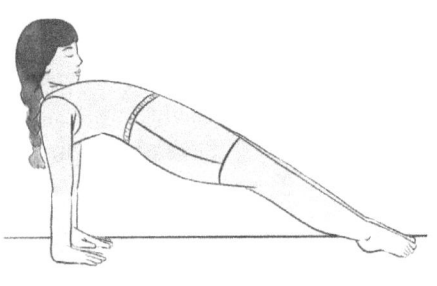

4) Back Platform Pose. Extend the legs straight forward and place the palms on the ground behind the back with the fingertips pointing towards the toes. Lift the chest and buttocks up until the body is straight with only the heels and palms on the ground. Bring the chin to the chest. Press the toes forward. Breathe naturally. Continue for **3 minutes**.

TO END: Inhale deeply, exhale, and apply Root Lock. Repeat 2 more times and relax.

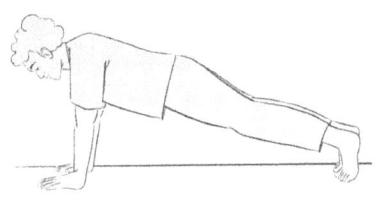

5) Push-ups. Lie on the stomach. Place the palms on the ground under the shoulders. Push up off the ground with the body straight until you form a front platform. Exhale as you slowly go down to the ground. Inhale as you slowly rise up. Do not apply Root Lock. Continue with deep, slow breaths **26 times.** Relax.

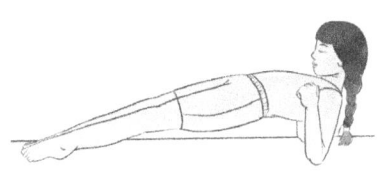

6) Back Platform Variation. Lie on the back. Rise up on the elbows; the elbows are aligned beneath the shoulders. Raise the buttocks up so the spine and body are straight. Chin is tucked. Only the heels and elbows are on the ground. Point the toes. Hold the pose with Long Deep Breathing. Continue for **3 minutes.** Inhale, then exhale completely, and apply Root Lock.

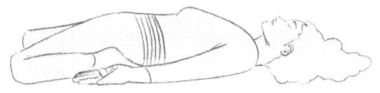

7) Celibate Pose. Sit on the heels. Slowly lean back until the head and possibly the shoulders are on the ground. The arms are relaxed on the ground beside the legs. Keep a light, constant Root Lock applied. Begin Long Deep Breathing and continue for **3 minutes.**

TO END: Inhale, exhale completely, and apply a strong Root Lock. Repeat 2 more times. Relax.

→

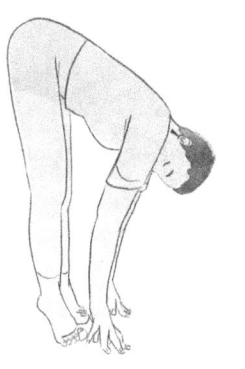

8) Frog Pose. Squat on the toes, with the knees wide and spine straight. Heels touch and are off the ground. Fingertips are on the ground between the legs and close to the body. The face is forward. Lift the hips and straighten the legs up on the inhale, keeping the fingertips on the ground. Squat down to the starting position on the exhale. Engage the Navel Point and use the fingertips on the ground for support. Keep the heels slightly off the ground throughout the exercise, and the knees always outside the arms. Continue this cycle **30 times.** Move rapidly and breathe powerfully.

9) Alternate Leg Lifts. Lie on the back. Relax the arms along the sides with the palms facing up. Raise and lower alternate legs to 90 degrees. Inhale, apply a slight Root Lock when raising, and exhale when lowering the leg down smoothly to the ground. Continue for **3 minutes.**

10) Meditate. Sit in a comfortable meditation posture. Pull in the Navel Point and apply Root Lock. Mentally view the entire body. Scan through each area and every cell systematically. As you do this, your mind will send many thoughts. The thoughts will be whatever is associated with the feelings and memories stored in that area of the body. The subconscious will also release thoughts. Reject any thought. Do not agree to the identification they invite. Free the body and cells to be neutral, present, and faithful only to your consciousness. Whether the thoughts are true or false does not matter. Simply assert your presence to be as you are and nothing else. If the thought is "I am sitting," think "I am not sitting." If it is "I am not sitting," reject that as well and just be. Let all thoughts release and resolve themselves into the vastness of your being, that includes all polarities. Each thought naturally invites you to action or identification. Stay neutral. You are not the body, mind, or spirit, but the consciousness that gives rise to and integrates them all. Continue for at least **3 minutes.**

Comments: This kriya is a good physical workout that requires flexibility and endurance and some familiarity with the basics of Kundalini Yoga exercise. The lower nerve plexuses are pressured, and the vital energy is raised above the diaphragm. If you experience chronic constipation or digestive problems, this set is of great value. If you want to stay steady under tense situations, this set is excellent. It frees your body from past patterns and opens you to the creative possibilities in the present moment.

◊
_____

KRI KUNDALINI RESEARCH INSTITUTE

CHAPTER 9

Yogic Enhancement #3:

More Helpful Yogic Concepts

In this chapter, we continue to reorganize your conceptual space into one in which your manifestation powers make sense, your doubts get removed, and you can fulfill your desires. The following ideas might be new to you. If so, I encourage you to embrace them for better manifestation. Or perhaps you've heard them before; in which case, bring them to the forefront of your mind to enhance your manifesting abilities.

THE MULTIVERSE. STEPPING INTO A NEW STATE

Spiritual processes like manifestation can happen very quickly. Zen Buddhism teachings say that even enlightenment can happen like a flash in any moment and is available to everyone. This is referred to as Satori in Japanese. A similar speed can occur with manifestation in two ways: your understanding of it can come suddenly, like the classic "aha moment," and you can actually manifest very quickly.

We can change our game of manifestation if we understand time in a new and different way. For instance, by looking at the concept of the multiverse or even at the Buddhist and Hindu teachings that say that time is an illusion. Both understandings teach us that time is not linear and that everything happens at the same moment, as if in parallel realities. If we take this invitation to understand time differently, we could subsequently think of the following in terms of what we already learned regarding manifestation techniques:

- » The desired state we want to manifest doesn't have to be created; it already exists. It equals one part of the universe, or one universe in the multiverse.
- » Because it already exists, we don't have to create it; we just have to access it. Entering a new state is not a question of action but of consciousness.

If everything exists at the same time, then the life and the objects we desire are already out there, and reaching them is not a matter of working towards them on a time-space continuum but of navigating a realm of timelessness or spacelessness, a multiverse. The potential rewards for manifestation seem enormous. Can we do it in our vehicles of mind, body, and spirit? The Bhagavad Gita reminds us that "Never was there a time when I did not exist, nor you, nor all these kings; nor in the future shall any of us cease to be."[76] And Neville Goddard, in the same understanding, writes that "all that mankind ever was or ever will be exists now. This is what is meant by creation."[77]

If it's true that everything already exists, why don't we know it's there? Do we need superhuman perception and a whole new set of senses to access this kind of expanded reality? Spiritual teachings suggest that it's all a matter of developing the faculties you already have, and it might be easier than you think.

Often, when we're filled with all those strong desires and related emotions, we don't see the forest for the trees. To avoid such a tainted vision, let's approach this from the other end: Would it be easier to get something that you really don't want at all? Ram Dass gives a useful example in his lecture "It's all Right Here," where he wants us to understand the totality of each moment by pulling something out of the present moment that we don't want — boredom in this example. He invites the audience to identify boredom from the current mix of sensations, experience it, and fully embrace that feeling. He then goes on to explain that, just like you extracted a feeling you were not feeling or noticing, you can consciously create and access any state you want in your present reality.

Now, sit down in meditation and become still. Instead of focusing on inner peace and relaxation, try to put your mental finger on the presence of boredom. And if this one quality can be extracted, why not something much bigger, including completely new states and realities? Think of it this way: the boredom you found is like a little speck of diamond, an indication that there are greater treasures to be discovered. Likewise, you can use your yogic tools and consciousness to excavate the reality you want at any moment.

---

76 *Bhagavad Gita: The Song of God*, Chapter 2, Verse 12, trans. Swami Mukundananda, 2014, www.holy-bhagavad-gita.org.

77 Neville Goddard, *The Power of Awareness* (Garden City: Dover Publications, Inc., 2013), 25.

Your ability to feel is the best tool for finding anything in your consciousness. That's how you discovered boredom just now: you felt it. And that's how you find everything else you want to bring into your reality — by feeling it. Once you feel its presence, it appears. But wait a moment, you'll say, boredom is just a feeling anyway; it's not an object; it's got to be different with objects! Yes and no. Boredom is a vibration that gives you a particular feeling. And we have established earlier in this book that everything is essentially vibration, which means that any vibration you choose to get in touch with, you can also feel. In other words, you can feel all objects, situations, and even people that you focus on. For example, house ownership has a particular vibration that you can feel, so extract that feeling out of the ocean of vibrations around you if you want to manifest a house. Being in a happy relationship has a particular vibration. Identify the feeling and activate it if a relationship is what you want. Being on the beach on a sunny day has a particular vibration; choose that tune and play it if you want to be at a sunny destination. All these felt vibrations are subjective. Of course, only you know what they feel like inside of you, but your particular feeling is all the qualification you need. The speed with which you bring these desires into the physical plane has everything to do with the purity, accuracy, and intensity you bring to conjuring the particular vibration. The following Patanjali's yoga sutra spells it out: "In the different fields of manifestation, the Consciousness, though one, is the elective cause of many states of consciousness."[78]

The sutra acknowledges the existence of many levels of manifestation. The "different fields of manifestation" can be anything — various situations or entire realities — and while the sutra probably refers to an individual, subjective experience of a yogi, it doesn't change the fact that any subjective experience is still a reality for that person, and that includes all physical manifestations. The sutra also talks about the origins of each of these manifestations, and the operative word here is "elective." It says that manifestations are different because consciousness has elected them to be like that. How so? By feeling it, by imagining the feeling, and then feeling the feeling. Or, as Neville Goddard says, by thinking feelingly. The feeling is the seed vibration around which the manifestation develops. The clearer the feeling, the faster the manifestation. Let me be clear: we are referring to feelings fueled by imagination. Do not underestimate imagination in the formula — the creative power of your mind in

---

78 *The Yoga Sutras of Patanjali*, sutra 4.5, trans. Charles Johnston (n.p., Prabhat Prakashan, 2021), 11.

imagination combined with the physical sensation in your body that you can and must create for successful manifestation.

This is a good time to remind you of the familiar philosophical thought experiment: "If a tree falls in the forest, does it make a sound?". If you are an experienced yogi who understands consciousness, you probably know the answer: only if there is a consciousness present to perceive the sound. And more broadly, absolutely everything only exists if there is a consciousness to be aware of it. But this also makes a case for the power of consciousness, and the sutra mentioned above emphasizes this power by saying that before anything can be perceived, it must be elected and imagined into existence by consciousness as well. So the cycle completes: consciousness brings it into existence, and then consciousness perceives it. All is one; all is consciousness.

Some even claim this process of manifestation can be instant. For example, in his famous book *Autobiography of a Yogi*, Paramahansa Yogananda mentions several remarkable manifestations. He claimed that in addition to once creating an amulet out of thin air as a gift for a friend, he and his guru, Sri Yukteswar, were both teleported to a faraway location by the guru's simple mental application. Moreover, he describes instances of healing and control of bodily function, like slowing down and stopping the heart — all surely physical manifestations.

It is very important to clarify, for our purpose of becoming skilled manifestors, that vibration and physical manifestation are one. They are just at different points on the scale of our perception, like different stations on a radio dial. While we might experience something, a house, for example, only as a visual blueprint in our mind's eye along with a vibrational sensation that we feel in our body, that doesn't make it less real than something that is in brick and mortar in front of us. This is saying that the spiritual, non-physical form of something is just as real as its physical form. Understanding and accepting this is crucial for the success of our manifesting efforts, because it will be hard to nurture something as it grows if we only believe it is real in its final physical stage. It would be like denying the realness of a sprouted acorn in the ground and only accepting it by the time it has become a tree, or dismissing the entire process of planning a house on paper and only giving meaning to the finished building.

If we can accept the non-physical, vibrational, and spiritual nature of anything as real and use this mindset for manifestation, we are effectively working with energy. Now we know we are actively shaping energy and universal elements into manifested forms. Yogis have the advantage of working with energy, as much of their experience is not tangible and form-based, like deep meditation or absorption in the sound of mantra. Now that we have established that everything exists on subtle, vibrational levels that are not yet physical and dense, let's come back to the idea of the multiverse. How do we reach another universe, another state, or another reality? By stepping into its vibration. Where do we find the vibration? In our imagination.

At the beginning of this section, we talked about identifying or imagining the vibration of boredom or of some other object. You might think that it's easy to conjure a singular object or a simple feeling and that imagining the vibration of a whole new reality is a whole different caliber. However, that's not true. You can immerse yourself in the vibration of a singular object just as easily as in the vibration of a complex system or world. Try this: first conjure the sound of a straightforward melody, then imagine a full orchestra playing a symphony. Both are equally easy to conjure. All that matters is the quality of your consciousness and your imagination, and both are infinite and not subject to time or space. Simply imagine the vibration of the state you want, no matter how complex and populated with things, people, colors, sounds, and smells it might be. Do you remember visiting a new city for the first time? While there are certainly many impressions, the entire visit can still be categorized as one experience, and this one experience had a particular vibration. Now create this particular vibration for the desired state and maintain the vibration. That's how you manifest. Everything that can be imagined already exists. This includes every state that you want. Are you getting closer?

This is a matter of linear thinking versus non-linear thinking. When you think of states you want to get into or out of — for example, from frustration and stuckness to flow and ease — you think of them as a linear process in space and time. You start out in frustration, and through some kind of progress, you gradually and over time enter a state of flow, calmness, or satisfaction, whatever the goal may be. A particular shade of frustration changes through gradations into flow, like the individual images of a flip book run together to show the story. That's what you have been thinking. But again, manifestation and spiritual teachings posit that states are eternal and already existing, not developing. The yogic concepts of "eternal present" and "timelessness" express this. As Neville Goddard summarizes it: "Creation is finished. Creativeness is only a deeper receptiveness, for the entire contents of all time and all space, while experienced in a time sequence, actually coexist in an infinite and eternal now."[79]

At this point, hopefully you accept that absolutely any state is possible. From here, accept that they all exist now. And here's the trick for rapid, effective manifestation: instead of developing a new state over time, you simply step into the new, desired state now, as if an elevator door opens and your new reality is right in front of you like the vast floor of a department store.

This is the practical aspect of being a yogi: If you are connected to everything, then you are also connected to every state there is. You don't create the new state; you access it by calibrating your consciousness. It's a key more than a tool. It's not a journey; it's one step with an instant arrival. A good analogy is the beaming of people, as it happens in science fiction movies like Star Trek. The beam technician presses a button, and a person is instantly transported to another place or planet. You can do this button-pressing on your own by changing your consciousness into one in which you already exist in the desired state and the state already exists in and around you. Out of all the possible universes, pick the one that is exactly like the reality you want, feel its vibration, and then bring it to yourself (as opposed to imagining yourself going there, which adds the layer of time and travel). With your self at the center, bring this universe into yours right now. Let the two merge until the desired universe covers all. Just like that.

By the way, stepping fully into an imagined state that feels absolutely real is the definition of the word "righteousness" as it shows up in the Bible. It has nothing to do with living by the law or being right when others are wrong. Just look at this quote from the Gospel of Matthew (6:33): "But seek first his kingdom and his righteousness, and all these things will be given to you as well."

---

79 Neville Goddard, *Neville Goddard - The Complete Collection: The Reference Book by Neville Goddard with All Books, Radio Lectures and Lessons* (self-pub., Tolino Media, 2023), 278.

KRI KUNDALINI RESEARCH INSTITUTE

Read it from the perspective of consciousness manifestation: "his kingdom" is the vibrational cosmos, the unified field of consciousness; "his righteousness" is the particular vibration that you accept as the reality of the new state; and voila, those exact things that you vibrate and assume as real "will be given to you as well." Neville Goddard adds this: "You can create nothing, but your assumption determines what portion of creation you will experience."[80]

Stepping into a new state, or simply immersing yourself in a new state, feels amazing. I do it all the time now, and when I do it, it feels like a breakthrough, and the other side that I am stepping into always brings a new level of clarity, sometimes just for a moment, but I can feel the metaphysical nature of this process. It is very similar to breaking through the surface after being underwater. It's like your life up to that point has been underwater, and the water might have been crystal clear, but there is always some distortion and blurry vision underwater. When you swim to the surface and your head breaks through, it's clearer above water than it was under it. It's like that for me when I decide to step into the alternative universe of my choice and succeed. The clarity is astonishing. It may not last very long, and you may be pulled back underwater into the previous reality, but you made the connection, and the vibration is active in you. The more you practice it, the easier it gets, and most of all, you'll have profound experiences of clear and undeniable manifestations along the way. Your manifestation skills are like a muscle that can be trained.

Ram Dass describes a version of an experienced manifestor in one of his lectures: "The final place one gets to is that one has a dial that is completely flexible, and you can bring in all levels at all times and see how it is at every level all the time."[81] In the same lecture, Ram Das talks about his guru, Maharaji, and how, when he first met him, Maharaji talked to him about Ram Dass' mother, who had died shortly before the meeting. Maharaji knew the cause of her death and he knew that Ram Das had been thinking about it the night before, even though Ram Dass had never talked to Maharaji about it. Ram Das explained his guru's ability to know as being one with everything: that in that moment, the guru is his mother and his mother's cause of death, and it's all interchangeable; it's all one. This is another example of being able to access any reality, to become something instead of thinking about it,

80 Neville Goddard, *The Power of Awareness: Includes Awakened Imagination* (Garden City: Dover Publications, 2019), 49.

81 Ram Dass, "Here We All Are," 1969, lecture, https://www.youtube.com/watch?v=20cqxk7zvH0.

to think from it, not about it. Ram Dass says, "It's a completely homogeneous field, which, when you're hooked up, you're in it all; you are it all." The Sanskrit term for this is *Sat Chit Ananda*, a state of living in interconnectedness with all creation, which brings joy and peace.

Goddard also mentions a Bible story as a wonderful example of stepping into an alternate universe if you interpret the story as a metaphor for manifestation. It's the story of Daniel in the lion's den. You might know the story: in ancient Babylon, a man named Daniel served under King Darius, who liked Daniel very much. Jealous officials manipulated the king into stating a law that forbade prayers to any god except the king for 30 days. Daniel kept praying to his God despite the law. The king then put Daniel in the lion's den as a punishment and closed it with a stone, but Daniel ignored the lions and instead looked up at the light coming through the stone. When the king opened the den the next day, Daniel was unharmed. If you think of the lions as stand-ins for danger or an unwanted situation, and Daniel's action of focusing on the light as a different vision of reality and as stepping into an alternative universe where there is no danger, the story makes perfect sense, and Daniel's success is our inspiration.

Here is a technique for stepping into another universe that came to me while I was out for a walk. It works beautifully, and I'd like to share it with you. This technique is like walking in your own new shoes as the person whose desires have been fulfilled. You can also think of it as a kind of stage, like a runway in a fashion show where people dressed in designer clothes become someone else just for a few moments, carrying a new skin or shell, literally walking in new shoes.

Here's how it works: While on a street or any place where you can walk comfortably, pick a point about 300–500 feet away, such as a lamp post or a tree. Walk towards this point while maintaining the consciousness of your fulfilled desire, and let your whole being express it as you are walking. For example, if you desire a promotion or a new job, walk as if you have already achieved it. Pretend you have stepped outside on the street after a job interview, during which you were told that you got your dream job and they'll pay you more than you asked for.

Now you are walking as the person you wanted to be — the person with the dream job secured, with any other blessings and possessions you desired, or with the new relationships you wanted already in your life. Once you reach the mark, do it over again, repeat the process, and try to make it more vivid. Or, walk in the consciousness of another fulfilled wish. You could do your whole list of things you want to manifest in one walk.

This walking meditation is excellent because it involves your entire being, body and mind. It's easy to feel the change in the way you walk and carry yourself. It's also enjoyable and a fantastic way to do your daily projections.

◊

THE NEUTRAL UNIVERSE & THE ABSENCE OF A JUDGING POWER

The concept of a neutral universe is immensely helpful for manifestation because it frees you from the fear of judgment. If you want your manifestations to sprout and mature in the unified field, it is more helpful to trust it, as opposed to fearing some higher force that disapproves of your plans. Unfortunately, the belief that there is some higher force watching and judging you is very common, and you might carry some version of it inside yourself. Even worse, this belief can block your manifestations.

The teachings of Christianity, Judaism, and Islam have for centuries shaped the dominant conception of the world in the West, as previously stated in a different chapter. In all three, there is an almighty God who watches you and judges you, and he has put iron rules in place that you must follow or else there will be some kind of repercussion. Even in Eastern religions, the concept of karma hints at some kind of cosmic judgment, at least in our Western understanding. It's no wonder that many of us live and act with a constant sense of being scrutinized, even when we're alone.

Here's a fresh and liberating viewpoint: Seeing the universe as a garden. Not only is it easy to imagine a garden, but it also allows us to glean insights into broader cosmic patterns. Since a garden is part of the universe, we can easily accept it as representative of the larger universe and look at what happens in it to understand larger patterns in the world. We've also already described the universe as a field of potential, and a garden is an image that captures this concept well.

Well, what happens when you plant a fruit tree or put seeds of vegetables like carrots or onions into the soil? With enough water, warmth, and proper care, these plants will grow and eventually yield nutritious food for you. No problem there. But what happens when you plant poison ivy, a thorn bush, or some other potentially harmful plant? The garden will treat it exactly like the fruit and vegetable plants; it does not discriminate. If that's what the small universe does as a garden, why wouldn't the large universe do exactly the same with the seeds you plant as thoughts in conscious manifestation? And as long as you don't use manifestation to harm others, the karmic repercussions might be neutral as well, or they might even be very positive and rewarding if you manifest for the benefit of others as well.

Here's another important point that comes out of the garden analogy: when you garden, the quality of the soil matters. Faith, trust, and patience are the ingredients that make the soil conducive to manifestation. Doubt and negativity are like pouring vinegar on your seeds.

A QUANTUM LEAP OF FAITH. COMPUTER ANALOGY

Sooner or later, you'll have to deal with doubt about manifestation teachings, and a voice in yourself or from someone speaking to you might sound something like this: "Do you expect me to believe that something will come to me just because I think about it? That the universe hears me and delivers what I want? That my thoughts can be received anywhere and set in motion a sequence that returns something to me without much effort? You are describing magic, and I think you are a fool to believe such nonsense. You will only get something through hard work, and things don't appear out of nowhere. Someone has to produce it, and someone has to pay for it. I am sorry, but that's how the world really works."

After which you can reply: "Thank you, my friend. Now show me your smartphone. Devices like that have only gained widespread popularity since 2007. How would someone have reacted if you told them before 2007 what you can say with certainty today, which is this, 'I am carrying a device that connects wirelessly to a cloud of information that spans invisibly all across the globe and throughout space and out of which I can retrieve any data, image, or even entire bodies of work and knowledge into the palm of my hand'? You can go on and say, 'With just a few movements of my fingers, I can access all the information humans have ever gathered and answers to all my questions within moments. I can order whatever I want, and it will appear in my hand or on my doorstep. Many people have acquired astronomical wealth through related code and algorithms that are immaterial, and much of the technology is free'. This would sound like utter nonsense to anyone who has never seen and used a smartphone or wireless Internet device, but no longer to you because you have the experience of using this modern technology. I have the experience of manifesting, and so can you."

This might shut them up or not, but the similarities between manifestation, modern telecommunications, and Internet technology are glaring. The internet and smartphones didn't happen accidentally; they were first imagined and existed as spiritual blueprints, just like AI was before it arrived. But it is no accident when you consider computers are conceived by the human mind, and the mind creates according to its nature and content. Voilà, modern technology is a mirror of the human mind as a unit and a part of the collective.

MAKE A VIRTUAL REALITY WORLD OUT OF YOUR FULFILLED DESIRE

In 2023, the tourism office of New York City collaborated with a candle maker to create a scent for promoting the city's Gay Pride events. To capture the essence of the festivities in Greenwich Village and beyond, they used the scents of jasmine and sandalwood. If you've ever been in the area on a Gay Pride Sunday and smelled the air, you might agree that their candle scent comes pretty close, or you might remember different smells and impressions. If you haven't been there, you'll find plenty of other scented candles and scents in the marketplace that try to transport you to another place through smell, like a blend of flowers from a summer meadow, a marine setting, or desert fragrances. Or just think of the last time you visited a city for the first time and found yourself surrounded by the specific life in it — a plaza in Cairo, a bazaar in Rishikesh, the downtown of an American city, for example — each has a distinct feel and flavor. Do you remember its scents, sights, sounds, and feelings?

Our goal here is to identify those sensory impressions that create the experience of your fulfilled desire and then switch on these made-up sensations inside of us to create the feeling that fuels the manifestation, because the felt experience of your imagined fulfilled desire is key to manifestation. Here again, it's the upside-down approach of yoga, as we create the feeling before the state and put the cart before the horse (as we've seen in an earlier chapter). A better word for feeling in this context might be atmosphere, as it describes something more holistic that emerges from a collection of ingredients as a new individual entity. That is also why the metaphor of a scented candle is limited, because it only engages one sensory organ.

The latest developments in virtual reality provide better examples, and "virtual reality world" is a term that comes closer to what I am describing. I invite you to make your own VR world movie that plays in your 3D headset, also known as your mind. To engage all your senses, create an utterly positive 3D movie in your mind of the particular atmosphere of what you want. And then, most importantly, step into and stay inside your movie for complete immersion. For example, the atmosphere of a vacation with a loved one could be one movie, or the atmosphere of a happy home or of a place of employment in which you perform your fulfilling work could be others. The central question is: What is the atmosphere like for your fulfilled desire? What's it like to see, hear, smell, touch, and taste it? What does the environment look like—the colors, the furniture, the vegetation, the architecture? Who are the characters, how do they engage, and how are they affected by your fulfilled desire?

Your task for efficient manifestation is to create this atmosphere inside your senses, to make it all up, and then feel it as richly as possible, complete with sights, sounds, movement, and breath. This is where you use the infinite resourcefulness of your imagination, put all the ingredients together, and then experience it from within. Living inside this 3D movie of your fulfilled desire is the transcendental bridge from a spiritual reality into one on the physical plane.

A good analogy would be the healing miracles described in scripture, where, for example, a paralytic walks again after Jesus blesses him (Gospel of Mark, Chapter 2, verses 1–12). This kind of miracle is often used to teach faith to followers of a religion, but it can also be a lesson in manifestation if you are inclined to scrutinize Jesus' healing powers and use your findings to imitate him instead of merely admiring him. So how exactly did Jesus do it? Maybe he projected a 3D movie of the man completely healed into the space and enveloped the man with this vision of total health. And through this spiritual image and the masterful skill of Jesus' projection (a great yogic skill!) — a nd, at last equally important, the acceptance of the new vision by the man — the manifestation followed almost instantly. This would be our manifestation process in a fast-forward manner.

Why could it happen so fast? Because of Jesus' expertise in manifestation techniques, the supreme quality of his *dhyana and dharana*, and the sharp focus of his projections. And consider this: Jesus also speaks to the paralytic right before the man walks again and says, "Son, your sins are forgiven." If you know that "sin" does not mean crime but simply an error in the choosing of your own identity, and "forgiving a sin" means an adjustment in attitude, so that the man no longer mistakenly thinks he is paralyzed (powerless) but healthy (powerful with godlike agency to change his condition), then this story really makes sense as an example of manifestation through mind projection and also as a metaphor for human beings' innate ability to heal on their own.

The following story from Hindu scripture could be an even better example of the effectiveness of replacing one reality with another by the sheer force of your own projecting powers. It's a story from the ancient Indian epic Ramayana. The story tells that Lord Rama's brother Lakshamana is in a battle and gets hit by an arrow, and Rama determines that Lakshamana can only be saved by an herb called Sanivani, which only grows on a particular mountain across the ocean. Another deity, the monkey-faced Hanuman, is sent to fetch the herb. Once Hanuman gets to the mountain, however, he cannot identify the herb, and instead of picking a random plant, he carries the whole mountain back to Rama and Lakshamana, including the herb, and Lakshamana is healed. Now think about this: the mountain is literally a whole other world that contains in it the healing ingredient and, technically, it took the entire mountain to make the miracle happen, not just one herb. Isn't "bringing the whole mountain" a great metaphor for the projection of your 3D movie onto a current situation to find through it the pathway (the herb) to get to the state that you want?

To my mind, both stories are primarily stories of gaining agency through imagination and resourcefulness. The diseases in each story are symbolic of the limitations of the human mind, but with the godlike gift of imagination and the projection of a desired reality onto another, an utterly new and improved state is achieved. I also see how easily both stories could be interpreted merely as stories of the superiority of other beings and the need to obey them instead of being inspired by them to apply your own powers. If you, like me, accept scriptures as representations of human psychology, the message of both stories is clear: You can do it too. Project a lifelike 3D movie of your desired state onto a current state to transform the latter into the first. Below is a meditation to practice this skill in simple form. I suggest that, before sitting to meditate, you do a physical yoga set as preparation, then sit down and create your own 3D movie of your desire fulfilled. Make it as vivid as possible.

The key aspect of this meditation is a prolonged projection of an imagined state, which is equal to the desired state in manifestation. You can also consider this meditation training for your creative imagination. It begins with an intense pranayama, then moves to a meditation in which you imagine yourself as a flame. Here again, the physical work is also the preparation for an improved meditative state. The breath relaxes you so that focus and imagination can be stronger. The mental image of the flame is both simple and all-consuming, which makes it ideal to train the imagination with your entire being at its center in just a few minutes

Sit in Easy Pose with a straight spine and a light Neck Lock.

Mudra: Place the hands on the knees in Gyan Mudra, touch the tip of the thumbs with the Jupiter (index) fingers, and keep the other three fingers extended straight. Arms are relaxed, with elbows slightly bent.

Eye Focus: Not specified.

Breath: Open the mouth and jaw wide, inhale and exhale deeply and powerfully through the mouth, continue for **3 ½ minutes**, then inhale deeply to end. Close the mouth and do Long Deep Breathing through the nose. Continue for **2 more minutes** while you meditate, purify yourself, and turn yourself into a flame of light.

Total Time: 5 ½ minutes.

To End: Inhale and exhale powerfully 3 times. On the third inhale, stretch up, suspend the breath for **15 seconds,** and shake the spine and the hands vigorously to equalize the energy.

◊

CHAPTER 10

YOGIC ENHANCEMENT #4:

ROUND UP YOUR CHAKRA SYSTEM

The chakra system is an excellent pathway to conscious manifestation, and this chapter shows you how. If you've practiced yoga for a while, you've probably come across some information about chakras. In almost all presentations of the chakra system that I have attended in yoga settings, the order of the chakras explained was always exclusively from the bottom up. The explanation often focused on the upward movement of the Kundalini energy, the energy of consciousness, after it gets activated in spiritual development and starts its travel from its resting place at the bottom of the spine, from the first chakra, through all the subsequent ones up the spine, to the 7th chakra at the crown of the head. However, it's the energy's downward movement in reversed order through the chakras that facilitates manifestation.

WHAT IS THE CHAKRA SYSTEM?

The chakras are energetic centers in the body that process certain life experiences and are used in yogic philosophy to explain the awakening of a person's consciousness to higher levels. Once again, we find a good analogy in technology: think of the chakras as apps on a computer that is your body, installed along the spine from chakra number one at the base of your spine to chakra number seven at the crown of your head. Most general chakra systems are explained with seven main chakras along the spine. There are exceptions, and studying the chakra system in depth is a good idea for all your spiritual practices, but for the sake of our discussion, we'll stick with seven chakras.

Each app is designed to assist you with specific tasks on an energetic level. Just like the output from various apps or software applications on a computer determines the overall functionality and quality of the user experience, your chakra system determines your life experience. Ideally, all chakras function well and are interconnected like a good modern computer with a solid operating system and relevant application software. I am sure you know the difference between using an old, cluttered computer versus a new, updated, and well-working machine, and just as the latter can give you ease in everything you do — work, play, entertainment, communication, etc. — a well-working chakra system can give you ease and flow in your life.

Organs handle specific physical tasks like digestion, detoxification, oxygenation, etc. When, for example, food enters the digestive system, the organs deal with it, extract nutrients, create fuel, and dispose of matter. And just like the organs work on the physical level, chakras work on the level of energy and experience, so both their input and output are energetic. For example, the first chakra at the base of your spine is like a processing center for issues that have to do with your place in the world and your sense of belonging. So if energy enters your body through your senses (for example, if you are in a crowd of people and you observe and interact with what goes on around you), the first chakra takes the input from your senses (people's behavior towards you, your attractions and aversions, your interpretations of social going-ons, etc.) and computes it into your particular perception and experience in relation to your place in the world. In this example, your particular filters, colored by emotionally charged concepts from your experiences, your fears, hopes, and beliefs, compute your particular state of being. Just like there are nuances in apps, from very sophisticated to poorly working ones, the state of your chakras affects how you feel as a person in the world.

To expand on the examples above, let's say you find yourself surrounded by people who want to talk to you. The input from your senses is computed by your first chakra and its particular composition of filters and concepts. With an unbalanced first chakra, you might feel threatened and very uncomfortable, as your chakra is not returning positive feedback. Or, with a strong and balanced first chakra, you cherish the sudden flow of people's attention towards you; it feeds you in a positive, uplifting way, and your sense of belonging in this world is confirmed and elevated through this chance encounter with new and interesting people.

Again, how well a chakra works depends on various factors, just like apps function on a number of factors like the quality of the code they're written on, the platform they're installed on, and how current they are. For chakras, the code would be your beliefs, opinions, and so on, the web of mental functions that makes the chakra compute on the spectrum between very positive and effective to dull, depressing, dark, or blocked, and the quality of the platform the chakra is installed on is equivalent to your physical body and its current condition, your health, your fitness, and your immune system. Many yogic practices are designed to optimize the chakra system, either all or select ones, as well as their foundation, the body.

Each chakra contributes its own energetic output: the second chakra in relation to sexuality and creativity, for example, the third chakra in relation to your sense of personal power, the fourth chakra (at the Heart Center) in relation to your level of connection and love for others and yourself, and so forth. When it comes to the ultimate goal of yoga, which is enlightenment and liberation through elevated consciousness, all chakras are balanced. Here, the Kundalini energy moves effectively through the entire system and facilitates the personal evolution of a person, from their primitive, animal nature at the bottom of the consciousness and chakra ladder to a more heart-centered human being at the fourth chakra, then to a being with a more highly evolved consciousness — an angel, or *bodhisattva*, if you will — at the top. After all, the awakening of consciousness is called Kundalini rising, not falling. Spiritual teacher Osho gives an alternative overview of the system in one of his books:

> "The ancient Buddhist scriptures talk about seven temples. Just as the Sufis talk about seven valleys and Hindus talk about seven chakras, Buddhists talk about seven temples. The first temple is the physical, the second temple is psychosomatic, the third temple is psychological, the fourth temple is psycho-spiritual, the fifth temple is spiritual, the sixth temple is psycho-transcendental, and the seventh temple and the ultimate — the temple of temples — is the transcendental." – Osho[82]

Patanjali's 45 and 46 Yoga Sutras support this notion when they say that "subtle substance rises in ascending degrees, to that pure nature which has no distinguishing mark" and "the above are the degrees of limited and conditioned spiritual consciousness, still containing the seed of separateness." You might have seen a pictorial representation for that, a thousand petals opening up at the crown of the head, symbolizing the opening of the human and the unification of their consciousness with the universal consciousness. For many, that's the ultimate goal of their yoga practice — the end all in their quest for higher consciousness. It's a bit like the happily-ever-after, with little attention to what comes after. What comes after could be, in an extreme case, a complete and final merger into the

---

82 Osho, *The Heart Sutra: Becoming a Buddha Through Meditation*, (**city**: Osho Media International, 2014), 5.

formless, also known as death, or it could simply be an awakened being returning to everyday life, getting up from the yoga mat, vacuuming the floor, calling their mother, and scrolling on social media before going to bed. As a Zen proverb says, "Before enlightenment, chop wood and carry water. After enlightenment, chop wood and carry water."

But wait, there's a lot more you can do with chakras than being an enlightened person chopping wood and carrying water. If the upward movement of energy through the chakras is you blossoming like a flower, the downward movement is you returning flowers to the world as you move Kundalini energy through the chakras, which materializes as your manifestations on the physical plane. When I learned that the downward movement is equally important for human life as it represents the manifestation process, it felt good to see a circle in my head instead of a line, and it gave me a sense of completion and closure within myself, one of the great rewards of a yoga practice. I hope you will feel it too.

Here is one of the few mentions of energy moving downward through the chakras. In his book *A Chakra and Kundalini Workbook*, Swami Anandakapila Saraswati (Dr. John Mumford) mentions this in the context of a definition of the symbol of Kundalini energy, the image of a snake coiled three and a half times: "The coil of the three represents the three states of energy (positive, negative, and neutral), while the half coil represents kundalini as always on the verge of changing from static to kinetic manifestation."[83] In my mind, there is no reason not to read this symbol also from potential and spiritual energy to manifestation in physical life. The following section explains the effects of both the upward and downward movements in more detail.

---

83 Jonn Mumford, *A Chakra & Kundalini Workbook: Psycho-spiritual Techniques for Health, Rejuvenation, Psychic Powers, and Spiritual Realization* (St. Paul, MN: Llewellyn Publications, 1994), 74.

UP-AND-DOWN CONSCIOUSNESS MOVEMENT IN THE CHAKRA SYSTEM

Let's compare the two directions, up and down, in the following summary, and the chart below will go into more detail in this chapter. It ends with a meditation for manifestation using the top-down path.

BOTTOM-UP FOR HIGHER CONSCIOUSNESS

Chakra 1: Base of your spine. You start your application of consciousness on the physical level. You get your bearings on the earth plane, develop a sense of who you are and what your environment is, whether you feel safe in it, whether it feels like a home or an inhospitable land. As much as your environment contributes to your feeling of safety and security, so do the people around you: your family, community, and tribe. Do you feel connected and supported by them, or do you feel alone? Do you want to stay where you are or leave? When you feel at home, trust, and enjoy the place and people around you, you have a solid base from which the energy can rise. You develop an interest in expanding yourself and your life in your established environment as your energy and personal evolution move up to the level and vibration of the next chakra.

Chakra 2: Sexual organs. Expansion includes procreation in the second chakra, and its energy becomes sexual as expressed through your sexual organs. But it also goes beyond physical lovemaking and procreation. Second chakra expressions can include the entire spectrum from very sexy to very creepy, attractive or repulsive, liberated or blocked. They determine your communication through your creativity and self-expression in the world. Healthy sexual relationships and the desire to merge with others could mark a balanced situation at the second chakra level. An unbalanced situation might be due to a lack of sexual drive and passion.

Chakra 3: Navel. The issues computed here concern personal power and the energy is related to the navel. It asks, How do you apply your strength and position in your environment? Do you assert your ideas and opinions, and how do you debate fairly, boss people around, or hide under the covers? Anything from great diplomacy to being a total jerk is possible with this level of behavior and communication. Your capacity to confidently and harmoniously blend into your physical surroundings and welcome relevant thoughts, deeds, and other contributions from your environment for improved standing characterizes a balanced situation at the third chakra level.

We have now covered the lower three chakras, and they are sometimes grouped as a subsystem, the lower triangle, because they all deal with some of the fundamental issues of personal and communal life: survival, procreation, and assertion. Or you can say money, sex, and power. According to yogic science, there are many more levels to human existence, and each level above is higher and more refined, which is why spreading a technology that gets you there — including yoga and manifestation — is a worthwhile mission. More and more people are moving beyond the lower three chakras, or at least sensing that it is possible, which is one reason for the growing interest in yoga and spirituality as entryways. Now let's see what lies beyond the lower triangle.

Chakra 4: Heart Center. At the heart level, relationships are everything. How you relate to others and yourself, and how much you can love everyone, including yourself. A balanced situation at the heart level can make you feel mostly compassion, not disdain, for others. Your heart is open and buzzing gently, like a purring cat, and you are ready for peaceful and open-minded interactions. You feel compassion for people no matter how similar or different they feel from your own life, and most of all, you can love easily and receive love. The fourth chakra is also the energetic center of your body, and as we move higher, the energy gets more etheric and refined.

Chakra 5: Throat. We have reached the fifth chakra, near your throat. This is the center of your truth and communication. How do you communicate on all levels, not just verbally but also and especially, through your art? How do you carry yourself? For example, if you are fearful, you might speak with a hushed voice and walk around with your shoulders hunched. Either way, it's communication. Is your voice audible, are your words well-chosen, and are your messages understandable? Do you understand your communications on a vibrational level, that your environment translates not just as literal content but as feelings and emotions? If yes is the answer to those three questions, you can call that a balanced fifth chakra situation. From your center of truth, you move to your center of intuition.

Chakra 6: The Third Eye. The third eye is located at the level of your pituitary gland, inside your skull, at the point between your eyes. This is your inner eye, often depicted in Hindu illustrations as a small, dark circle on the forehead. How clear is your inner vision? Is it easy for you to see something in your mind's eye and hold that vision? Can you read between the lines? And how is your intuition? Intuition is the ability to form a big picture from scattered signals and information you get at any point. It is knowing something without knowing why you know it. With your energy well developed in the sixth chakra, you compute the input from your senses and your mind into a coherent perspective that includes past, present, and future, which helps you develop a strategy for dealing with anything.

Chakra 7: The Crown Chakra. You have reached the crown of your head at the opposite end of your first chakra, your connection to the earth, and here you are connecting to the ethereal realms. You feel part of something bigger. The seventh chakra is your door to the cosmos. When people report a sense of being supported by something greater than themselves, a bigger spirit, or God, they are expressing a seventh chakra experience. Equally, a person who cannot see and believe anything beyond what they pick up from the physical world most likely does not have an active seventh chakra, and their energy has not moved higher than any of the lower chakras. A highly developed seventh chakra could lead to a sense of complete merger with the cosmos, a state sometimes referred to as *samadhi*, the oneness of the self with the universal self that is at the heart of yogic teachings.

You can see how a balanced chakra system is represented in a balanced life where a person feels at home in the world and beyond it, a healthy sense of being in this world but not of this world, and is very comfortable in all environments and with everyone around them. This is perfectly attainable for everyone, and most comprehensive yoga practices, especially Kundalini Yoga as taught by Yogi Bhajan with its emphasis on mental, physical, and spiritual balance, are designed to balance the seven chakras for optimum life quality.

THE EIGHTH CHAKRA — YOUR POINT OF ATTRACTION

In Kundalini Yoga as taught by Yogi Bhajan, there is also the concept of the eighth chakra, your energetic field, which can be explained as the sum of all individual chakra functionalities, a vibrational cocktail, if you will. It's also called the aura, or electromagnetic field. If manifestation is attraction and creation through the interaction of your being's energetic activity with the elements of the universe, then you can think of your electromagnetic field as your particular calling card for the universe. Or, to use a tech analogy again: all your being's energetic and mind activity is the input for the algorithm, and your electromagnetic field is the output. If you study the teachings of Abraham Hicks, you will hear the term "point of attraction" often. This is the yogic equivalent, your particular kind of magnet that buzzes it's cosmic signal on your very personal frequency and touches equal vibrations, like-minded energy, if you will, which will be the things, people, and situations you attract. The more you develop your awareness for manifestation and the more you understand your particular vibrational mix, the more you will recognize what shows up in your life as elements with the same vibrational frequency, even if on the outside they appear as completely different situations. For example, one day as I was writing a page for this book, I sat in a new place that had everything I wanted that day: nature, solitude, closeness, perfect temperatures, and all of that in the middle of a very busy city — just a very improbable mix that boggled my mind that day. And I sat there with my heart full of gratitude for being served this perfect cosmic cocktail that day. That's when a friend texted me after he had just learned that the cruise he had booked for his family had been delayed and their cruise ship had been parked for a few days on the arm of a river, where they happened to be just steps away from an annual summer fair with plenty of great rides. Cruises and amusement parks are the two favorite things for this family, but these two things almost never coexist, as a park requires a large piece of land and the cruise ship a deep body of water. But there they were, with both pieces in the same place, and feeling very lucky. Do you see how our vibrations equaled? We both found ourselves in a situation that included very unlikely combinations of our favorite things, and we both felt happy about this unusual gift.

If you practice the techniques in this book and develop a sense of their workings, you too will be able to identify more and more of what the universe delivers in response to your particular frequency. It's a bit like speaking a new language and seeing it integrated into your environment as people respond to your communications, and your understanding of signals and signs around you grows. As far as the aura goes, some people can see it, often as colors around a person or as a general "vibe" you get from a person. The more sensitive you become as a yogi, the more you understand people's level of energy and read their energy. To assess a person and their situation as a teacher, therapist, or in any encounter, you often need nothing but what you receive from their aura. As you learn to identify the different energetic levels that people function on, you'll understand more and more the environments they create and, of course, your own. So let's work creatively with the chakra system as we move downward for the sake of manifestation.

TOP-DOWN FOR CONSCIOUS MANIFESTATION

We begin with the crown chakra to merge with the cosmos, and like opening a skylight in your ceiling, we open the chakra to receive what comes in from the beautiful soup of the universal cosmic consciousness — signals, messages, and visions. You can simply call it getting an idea. By the way, meditation is one of the best ways to open this portal, and in the stillness of your mind, ideas come in. Many people report getting their best ideas in a still and relaxed state. Many scientists and artists report this, and even Einstein says he had some of his most profound insights while sitting quietly in a bubble bath. To me, any good art is what someone has received from this cosmic exchange and captured in their art medium as a pure expression of infinity.

That idea or spark of energy that manifested in the seventh chakra now moves down to the sixth chakra, so you can use your inner eye to draw the idea into a clearer form with colors and movement. A thought becomes a fuller vision, a blueprint of future manifestation. The clearer the image is in your mind's eye, the better the quality of the blueprint, and the better the chances of manifesting exactly what you see. Allow time here to fill in the blanks with aliveness, like a three-dimensional paint-by-numbers or a very clear movie playing in your head, with the main plot and actors all showcasing the positive aspects of the desire you want to manifest.

Let your vision drop and move from your third eye to the fifth chakra, the center of truth and communication. Here, you give it meaning and expression in alignment with your inner flow. On the level of language, you name it and describe it. Moreover, you articulate your truth about the idea, why it makes sense for you to pursue it, how it aligns with who you are, and your wishes for your life.

As your idea becomes a plan and a strategy, you take it to your heart. How do the central issues of the fourth chakra, love and relationships, relate to your idea? Here, you define who can be involved and why. Who are the people with the right resources — your collaborators and partners, suppliers, contractors, and artists — who know how to flesh out your idea? Just as importantly, who will benefit from your idea? Who will love the finished thing? Your heartfelt expression of your idea can be a magnet for the right relationships in your project.

The third chakra is next, as your idea becomes more and more solid. At the level of your personal power, you bring your idea into the world with more assertion. You carve out a space for it, find a location, buy some land, rent a space, and create a PR, marketing, and sales campaign. You pitch the idea to investors, builders, media, friends, or students to cement your power and your foundation through funding or any other support.

In the second chakra, you merge with your idea in a sexual dance with the elements of the universe. Everything you have accumulated on the way down so far is like an egg, and adding second chakra energy is the insemination. The egg is fertilized, and it is ready to grow and get fleshed out like a baby in the womb. You build, add layers and limbs, and in the allocated time, your idea grows into a complete thing ready to be born.

And finally, after you've conceived the cosmic spark and nurtured it through the chakra system from an etheric state into a solid one, you let it out into the earth. At the level of the first chakra, your project is born into the world. The building is built, the product is finished, the person is sitting next to you, the community around you. Cut the ribbon, uncork the champagne, and give your new friends a hug.

Please refer to the chart below for a new look at the chakra system: the line of ascension as the line of manifestation.

UPWARD MOVEMENT EVOLUTION	CHAKRAS KEY ISSUES	DOWNWARD MOVEMENT MANIFESTATION
STEP 7: Expand beyond your physical boundaries, connect to the universal consciousness, and understand and live your reality in oneness.	**SEVENTH CHAKRA:** Cosmic connection, identity in spirit, and oneness.	**STEP 1:** From your connection to the universe and infinite creativity, receive ideas and impulses for a new reality.
STEP 6: Use your vision and intuition to understand the world with subtlety.	**SIXTH CHAKRA:** Vision, ideas, intuition, and seeing the unseen.	**STEP 2:** Refine the vision in your mind's eye. See the full manifestation as a complete blueprint.
STEP 5: Express your truth and creativity in a unique and integrative way.	**FIFTH CHAKRA:** Center of truth, language, and creative expression.	**STEP 3:** Express it in words, images, and concepts. Make the blueprint communicable.
STEP 4: Share your wisdom and joy with others, and let them share with you.	**FOURTH CHAKRA:** Human connection, community, and love.	**STEP 4:** Bring other people into your plans.
STEP 3: Connect to your personal power of projection and action.	**THIRD CHAKRA:** Personal power and projection.	**STEP 4:** Use your personal power to allocate the resources, team up and delegate with your allies.
STEP 2: Explore your creativity in sexuality and other forms of co-creating.	**SECOND CHAKRA:** Sexuality, conception, and creativity.	**STEP 5:** Flesh it out in the physical world. Build it, write it, put the pieces together, and orchestrate the universe.
STEP 1: Become secure and established where you live, with the people around you and your environments.	**FIRST CHAKRA:** Grounding, belonging, and existence on earth plane.	**STEP 6:** The manifestation arrives on the physical plane. Integrate it in the physical world.

This meditation is great to do as a guided meditation for an individual, a group, or on your own, ideally after a good yoga set or other physical preparation for meditation, especially one that activates the chakra system, including the eighth chakra. Think of this meditation as an enhanced visualization technique for wish fulfillment. You visualize each step as you go down the chakra ladder and infuse your creation with the particular chakra energy at each level. Spend several minutes with each chakra, or as long as you need to feel that the specific task at each chakra is complete. You are actively assisting the universe in adding layers of density and physical reality. Your additional attention and targeted mind activity clarify and accelerate your manifestation. What is it you want to manifest? I will simply call it "THAT."

1. Begin in deep meditation. Focus on the crown of your head. Visualize an opening, like a skylight — a fusion between your crown and the cosmos. Feel the connection between the heavens and your skull, the cosmic energy all around you and entering you through your crown chakra. If you already have an idea, let it float right above your head for exposure to the cosmic energy, a kind of marinade, the universe taking another look by shining a light on it. Stay there and be open. Does THAT feel complete, or does THAT need adjustments? Feel yourself into the best starting point for your idea. Move to the next step when you are ready.

2. Pull THAT to the level of the sixth chakra. You can think of this stage as your graphic department executing your written plan into a model. Make it a full 3-D model with color and movement. See every detail of the thing or the situation from all sides; let it breathe and move. Pay attention to the details. What do you see? What are the surfaces and textures like? Is there odor and taste? How does THAT fit into its environment? How do people react to it?

3. Pull THAT to the level of the throat to infuse it with the energy from the center of your truth. Begin with adding language. Describe THAT in the most accurate way. Add a title or a name. Articulate an elevator pitch in your mind. How would you describe it to someone in a few sentences so that it makes total sense? Explain why this manifestation should happen. Qualify it with your words in a way that feels true and just. In the beginning was the word, and words become things.

4. Here, just love THAT. Shower your baby with love, and surround it with your green heart energy. Also, think lovingly and specifically of the people involved, both collaborators and beneficiaries. Think of all the people whose lives will be touched by THAT and see and feel the joy they radiate. It fills your heart with joy and love for your project, for you, and for everyone around THAT.

5. Now enter the lower triangle, where density and weight increase. But first add your navel energy, your power, to THAT. Seek a place for it to open up in the world and claim it. Confirm that all permits and blessings for your project are granted, that it has been qualified, that all materials, people, and resources are confirmed and approved, and that the building with solid materials can begin.

6. You are at the second chakra. It's love-making by loving what you make with your mind and your hands. See that your thoughts and actions are adding layers and life to THAT. See it developing in your mind's eye like a fast-motion film of a human fetus growing into a baby to be born, or a construction site turning into a full-scale building, or an entire world being born into existence.

7. THAT is on the earth now. Spend several minutes experiencing the physical reality of THAT in your whole body. How does it feel to have it, be around it, interact with it, and live with it? Shake people's hands and invite them in. Hear their comments; let them test drive while you do the same. This part is a turbocharged visualization, a deluxe version of the core manifestation teaching.

After the journey through the chakras with your imagination in full swing, this visualization of THAT may become one of the most profound, embodied manifestation experiences you've ever had.

CHAPTER 11

Yogic Enhancement #5:
Live In The Present With Your Future

FOCUSING ON THE PRESENT VERSUS THE FUTURE

"Patience is a projected mythology of advancement." –Yogi Bhajan[84]

While you have been reading up to this point, you might ask yourself: If one key to manifestation is the constant projection of a fulfilled future, isn't that a contradiction to my effort to live in the present moment? Isn't being fully present and operating in the now the gold standard for spiritual caliber?

I completely understand if you see a red flag here, as there is hardly any advice you'll hear more often these days than "Just be present." It's a piece of advice we widely accept as a truism and give without a second thought, similar to "Just be yourself." It has been so vividly associated with the basics of spiritual practices that several books and quotes related to this idea have gained considerable traction in the collective psyche, and most people have heard: "Wherever you go, there you are," from Jon Kabat-Zinn, founder of the Center for Mindfulness at the University of Massachusetts Medical School, or the famous title of the 1971 book *Be Here Now* by Ram Dass, an American author and spiritual teacher. When Eckhart Tolle's book *The Power of Now* appeared in 1999, the concept of present-moment awareness received another boost and entered the mainstream.

The Power of Now was the first spiritual book I read in 2003. After seeing the title online and being interested in it, I borrowed it from a library. On the way over to a friend's house on a Saturday night with the book, I read the first pages, and instantly I felt a shift in the quality of the world, as if life was a giant wave and I was surfing on it with absolute ease. The feeling lasted all night, and I welcomed it quietly and didn't talk to anyone about it. It catapulted me into spiritual studies and eventually into yoga. In this chapter, my focus will also be on Tolle's teachings,

---

84 Yogi Bhajan, "Patience Pays," (lecture, Los Angeles, October 20, 1985).

as they serve as an accessible bridge to manifestation. I find his teachings about present-moment awareness unmatched in clarity and contemporary accessibility and also very useful for this discussion. Tolle's teachings are entirely yogic, as he believes that the now is an entryway into the spiritual dimension and offers the same reward as yoga practice: oneness with all. He defines enlightenment as "your natural state of felt oneness with being." Tolle explains not only the outcome of being present but also that of meditation. "You can create a gap in the mindstream by directing your focus to the now. Just become intensely conscious of the present moment. This is deeply satisfying and draws consciousness away from mind activity, creating a gap of no-mind where you are highly alert and aware but not thinking. This is the essence of meditation."[85]

In everyday use, being present usually helps you cultivate inner peace, aliveness, and vibrancy in your life. It gives you access to higher intelligence and greater success as a human being. The difference between working in the world from a connection to the present moment and from a disconnected state is immense and noticeable for everyone. For example, when you speak with someone who is connected to the present moment, the interaction is usually much more enjoyable and engaging because that person listens very well and communicates with clues from the present moment. A good comedian in front of an audience seems to pull jokes out of nowhere and they land well because they fit the moment and feel fresh and relevant. That comedian is fully present, but if they weren't, the jokes would feel rehearsed and flat. Likewise, talking with someone who works mostly with generic statements and tried responses is a joyless experience that can leave everyone feeling frustrated and lonely. Where is this freshness coming from in the communications of someone in the now? From the universal consciousness, from a direct connection to the source: the essence of all spiritual teachings and religions.

Tolle puts this connection and its usability in these practical terms: "Should a situation arise that you need to deal with now, your action will be clear and incisive if it arises out of present-moment awareness. It is also more likely to be effective. It will not be a reaction coming from the past conditioning of your mind, but an intuitive response to the situation."[86] When you focus on the present

85 Eckhart Tolle, *The Power of Now: A Guide to Spiritual Enlightenment* (Novato: New World Library, 2010), 20.

86 Tolle, *The Power of Now*, 66.

moment, you divert mental energy from those things in your life that you label problems, because 'problem' always refers to something that has happened in the past and calls for resolution, or to something you believe will happen in the future and require your resources. In the present moment, usually, there is none of that, unless your mind drops it on you. To put it bluntly, unless you are confronted with something that needs your immediate action — say, you have an arrow stuck in your leg or a bull stampede is coming down the street — your so-called problems have no business being in the present moment.

Tolle mentions in his book that this is precisely what Zen is all about: clearing the mind of anything that has no business being in your mind at the present moment. He says: "The whole essence of Zen consists in walking along the razor's edge of Now — to be so utterly, so completely present that no problem, no suffering, nothing that is not who you are in your essence, can survive in you. In the Now, in the absence of time, all your problems dissolve."[87] He mentions in this context the Zen master Rinzai and his method of bringing students into the present moment by asking them, "What, at this moment, is lacking?" It is a brilliant question that, in most moments, we can probably answer with "nothing." Try it for yourself; ask yourself what in this moment is lacking, and you can almost hear your problems falling away, cut off from the constant mind attention we give them, whether or not we are aware of doing that. This constant something-in-the-back-of-your-mind-pulling-you-out-of-the-present is something I want you to work with because it is the ideal target for the upside-is-downness that makes yoga so effective, plus it eventually leads to a new foundation for effective manifestation. But first, let's look at the power of your attention in the context of focusing on the present.

---

87 Tolle, *The Power of Now*, 52.

INTEGRATED FUTURE. ENHANCED NOW FOR BETTER MANIFESTING

We have established that applying mind activity to your seed desire is crucial for its development into full manifestation. A simple way of saying this is: What you give your attention to will grow. However, if you are not aware of where you put your attention, the default object is usually that which is already manifested —those things and situations right in front of you or going on right now. If you give your attention to what is, what is will grow instead of your desire, which does not receive the full nourishment of your attention. Attention is like water in a watering can. If you pour all of it on the plants above ground, the seeds underground will die. Patanjali's Yoga Sutras elaborate on this dilemma, and we can relate it to manifestation:

> "To him who possesses discernment, all personal life is misery, because it ever waxes and wanes, is ever afflicted with restlessness, makes ever new dynamic impresses in the mind; and because all its activities war with each other. (2.15)

> This pain is to be warded off, before it has come (2.16)

> The cause of what is to be warded off is the absorption of the Seer in things seen. (2.17)

> Things seen have as their property manifestation, action, inertia. They form the basis of the elements and the sense-powers. They make for experience and for liberation. (2.18)"

> – Patanjali, Yoga Sutras[88]

These four sutras talk about the nature of life, that everything changes eventually, and the pain this causes us as the mind fluctuates according to what it perceives in its surroundings. The cause of the pain is that we get too absorbed in the things we see and experience. When you reflect on your own life and that of your loved ones, you'll notice that the situations that endure are often those that receive ongoing attention and conversation. The general solution is to manage your attention and withdraw it from the present situation by practicing detachment from the external world and cultivating inner peace and stillness through practices such as

---

88 Patañjali, *The Yoga Sutras of Patanjali – The Book of the Spiritual Man: In Large Print*, trans. Charles Johnston (n.p.: Outlook Verlag, 2022), 39–40.

meditation and self-reflection. Now let's get back to the initial question: What kind of present-moment awareness is more effective for manifestation?

There are certainly enough reasons to cultivate present-mind awareness even if you don't intend to manifest — feeling alive, experiencing the world as vibrant, and having access to greater intelligence for all your communications and tasks — just as it makes sense to keep this type of awareness turned on all the time. However, there is more to it than simply flipping the switch. A present-focused mind has varied degrees and applications, just as becoming a yogi entails more than just meditating on a pillow. While the present mind is a versatile tool that can be applied to every situation, it is utilized for various purposes in the same way that different screwdrivers are used for different tasks. Eckhart Tolle discusses variation in the use of the mind while "enlightened," which is simply his way of being connected to the universal consciousness, the eternal isness, or "Being," as he calls it:

> "Enlightenment means rising above thought, not falling back to a level below thought. In the enlightened state, you still use your thinking mind when needed, but in a much more focused and effective way than before. You use it mostly for practical purposes, but you are free of the involuntary internal dialogue, and there is inner stillness. When you do use your mind, and particularly when a creative solution is needed, you oscillate every few minutes or so between thought and stillness, between mind and no-mind. No-mind is consciousness without thought." Eckhard Tolle[89]

Picture yourself in a plane's cockpit in flight, and the hardware and software that keep the plane in the air is your mind. You are the captain in charge of the controls that make the mind do what is needed for every phase of the flight. You'll use different switches for takeoff, landing, and flying through calm skies or turbulence. A good yogi is masterful inside the cockpit and can fly the plane with the mind as support, but never allows the mind to take over and fly the plane instead of you. A master always understands degrees and variations; that's what makes them masterful, and the mental tool for manifestation I want to add to your palette is "present mind plus projection of desired outcome."

You can call it an enhanced being in the Now, and it might strike purists as a dilution at first, but please bear with me. Nothing of what I am about to propose

---

89 Eckhart Tolle, *The Power of Now: A Guide to Spiritual Enlightenment* (Novato: New World Library, 2010), 25.

contradicts or weakens original spiritual teachings. It's just another instance where yoga and manifestation techniques fit seamlessly and become more effective when put together. For example, if you want to manifest a new home and you are sitting down to eat, and you want to be fully present and eat mindfully to enjoy the full flavor and sensations of the meal, you would sit down in your projected new home and eat your meal there. In your imagination, your surroundings would morph into the new place that you want, and you would see its form and feel its energy while enjoying the food in the physical space you are in at the moment. Think of it as a three-dimensional visualization of present-moment awareness.

The technique I'm describing here is the same as that found in the teachings of Goddard, Abraham, and even the Bible, where you visualize and feel your desire fulfilled. However, this book is about enhanced manifestation through yoga, and the process of projecting the fulfilled desire into the present moment is definitely enhanced from a yogic perspective and elevated consciousness. For a yogi who has observed their mind, understands the mechanics and patterns of their thinking, and knows how to manage these patterns, approaching manifesting through mind and thoughts in the same way is as though an experienced cook, who creates a new dish by applying the expertise and finesse gained from cooking many other meals.

But wait a second, you may say, isn't this exactly what we don't want? Bringing the future into the mix and diverting the mind with something that isn't really here? The answer is no, because there is no future involved in any of this. Do not confuse the future with the fact that the manifestation on the physical plane has not yet happened. If what you are bringing into the mix is the spiritual version of this manifestation, then it already exists right now. It is easy to confuse the future with the desired state because you may think of the desired state as something that happens in the future. However, the idea is to bring the desired state into the present.

Let's go back to the example and break the process down. Again, you are sitting at the table, mindfully eating a bowl of your favorite meal inside the spiritual version of your new home. All of this is the present moment. Remember how Tolle describes the process of the present mind in action: "When you do use your mind, and particularly when a creative solution is needed, you oscillate every few minutes or so between thought and stillness, between mind and no-mind."[90] What does this look like in this example of a manifestation session for a new home while eating a meal? You sit down and begin with a thought, thinking about how the desired home fits into your space. Where are the walls, what color are they, and what is on them? You see the furniture, windows, and what lighting is there. Then you hold all this and oscillate to no-thought, which is the feeling of all these ingredients together as the new surroundings of your present moment in which you enjoy the food as real as possible in the now. There is the flavor of the food, the surroundings of your imagination, the ambience, your corresponding feelings and enjoyment, and then you stay in this space for as long as possible.

A mind trained in yoga and meditation can hold this projection much longer, but it is true for most yogis, except the true masters, that we cannot turn the mind off and remain in an all-feeling state all the time. That's fine, and eventually you'll drop out of the lived imagination into a segment where thought is dominant again. Go with it and use the new segment to apply your thoughts to make adjustments in your projection. What do you need to make it better now that you've lived in it for a little while? Better lighting? Inspiring art on the walls? A glorious view from the windows that you didn't see before? Are people joining you at the table and expressing their awe at the new reality? Just keep going with additions and modifications, then go back into being in the space as long and deeply as you can. And repeat this process several times.

Do you recognize this process from something you learned during your first meditation instruction? You were instructed to observe your thoughts without reacting to them, and whenever a thought caught your attention, to bring yourself back to observing, to being the seer detached from the thoughts floating by, like watching clouds in the sky and remaining steady as they move and change. The basic process here is the same, but it's a more complex version with a practical application beyond quieting the mind. It puts the mind to use and supports you while you and your fulfilled desire exist entirely in the present moment. It's advanced meditation, or an advanced application of the meditative mind for the purpose of creating. The mind takes you to the space, but then you

90 Tolle, *The Power of Now*, 23.

switch to no thought and experience the ideas not as mental concepts but as a felt reality. The present, future, and past are relevant for the entire process, but they play different roles at different times. This is the applied mind for practical purposes. As Tolle describes it, "any lesson from the past becomes relevant and is applied now. Any planning as well as working toward achieving a particular goal is done now. The enlightened person's main focus of attention is always the Now, but they are still peripherally aware of time."[91]

In the previous example, the desired future is still present in your mind, as you are aware that it exists in the spiritual realm but not yet in the physical world. However, this awareness is just one thought among many in your mind, and you learn to detach from it and let it pass without engaging with it. Instead, you focus on the feeling of having the fulfilled desire in the present moment.

If you still have doubts about this process, you might think that adding an imagined home or fantasy to your meditation practice would be counterproductive and make it more difficult to achieve clarity and stillness. However, it's essential to realize that this resistance to positive projections might reflect how challenging it is to maintain a positive outlook in a world that bombards us with negativity. The truth is, we already carry negative constructs in our minds all the time, such as problems that we carry with us constantly or the news we consume daily. By contrast, a projected fulfilled desire is a positive and intentional projection that we can choose to focus on. So, while some might argue that it's unnatural to inject another dimension or reality into the present moment, it's fair to say we are already doing this, just negatively. Tolles explains that we create a problem and thus create pain for our lives when we mentally dwell in a situation without having the intention to take action now. It means "you are carrying in your mind the insane burden of a hundred things that you will or may have to do in the future instead of focusing your attention on the one thing that you can do now."[92]

I am sure this sounds familiar to you. Most of us are already carrying our problems around all the time. But we've been doing it for so long that it feels

---

91 Tolle, *The Power of Now*, 57.

92 Tolle, *The Power of Now*, 65.

normal. What I am proposing is the same process, just conscious and with chosen cargo. Instead of unconsciously making a permanent space in your inner world for negative subjects, you do the radically uncommon thing of consciously holding positive subjects there. It is simply a reversal of habitual mental processes, and the reversal is complete. You choose what you hold there, and you want it there. It's beautiful and positive, and your mind is helping it grow in the physical world. It's your call. Tolle says that is a very radical choice, although also simple: "All it takes is a simple choice, a simple decision: no matter what happens, I will create no more pain for myself. I will create no more problems."[93] He also talks more about our containment of problems. He explores it in the context of becoming present for a better life, but at the core of this message, to my mind, is also manifestation:

> "If all your problems or perceived causes of suffering or unhappiness were miraculously removed for you today, but you had not become more present, more conscious, you would soon find yourself with a similar set of problems or causes of suffering, like a shadow that follows you wherever you go. Ultimately, there is only one problem: the time-bound mind itself."[94]

What he is describing here is unconscious manifestation due to mind patterns. Your mind manifests, whether you do it consciously or not, and most people do it unconsciously or refuse to believe that there is such a thing as conscious manifestation. If the mind operates in a particular pattern and does so unchecked, the same things will keep appearing in one's life. You might agree with it based on your own experience or working with clients and students. Now let's create solutions instead of problems — solutions that are manifested desires.

STRENGTH OF SPIRIT TRANSLATED FOR MANIFESTATION

This is a good time to define something that is often heard but is just as often misunderstood. What exactly does it mean to have a strong spirit? It's simple: if you have a strong physical body, you can move a bunch of boxes easily. If you have a strong spirit, you can mold and hold spiritual objects easily.

---

93 Tolle, *The Power of Now*, 65.

94 Tolle, *The Power of Now*, 61.

Here's an illustration: Imagine yourself in a difficult situation, for example, a room in which there is a fight going on with screaming and yelling and lots of stress. So you decide to walk out of the room into another room, and you close the door behind you. Now, in the second room, it's just you, and the space is open for you to relax. However, you can relax only if you have left the first room completely. And here is the difference between a strong spirit and a weak one: the person with a weak spirit is physically in the second room but still under the influence of the first room. The strong spirit inhabits the new space without any mental pieces from the first room. None of it is there, and the escape from the stressful situation is complete. Now take this analogy a step further. Instead of leaving a room on a time-space continuum, you simply use your mind power to access a different room. Then you live in it. This well-known Zen story serves as an illustration of this idea:

Two monks walked on a muddy road and saw a woman attempting to cross without getting her robes dirty. One monk offered to carry her across, which he did. They continued their journey in silence until the other monk spoke up, angry that the first monk had touched a woman, as monks are not supposed to touch women. The first monk replied, "I put her down hours ago, but it seems like you're still carrying her."

If spirit is a term for everything formless, then having a strong spirit is the ability to be strong in the realm of the formless. In manifesting, it means that you are strong in keeping the image of your desired state in its spiritual form. Check your own spiritual constitution: can you easily project and hold your desired state within your reality? Are you able to walk in the world in which your desire is manifested? Or do you fall out of it easily, pulled back by your attention to what is?

The alternate universe of your imagination is always available for you to step into. But, granted, it's also simple to fall out. Any spiritual path is a constant in and out of elevated states. Spiritual teacher Ram Das gives an excellent, relatable example of a common cause for falling out of an elevated state. He said, "You think you're so spiritual. Just spend a weekend with your family." He's right. Whether it's your family or anyone around whom you feel weak or who brings out childish patterns in you, some people and events can bring you down quickly from an elevated state. It's like that with manifestation. You spend a few minutes in the imagined state of having millions of dollars, but then you come home to your shabby little apartment, and the reality of it pulls you back down into the universe in which you can barely pay your rent.

With a strong spirit, you *stay* in the desired state. Having a strong spirit also means becoming what you want to attract. This is a feat, a projection of a reality that exists in the formless realm. It means holding your consciousness in a state with conditions that exist in your imagination. It's like being the skilled operator of the 3D sci-fi holodeck you are creating for yourself. It's a muscle that you build when you bring yourself back into an elevated state, when you meditate, and when you strengthen your body and mind through your practice so that you can apply yourself in the ethers with consistency and stamina.

There are excellent meditations and sets for strong spirit at the end of this chapter.

September 21, 1985

Sit in Easy Pose with a straight spine and a light Neck Lock.

Mudra: Push the thumbs into the base of the cheekbones. Push in and up. Put the tongue on the upper palate, just behind the teeth. Keep the tongue on the upper palate.

Eyes: Third Eye Point.

Mantra & Mental Focus: Become a pouch of water; dissolve your muscles and your bones. Your skin is nothing but a pouch of water. Pull your meridians up, concentrate, and let the hypothalamus work. Repeat the mantra, **I AM ALL, ALL IS ME.** Continue for **1 minute.** Continue applying pressure and think these thoughts: "Because God cannot come to Earth and shake hands with you, God gave you a chance to make you as you. You are the best. If God could have produced better than you, He would have. It's Almighty God. He produced you; accept it — and accept it now." Consciously talk to yourself. Turn yourself into the *tattva* of water. Plug into the central nervous system and just turn yourself into water. Concentrate in this position and let the energy flow. Let it rinse from you the deficiencies and defects that you create because of other people and their thoughts about you. Continue for **8 more minutes**

To End: Inhale deeply, suspend the breath for **15–30 seconds**, and feel good. Exhale, and relax. Shake out your hands. Relax.

Comments: Give yourself a chance. Try to understand, in a conscious way, that you can totally eliminate all your neuroses — now. Because you have stimulated the central channel and forced that energy through the hypothalamus. You have activated both the Ida and the Pingala. All you have to do is understand that you are you. If it is true that you are born in the image of God, first believe. It's a belief system. Then you are born to succeed. This therapy has been known to mankind for thousands and thousands of years. Water keeps all levels equal, so neurosis and wisdom will come into equilibrium.

◊

February 3, 1977

Sit in Easy Pose with a straight spine and a light Neck Lock.

Mudra: Rest the hands in a comfortable position of your choice; you may rest them in the lap or in Gyan mudra on the knees.

Eye Focus: Closed.

Breath: Breathe normally.

Visualization: Imagine you are on a mountain and you are looking down at the town or city that you live in. Understand that what you are seeing is really inside of you. Imagine what size your head must be and think of how much it can contain. Now go up in the air until you can look at the entire United States. Go beyond this and see the entire Earth. Understand that the entire planet is in your head. Expand and see the solar system. Then see the entire universe. Become the entire universe, but still be in the body. Feel the vast amounts of energy flowing through the body. Expand the little "I" into a big "I." Go beyond time and try to grab infinity. Just expand into the vastness of yourself. In this vastness, see the light of purity. It is a glittering, simple, soft light. Now imagine that this glittering, soft, beautiful, pure light is in the center of your head. Focus on it. That is where the pineal gland is located. It is the most precious gem that God has put there. See nothing but light. It is blue light.**To End:** Inhale deeply and exhale completely. Repeat **2 more times**. Then inhale, suspend the breath, and exhale.

Comments: Concentrate very humbly, because when there is concentration, the glands overwork and oversecrete. Due to this stimulation of the endocrine system, this is a good meditation to practice on the day of the full moon. It will enhance your inner radiance. It is subtle, warm, and pure. Become pure light. Understand I am, I am.

◊

PART 4 **PRACTICE TIME: THE YOGA SCHOOL OF MANIFESTATION**

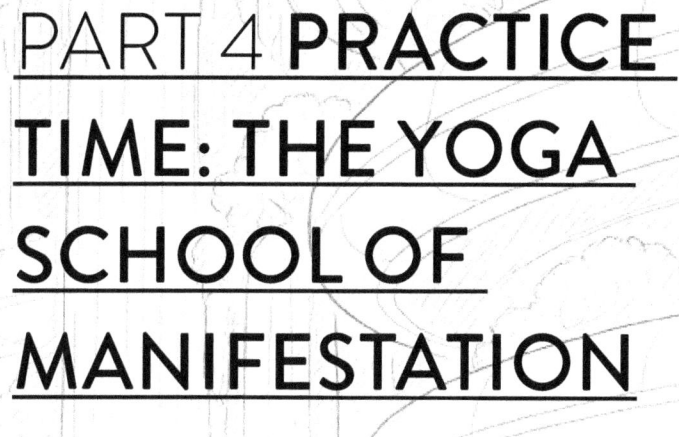

MANIFESTATION BOOT CAMP FOR YOGIS

"Yoga is skill in actions." - Bhagavad Gita (2.50)

This fourth part contains the yoga and meditation tools that take your manifestation skills to the next level. Most of the techniques presented below are yogic tools like sets (kriyas), meditations, pranayama, and relaxation techniques that have been around for a long time. I found them to be excellent manifestation enhancers, and they can help you get into the ideal physical, mental, and vibrational space for advanced manifestation.

However, their effectiveness for manifestation is not always obvious from their names and descriptions, which means these tools are diamonds in the rough for our purposes. Let's discover how we can make them shine with manifesting power. Your adjusted perspective is the only change necessary for most of these ancient tools, and all we need to do is apply them with new and enhanced intentions. Consider it a new adventure in yoga.

I am also introducing several new techniques to bring manifestation to spaces where they have rarely been used before, especially in group situations. As far as I know, all the classic and popular manifestation techniques mentioned in this book focus on the manifestation for and by an individual. Yet, if all is connected and we are all one, the collective application of manifestation techniques could multiply their power exponentially. This part is subdivided into three parts: 1) Basic training for manifestors; 2) Classic yoga tools repurposed for manifestation; and 3) New spiritual techniques for manifesting in our times.

KRI KUNDALINI RESEARCH INSTITUTE

CHAPTER 12
Time to Get Physical in Manifestation

Your directed mind performs internal work in the process of manifestation. It's a form of meditation, and as we established in earlier chapters, there is no better preparation for deep meditation than physical yoga, because that's exactly what most physical yoga has been designed for since ancient times. I won't say that you can't meditate deeply without physical preparation, but I believe almost every meditation can benefit from a good physical preparation of the body and the mind through a good yoga set or even some simple exercises and pranayama. The classic texts agree. In Yoga Sutra 2.46, Patanjali explains that the practice of asanas is a preparation of the body and mind for deep meditation. The Sanskrit words in this sutra, *Sthira Sukham Asanam*, say that a steady and comfortable posture allows the mind to become clear, quiet, and focused. In Chapter 6, Verse 11 of the Bhagavad Gita, the ancient Hindu scripture, Lord Krishna talks to Arjuna about bringing the body under control for effective meditation.

These yoga and meditation techniques are hardly mentioned in most contemporary manifestation materials, which is yet another strong reason to integrate them into our practice for ultimate manifestation success through optimized mind and body. The following techniques described in the following pages are excellent preparations for deep meditation.

SIMPLE WARM-UP WITH KUNDALINI YOGA PRACTICES

Please do not underestimate the effects of a good physical warm-up on your manifestation powers. With physical preparation, you'll be able to carry out all the spiritual work necessary for manifestation — isolating, planting, holding, and nurturing the spiritual seed of your manifested desire — much more easily, and the intensity of the inner experience might surprise you. Moreover, the sets provide additional health benefits for your whole body, a true win-win. So before engaging in the internal manifestation work, try any of the following exercises and sets. You'll see four options below to choose from, depending on how much time you have and how deeply you want to go. I use all of them regularly and love what they do. For extra deep meditation, try the two Kundalini Yoga sets below. They require a greater time investment, but they are well worth it. If you've never combined meditation with a good yoga set, you're in for a treat.

1) Frog Pose. Squat on the toes, with the knees wide and spine straight. Heels touch and are off the ground. Fingertips are on the ground between the legs and close to the body. The face is forward. Lift the hips and straighten the legs up on the inhale, keeping the fingertips on the ground. Squat down to the starting position on the exhale. Engage the Navel Point and use the fingertips on the ground for support. Keep the heels slightly off the ground throughout the exercise, and the knees always remain outside the arms. Continue this cycle **21 times.** Move rapidly and breathe powerfully.

2) Spinal Twist. Sit in Easy Pose with a straight spine and a light Neck Lock. Interlock the hands behind the head at the hairline (under any loose hair) and twist the body powerfully from left to right. Keep the elbows stretched to the sides. Continue for **1 minute.**

This exercise helps move the lymph fluid through the lymph vessels and lymph nodes. This vigorous movement creates a flushing action for the aura, moving out old stagnant energy. It activates and flushes the spleen through a meridian point beneath the armpit.

◇

9 - MINUTE SET FOR AN AGREEABLE MIND

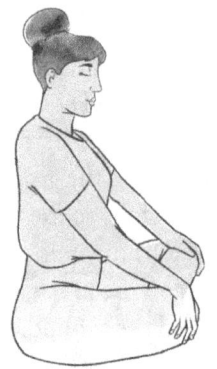

1) Spinal Flex. Sit in Easy Pose with a straight spine and a light Neck Lock. Grasp the knees firmly. Keeping the elbows straight, flex the upper spine forward and lift the chest on the inhale; flex the upper spine backward on the exhale. The movement is at the level of the upper thoracic spine in the heart area. The head is still and remains in Neck Lock. Continue at a moderate pace for **3 minutes**.

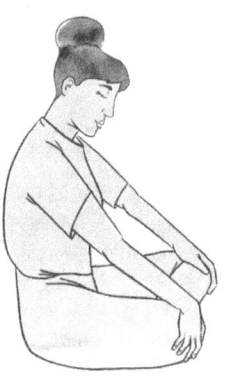

This exercise is for the lymph area. If done correctly, it will create an unusual pressure behind the ears on the neck. It means your whole nervous system and central nervous system, the Shushumna, are stretching. It should create sweat on the face.

2) Sat Kriya. Sit on the heels in Rock Pose with a straight spine and a light Neck Lock. Interlace the fingers with the Jupiter (index) fingers pointing up and the thumbs crossed. For working with masculine, projective energy, place the right thumb over the left. For working with feminine, reflective energy, place the left thumb over the right. Keep the ribcage lifted and the shoulders down; the shoulder blades are drawn down and wide. Chant SAT and pull the Navel Point in and up. Chant NAAM as you release it. Continue rhythmically for **3 minutes**.

TO END: Inhale, apply Root Lock, and squeeze the muscles tightly from the buttocks all the way up the spine. Suspend the breath briefly as you concentrate on the area just above the top of the head. Mentally allow the energy to flow through the top of the skull. Exhale completely. Inhale, exhale, suspend the breath for **5-20 seconds**, and apply all three locks, the Great Lock (Root Lock, Diaphragm Lock, and Neck Lock). Inhale and completely relax. Ideally, the relaxation is twice the length of time that you practiced Sat Kriya.

3) Alternate Shoulder Shrugs. Sit in Easy Pose with a straight spine and a light Neck Lock. Place the hands on the knees. Raise the left shoulder up as you lower the right shoulder on the inhale, and raise the right shoulder up as you lower the left shoulder on the exhale. Continue moving one shoulder up as the other comes down for 1 ½ minutes. Then reverse the breath, raise the right shoulder up, left shoulder down on the inhale and raise the left shoulder up and the right shoulder down on the exhale. Continue for **1 ½ minutes.** Breathe powerfully.

◊

◇ Kundalini Yoga Kriya to Correct Nerve Shallowness

June 6, 1984

1) Half Wheel Pose. Come into Half Wheel Pose by lying on the back and bending the knees to bring the feet flat on the floor, hip joint distance apart. Feel two parallel lines between the hip joints, knees, ankles, and feet. Lift the chest up and keep drawing the shoulder blades down the back. You can interlace your hands under your back to keep the chest open until you are strong enough to place them under your shoulders and can lift the torso all the way up. Do a heavy Breath of Fire through the mouth for **1 minute.**

This exercise benefits the nervous system.

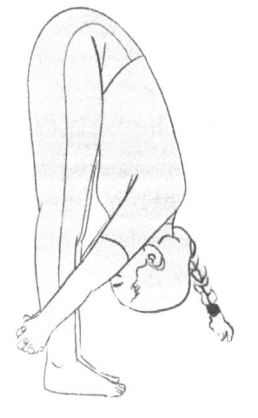

2) Forward Bend Variation. Stand up and bend forward, stretching your spine and bringing your head toward your knees. Keep your legs straight and interlace your hands behind your legs. Place your head through the legs if possible. Inhale through the mouth and exhale through the nose. Breathe quickly for **3 minutes.**

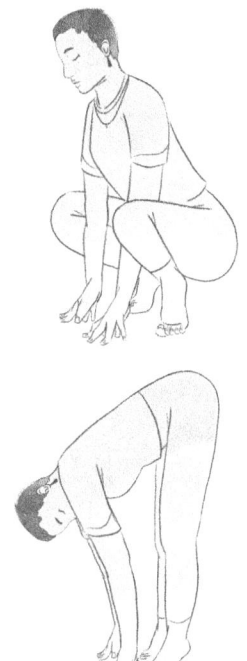

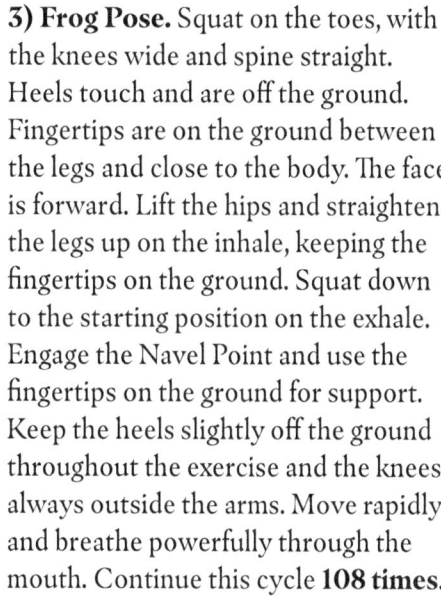

3) Frog Pose. Squat on the toes, with the knees wide and spine straight. Heels touch and are off the ground. Fingertips are on the ground between the legs and close to the body. The face is forward. Lift the hips and straighten the legs up on the inhale, keeping the fingertips on the ground. Squat down to the starting position on the exhale. Engage the Navel Point and use the fingertips on the ground for support. Keep the heels slightly off the ground throughout the exercise and the knees always outside the arms. Move rapidly and breathe powerfully through the mouth. Continue this cycle **108 times**.

4) Spine Circles. Sit in Easy Pose. Fold the arms across the chest, grasping the upper portion of the opposite arm. Rotate the spine around the hips, moving heavy and fast. Move "as if you are grinding at the sides." Continue for **2 minutes.**

→

5) Sit-ups Variation. Lie down on the back with the hands on the chest. Inhale through the mouth and raise the torso, bending forward, bringing the forehead to the knees. Exhale through the nose and lie back down. Continue for **3 ½ minutes.**

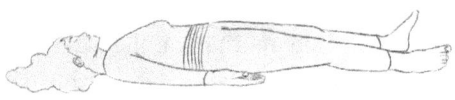

6) Lie on the Back with Breath. Remain on the back. Inhale deeply and quickly (1-2 seconds) and exhale long and slow (12-15 seconds). Continue for **3 minutes.**

TO END: Stretch and wiggle the body.

7) Knees Bounce. Sit in Easy Pose, hold your front shin with both hands and raise and lower the knees. Move fast and bounce the knees as high up and as far down as they can go. Continue for **1 ½ minutes.**

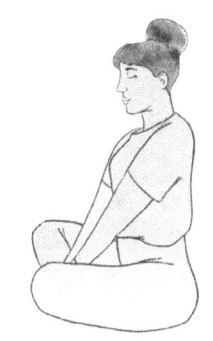

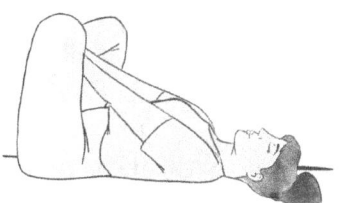

8) Back Roll Variation. Remain in Easy Pose, grasping the front shin with both hands, roll all the way back on your spine, and return to a sitting position. Continue rolling back and forth for **1 minute.**

Comments: When the nervous system acts extraordinarily weakly, the capability to be effectively calm and active becomes very shallow. It is not you who makes mistakes or who suffers. It is the nervous shallowness. Yogic science calls it 'slow wave contact.' The nervous authority, nervous center, and nervous self are not effectively strong enough to communicate their own duties about the physical identity. Your physical identity has a frequency, and your nervous center must correspondingly respond to it, and when that is not coordinated well, life is foggy. And mostly, such a life is based on the emotional self, emotional extension, and emotional satisfaction. The problem with emotional satisfaction is that, as much as you emotionally want to satisfy yourself, that feeling will be shallow and empty. Because once you let the emotions rule you, there are millions of them. There is one consciousness and millions of emotions.

◊

◊ Kundalini Yoga Kriya for Lungs, Magnetic Field & Deep Meditation

November 27, 1974

1) Whistle Breath. Sit in Easy Pose. Stretch the arms straight over the head with the palms together. Pull the spine up and tilt it back as far as you can gracefully maintain balance, applying a light Root Lock. Breathe consciously through the puckered mouth in a long whistle on the inhale and exhale. Continue for **5 minutes**. Relax for 30 seconds.

2) Arm Extensions. Remain in Easy Pose and interlace the fingers in front of the Heart Center with the palms facing forward and the thumb tips touching. Inhale and stretch the arms forward, parallel to each other and to the ground. Exhale as you bend the elbows and bring the back of the palms near the chest at the level of the Heart Center. Move quickly and breathe powerfully for **2-3 minutes**.

TO END: Inhale and suspend the breath with the arms extended briefly. Relax the breath and maintain the position to begin the next exercise.

3) Arm Pumps. Remain in Easy Pose. Inhale with the hands interlaced, arms extended forward, and palms facing away from the body. Suspend the breath in, and pump the arms up over the head and back down parallel to the ground. Then exhale, bringing the hands near the chest. Quickly inhale back into the first position and continue the sequence in a steady rhythm for **2-3 minutes**.

TO END: Inhale, extend the arms, and suspend the breath briefly for **10-15 seconds**. Exhale and immediately begin the next exercise.

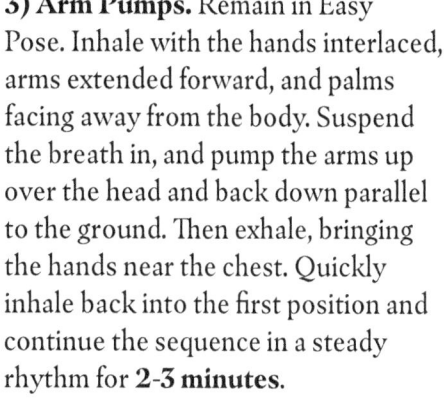

4) Arm Pulling. Remain in Easy Pose. Extend the arms forward parallel to the ground at a 60-degree angle to the body, with the palms facing each other and the elbows straight. Inhale deeply and slowly as you clench the fists. Suspend the breath in, slowly bend the arms, and bring the fists toward the chest, creating tremendous tension in all the arm and hand muscles. Pull as if you were dragging a thousand-pound weight. When you finally touch the chest, release the breath and the fists with an explosive exhale. Continue for **3 minutes**. Maintain an emotional and facial posture of anger and determination throughout the exercise.

➔

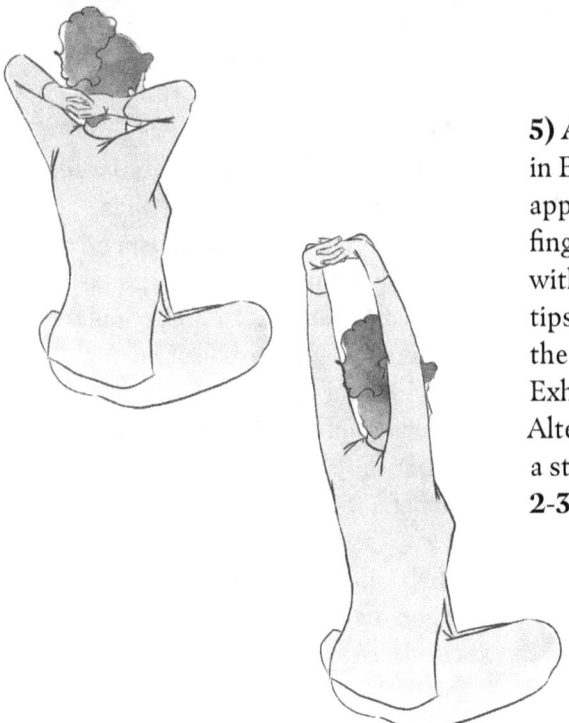

5) Arm Pumps Variation. Remain in Easy Pose with a straight spine and apply a light Root Lock. Interlace the fingers an inch (3 cm) behind the neck with the palms facing up and thumb tips touching. Inhale as you stretch the arms straight up over the head. Exhale back into the original position. Alternate rapidly, up and down, with a strong, smooth breath. Continue for **2-3 minutes**.

6) Torso Twists. Immediately stretch the arms straight up, hugging the ears with the palms flat together and the thumbs crossed over each other to lock the hands together. Inhale as you twist the torso and head to the left. Exhale as you twist toward the right. Rotate side to side at a steady, quick pace for **2-3 minutes**.

TO END: Inhale at the center, suspend the breath, apply Root Lock, and exhale.

7) Hand Pumps. Interlace the fingers in front of the Heart Center with the hands facing down and raise the elbows so that the forearms are parallel to the ground. Inhale as you raise the hands and forearms at the level of the Third Eye, keeping the arms parallel. Exhale down into the first position. Create a rapid, pumping motion and a strong, steady breath. Continue for **2-3 minutes**.

TO END: Inhale, suspend the breath for **10-15 seconds**, and exhale.

8) Spinal Twist. Remain in Easy Pose with a straight spine and a light Neck Lock. Grasp the shoulders with the fingers in front and the thumbs in back. Twist to the left on the inhale and twist to the right on the exhale. Keep the upper arms parallel to the ground, elbows pulled back to open the chest. Initiate the movement from the Navel Point, not the arms. The head moves last. Continue for **2–3 minutes**.

TO END: Inhale at the center, apply Root Lock, suspend the breath for **10-15 seconds**, and exhale.

→

9) Shoulder Shrugs. Remain in Easy Pose with a straight spine and a light Neck Lock. Rest the hands on the knees. Raise both shoulders up towards the ears on the inhale, and drop the shoulders down on the exhale. Continue for **2-3 minutes.** Move and breathe powerfully.

10) Spinal Flex (Camel Ride). Sit in Easy Pose with a straight spine and a light Neck Lock. Grasp the shins or ankles with the hands. Tilt the pelvis forward on the inhale and backward on the exhale. Only the pelvis and lower spine move. The rib cage, shoulders, and head remain still and over the hips. The motion is fluid and continuous. Continue for **2-3 minutes.** Breathe powerfully.

11) Meditate. Roll the eyes up as far as possible. Concentrate at the top of the head. Meditate for **15 minutes.**

Comments: This kriya begins by purifying the blood and expanding the lung capacity. Then the circulatory system is stimulated. The thyroid and parathyroid secretions are added to the increased circulation, and the upper magnetic field of the body is increased. This is an excellent preparation for beginners who need to learn deep meditation.

PRATYAHARA AND DHYANA. TRAINING FOR FOCUS AND ABSORPTION IN MENTAL STATES

Masterful manifestors can use their imagination optimally to transport themselves to the desired state and stay absorbed in it for an extended period of time. *Dhyana*, or deep meditation, represents this skill, which is one of the eight limbs of yoga, as we've seen in an earlier chapter. In *Dhyana*, the practitioner is completely absorbed in the meditative state, which can include focused, consistent, crystallized imagination. You can think of Pratyahara, or withdrawal of the senses, as a preparation for *dhyana*, a disconnection from external stimuli, attention turned inward, and a concentration on a state and object of meditation without distractions. *Pratyahara* and *dhyana* are skills that anyone can develop, like endurance and precision in other aspects of life. Two meditations you can practice that are excellent for entering and being in a deep meditation state are A Pure Flame of Light (Chapter 9, page 169) and Meditation to Turn Yourself Into Water (Chapter 11, page 196).

A Buddhist meditation practice is worth mentioning here because it is another example of a practice for intense creative visualization and one-pointed focus, the meditation practice called "Pure Land Buddhism." Its goal is to facilitate rebirth in a spiritual realm called Pure Land, also known as the Paradise of Amithabha Buddha, the Buddha who is believed to have created this special realm, a land of pure bliss and liberation. A major aspect of the practice is to imagine Amitabha Buddha and picture the Pure Land. This is an advanced practice that is best done under the guidance of a good teacher, although Pure Land is said to be open to everyone, regardless of skill and background. If you wish to learn more, you can find extensive information in the book *Buddhism of Wisdom and Faith: Pure Land Principles and Practice* by Thich Thien Tam.

To set the stage for deep meditation outside and in, most asana practices are excellent, as mentioned before. For strong focus, all standing Hatha poses are there to serve you, and you'll find some below. Your absolute balance is required to hold these standing poses, which is key in switching your focus on and often faster than many other yoga practices. With some of these, the potential for injury is significant, so please practice with caution or under guidance, and always according to your level of experience. Practice one or several for a practice for 3–11 minutes, then go into meditation.

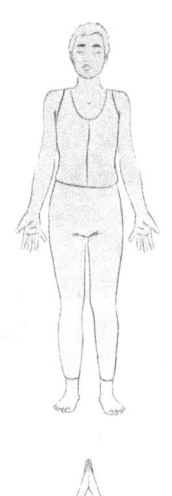

◊ Mountain Pose (Tadasana)

Stand tall with your feet together or hip wide apart, the arms relaxed by your sides, then twist the palms facing forward, tuck your tailbone under, and lift your chest.

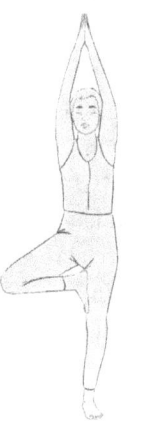

◊ Tree Pose (Vrikshasana)

Balance on one leg, the sole of the other foot against the inner thigh or calf of the other leg. Bring your hands in a prayer pose in front of your heart center or with your arms raised overhead.

◊ Warrior I (Virabhadrasana I)

Step one foot back into a lunge, the other leg in front with the knee bent at a 90-degree angle. Raise your arms overhead with palms facing forward or each other.

◊ Warrior II (Virabhadrasana II)

The same feet and leg position as Warrior I, but here, the hips and shoulders are open to the side of the back leg. Stretch the arms from the shoulders and parallel to the ground and legs, palms facing down, then look across the front hand.

◊ Eagle Pose (Garudasana)

Balance on one leg and wrap the other leg around it. Cross the arms in front of your chest, then press the palms together with the fingers pointing upward.

◊ Chair Pose (Utkatasana)

With the feet touching each other on the floor, come into a squatting position as if you are sitting in an invisible chair, your hips parallel to the ground. Stretch the arms upward and forward for balance.

◊ Extended Side Angle Pose
(Utthita Parsvakonasana)

Set up as in Warrior II, then rest the
forearm of the arm on the same side
as the front leg. Stretch the other arm
overhead, creating a diagonal line
from the side of the body.

◊ **ADVANCED**

◊ Warrior III (Virabhadrasana III)

Balance on one leg while the other leg and
torso are extended parallel to the ground,
forming a T shape with your whole body.
The arms either reach forward or behind
you like a superhero in flight.

◊ Extended Triangle Pose
(Utthita Trikonasana)

Stand with your feet about 3-4 feet
apart. Turn the right foot outward,
the left foot slightly inward. Bring
your arms parallel to the ground and
in line with your shoulders. Open
your hips slightly to the left, then
place your right hand outside your
right foot or on your shin or ankle.
The left arm is extended up, in line
with your right arm and shoulders.
Reverse the pose for the other side.

February 26, 1979

Sit in Easy Pose with a straight spine and a light Neck Lock.

Mudra: Rest the elbows at the sides and bring the forearms perpendicular to the ground with the hands at the level of the shoulders. Make a solid fist of the right hand with the palm facing forward. Bend the left wrist so that the hand is parallel to the ground, facing up with fingers together and straight pointing to the left.

Eye Focus: Tip of the Nose.

Breath: Long, slow, deep breath. Inhale and exhale consciously, with control. On the exhale, suspend the breath out for as long as you can, with the Navel Point pulled in firmly and the diaphragm lifted. When you can no longer hold the breath out, and before you experience any strain, inhale deeply and slowly.

Time: 11 minutes. You can gradually extend this time to **31 minutes** to deepen its effect.

To End: Rapidly inhale and exhale (2 seconds inhale, 2 seconds exhale). Repeat 1 more time. Then inhale, suspend the breath for 10 seconds, stretch both hands up and tighten the body, exhale, and relax.

Comments: Consciously hold the mudra. The left hand will tend to relax from its position, but keep it steady. Honest effort will bring the best results.

◊

___

CREATE YOUR OWN MANTRA FOR MANIFESTATION

Do you remember the first step in manifestation from the earlier chapter 2.1 "The Simple Truths"? Now that you know how mantras work, we can make this first step synonymous with creating your own mantra. In the same section, we also discussed that the key to finding the seed is to be as concise and accurate as possible in your articulation. Using "lake house" alone is more effective than saying "I want a lake house" because it has more space and potential to be filled with your feelings and visions. Saying "I want a lake house" is pretty clear but blunt and flat. The simple "Lake House," on the other hand, can be buzzing with anything you want inside and around it. That's why in the meditation below, you chant just "Har" and not "I am projecting Har." If you look at the meaning of most mantras, it's almost always just a term, not a sentence, and I suspect it's for that reason: to allow it to be fleshed out as a personal experience in any way possible and without the concept limitations that come with additional words.

So make the first step of your manifestation process like a mantra — a brief, concise container that carries most of its meaning in the feelings and interpretations you bring to it. That's what makes it creative and alive. Here's one example that came to me in meditation while writing this book. It's silly, but bear with me: "Unicorn forest with watermelon juice fountains." Repeat it a few times and check in with yourself to see what happens in your inner world. Is something becoming alive in your mind's eye? Are colors, shapes, motions, and feelings coming up? Are unicorns beginning to jump around in your mind's eye, drinking watermelon juice from fountains? Hopefully this little fun exercise shows you what can happen if you state your desire as a potent mantra that can burst into life through the mere repetition of sounds and the associations in your mind.

Now go ahead and create your own mantra based on your desire. Find the concise term that nails your desire. Let it become a container for the feelings that come with having your desire fulfilled, and awaken it by chanting it a few times. Keep it in a pocket of your mind and pull it out whenever you like to bring the feeling of your fulfilled desire into the space. Using the mantra is equivalent to nurturing the seed of your desire into manifestation.

June 21, 1996

This exercise is part of Subagh Kriya and can also be practiced as a stand-alone meditation. Sit in Easy Pose with a straight spine and a light Neck Lock.

Mudra: Rest the elbows by the sides; raise the forearms angled up and outward with the fingers at the level of the throat and the palms facing down. Alternately hit the sides of the hands together. The Mercury (little) fingers and the Moon Mounds (located on the bottom of the palms) hit when the palms face up. When the palms hit facing down, the sides of the Jupiter (index) fingers touch, and the thumbs cross below the hands, with the right thumb under the left. Chant **HAR** as you alternately hit the sides of the hands.

Eye Focus: Tip of the Nose, 1/10th open

Mantra: Chant **HAR** from the Navel using the tip of the tongue. (Tantric Har recording was played in the original class

Time: 3-11 minutes.

Comments: "This meditation stimulates the mind, the moon center, and Jupiter. When Jupiter and the moon come together, there is no way in the world you will not create wealth." — Yogi Bhajan

◇

POSITIVITY FROM ARCHETYPICAL POSES

The universal field is the garden for your manifestation seeds, but you still need to pick the best plot before you plant. Positivity is the plot with the most sunshine, richest soil, and cleanest water. Negativity is like the shady plot next to a dumping ground or a gas station, with crusty soil and toxins leaking into it. So arrive positive at your plot first before you manifest. And by "positive," I am referring to both your state of mind and the nature of your desire.

Let's be very clear: if you want to manifest improvements in any aspect of your life, the process starts with positivity and all its sisters and brothers under the same umbrella: optimism, enthusiasm, confidence, happiness, as well as gratitude, vitality, and compassion. Positivity is the compass for all steps in your manifestation endeavor. Remember from the eight limbs of yoga the *Yamas* and *Nyamas*, the do's and don'ts on the spiritual path, and manifesting for negative purposes would fall under *Ahimsa*, one of the *Yamas* or restraints: cultivate a mindset of love and compassion for others and avoid harm to others and yourself

If you can't find the positivity in you, wait until you can. In yoga, everything begins with the self, and if it's not on the inside, you won't find it on the outside. If positivity is your dominant and default state with all steps in the manifestation process, you'll have a wonderful time from beginning to end.

There are also many specific tools in yoga for feeling positive, and some are among the simplest yogic practices you can do. The next time you need a quick boost, try yogic movements that express positive emotions. I refer to these movements as "archetypes of emotional expressions" because they are universally recognizable without needing an explanation. For example, if you saw someone raising their arms up in the air with a smile, even just as a stick figure in a cartoon, you would most likely identify the expressed emotions as exuberant joy with no further information. In a 2015 study at the University of Geneva called "Emotion regulation through execution, observation, and imagery of emotional movements," researchers studied if emotional movements like those described above could be used as a method for managing emotions, and the study results clearly showed that expressions of these emotional movements, which include performing, observing, and visualizing them, were effective in changing emotions. This is equally true for movement expressions of positive emotions and those of negative emotions, like clenching your fists in anger or letting your head hang down in sadness. With this information, you can create your own positive-emotion warm-up for a better manifestation session. Take any or all of the following, or come up with your own movement that best expresses the emotion that goes along with your manifestation.

1. Begin with your hands on your heart center and move your arms up into victory pose at a 60-degree angle and down again. Repeat for several minutes while feeling victorious. You can do this sitting or standing up and move your legs with it as well.

2. Do a dance of joy as you might after receiving wonderful news, like winning a big prize at a raffle, for example.

3. Bring your hands to your cheeks in astonishment, like the kid from the movie *Home Alone*, except that your expression and attitude are exclusively of positive astonishment, or awe.

1. Sit down and go into manifestation mode by imagining and feeling. You might find that imagining your fulfilled desire in the most positive way is easier than ever before.

Achieving a positive mindset is one of the most important foundations for successful manifestation, so we are offering more related yogic techniques from the Kundalini Yoga toolbox on the following pages. They all approach positivity in different ways, so try the approach that resonates most with you or try each to identify the one(s) that work best for you. By the way, Kundalini Yoga uses the concept of archetypal expressions all the time and employs a lot of these in both sets (called kriyas) and meditations. Practitioners frequently practice them for longer periods, anywhere from 3 to 31 minutes or more, so that they can really milk the essence of these expressions and let them sink into their being. Below, I have selected a few practices with this goal. Before that, however, I want to share another technique that helps you in the process of replacing a negative seed with a positive one. It comes from Tibetan Buddhism.

APPROACH	KRIYA OR MEDITATION
Positivity from archetypical pose	Kriya Developing the Power to Win, page 231
Elevating your vibration	Kriya for Elevation, page 233 Meditation for Positive Mind, page 241
Generating joy for the practice	The Enthusiast Meditation, page 243
Dissolving productivity blocks	The Producer Meditation, page 244

In his book *The Diamond Cutter*, author Geshe Michael Roach describes a custom that Tibetan monks follow to set the right tone for the day and for success. It is also a great preparation for successful manifestation. The process is called Prenpa Tan, and one meaning of it is "shooting an arrow." You can think of it as fixing a particular outcome for the day by preparing yourself physically and mentally. The process is like creating the conditions for deep meditation. You dedicate a quiet space in your home. If you already have a meditation spot, just make sure it's not in your bed or close to where you sleep, so you won't transfer the energy of the night

You get up and, just like the Tibetan monks do, splash water on your face and blow your nose hard so you can breathe smoothly, then sit comfortably and go into absolute silence. Michael Roach says that the Tibetan monks emphasize the posture, just like many yogis do, and that sitting up straight engages your nervous system in the best way and supports the silencing of the mind.

Then you start with about 10 deep breaths, a practice the Tibetans call "joint-ngoop." The idea is to clear your mind by placing the mind on the breath and shutting out any thought or experience. The task is not to let your mind wander for ten breaths, and each time it does, start over. Like a muscle, your ability to focus will get stronger with this daily practice.

The next step after the ten breaths is to focus on the issue at hand and look closely at it. Roach says this is when you understand that the problem grew out of a negative seed in your mind, and the solution is to replace the seed or plant a positive seed that will grow into success. The session ends by visualizing yourself and your day with the most successful outcome. This is a Tibetan way of preparing yourself for optimum manifestation. You become still, recognize the path of negative manifestation the mind is on, and redirect it, visualizing the positive manifestation instead.

◇

April 2, 1986

1) Arms Raises. Sit in Easy Pose with the arms extended straight forward and angled downward. Interlock the fingers with the Jupiter (index) fingers extended and the thumbs crossed. Inhale and lift your arms straight up over the head, exhale and lower the arms back to the starting position. Continue for **1 minute.** Start Breath of Fire, inhaling and exhaling as deep as you can and continue for **15 more minutes.**

The index finger represents the flow of Jupiter energy. It is your projection, just like pointing. Magnetizing the Jupiter finger while energizing your navel center gives you focus, confidence, and victory.

2) Shoulder Twists Claps. Inhale, twist the shoulders to the left and exhale as you clap at the left side. Inhale, twist the shoulders to the right side, and exhale as you clap at the right side. All the twisting movement is done with the shoulders. Continue for **5 minutes.** Move to the rhythm of *I Am Thine* by Livtar Singh.

→

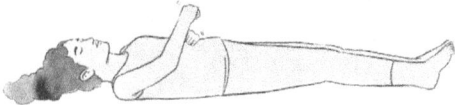

3) Navel Activation. Lie on the back and pump your navel in rhythm with *I Am Thine*. Lightly and rhythmically beat your navel with alternate hands. Continue for **3 minutes.**

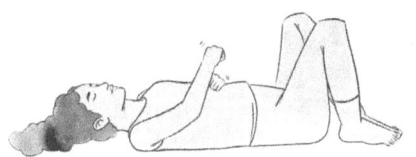

4) Butterfly Variation. Remain on the back, bend the knees, and keep the heels together on the ground. Open and close the knees while continuing to pump the navel and beat it with alternate hands. Continue for **1 ½ minutes.**

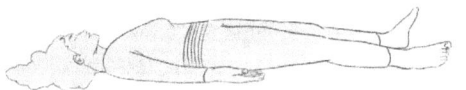

5) Relaxation with Chanting. Remain on the back in Corpse Pose and completely relax. Listen to *I Am Thine* for **4 minutes,** then sing along with the recording for **3 more minutes.**

Comments: The highest mental power of a human being is when they are confronted with a condition that is infinitely beyond their control and they have the will and strength to face it and come through it.

◊

Originally published in The Aquarian Teacher Yoga Manual

1) Ego Eradicator. Sit in Easy Pose with a straight spine and a light Neck Lock. Roll the shoulders down and open the shoulder blades wide. Raise the arms up and straight to 60 degrees. Curl the fingers onto the mounds at the base of the fingers and stretch the palms wide, pulling knuckles back. Stretch the thumbs away from the fingers and point them straight up. With eyes closed, focus on the Third Eye Point, while concentrating above the head. Continue for **1-3 minutes** with Breath of Fire.

TO END: Inhale, suspend the breath, and touch the thumb tips together over the head. Open fingers wide. Exhale and apply Root Lock. Inhale, exhale, and slowly lower the arms. Relax.

This helps open the lungs, brings the hemispheres of the brain to a state of alertness, and consolidates the magnetic field.

2) Spinal Flex. Sit in Easy Pose with a straight spine and a light Neck Lock. Grasp the knees firmly. Keeping the elbows straight, flex the upper spine forward and lift the chest on the inhale; flex the upper spine backward on the exhale. The movement is at the level of the upper thoracic spine in the heart area. The head is still and remains in Neck Lock. Continue at a moderate pace for **1-3 minutes**.

This exercise is for the lymph area. If done correctly, it will create an unusual pressure behind the ears on the neck. It means your whole nervous system and central nervous system, the Shushumna, are stretching. It should create sweat on the face.

3) Spinal Twist. Remain in Easy Pose with a straight spine and a light Neck Lock. Grasp the shoulders with the fingers in front, thumbs in back. Twist to the left on the inhale and twist to the right on the exhale. Keep the upper arms parallel to the ground, elbows pulled back to open the chest. Initiate the movement from the Navel Point, not the arms. Allow the head to move with the spine. Continue for **1-3 minutes.**

TO END: Inhale deeply at the center, suspend the breath, exhale, and relax.

This stimulates and stretches the lower and mid-spine.

4) Front Life Nerve Stretch. Sit with the legs stretched forward, a straight spine, and a light Neck Lock. Grasp the toes of both feet, inhale and elongate the spine, exhale, and stretch down, bringing the chest to the knees. Heart leads and the head follows. Inhale, come up to the center. Hands hold the toes throughout the movement. Continue for **1-3 minutes**. Breathe powerfully.

TO END: Inhale up and suspend the breath briefly.

This works on the lower and upper spine.

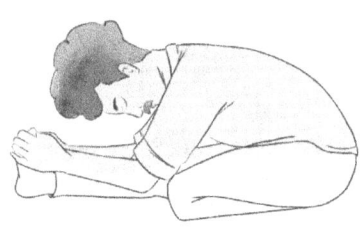

5) Modified Maha Mudra. Sit on the right heel with the left leg extended forward and a light Neck lock. Sit tall with the right heel tucked into the perineum. Sit with a straight spine and a light Neck Lock. Stretch the legs forward and wide apart as much as possible, with thighs rolled inward. Inhale and stretch the arms straight up. Exhale, stretch down and over the left leg, grasp the toes. Elongate the spine as you stretch down from the hip joint. Do not let the spine collapse. Heart leads and head follows, bringing the elbows towards the ground. Continue for **1-2 minutes** with Breath of Fire.

→

TO END: Inhale, exhale, and stretch the torso forward and down; the head follows last; suspend the breath out briefly. Inhale, switch legs, and repeat the exercise for **1-2 more minutes.** Relax.

This helps elimination, stretches the sciatic nerve and brings circulation to the upper torso.

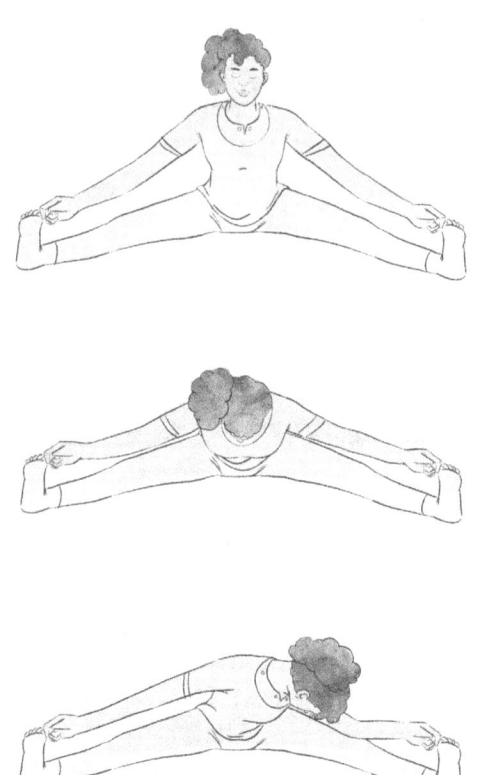

6) Life Nerve Stretch. Sit with a straight spine and a light Neck Lock. Sit tall on the sit bones, with the legs stretched wide apart, pelvis tilted slightly forward and thighs rolled inward. Grasp the toes of both feet. Inhale, elongate the spine, exhale, and stretch down and over the left leg, grasping the toes. Elongate the spine as you stretch down from the hip joint. Do not let the spine collapse. Heart leads and head follows. Inhale, come up to center; then exhale and stretch down and over the right leg. Continue alternating sides for **1-2 minutes.** Breathe powerfully. Then inhale, elongate the spine, exhale, stretch down, bringing the chest to the ground. The heart leads and the head follows. Inhale, come up to the center and continue to move up and down for **1 more minute.** Hands hold the toes throughout the exercise.

TO END: inhale up, stretching the spine straight. Exhale, bring the chest and forehead to the floor. Hold the breath out briefly as you stretch forward and down. Inhale, exhale, and relax.

This exercise develops flexibility of the lower spine and sacrum, and charges the magnetic field.

7) Cobra Pose. Lie on the stomach, place the hands on the ground under the shoulders, and push up into Cobra Pose by elongating the spine, lifting the Heart center, and dropping the shoulders away from the ears. Shoulder blades reach down and wide. Elbows are stretched but not locked. Continue for **1-3 minutes** with Breath of Fire.

TO END: Inhale, elongate, and arch the spine to the maximum, exhale and hold the breath out briefly, applying Root Lock. Inhale, exhale slowly, lower the arms, and relax the spine, vertebra by vertebra, from the base of the spine to the top. Relax, lying on the stomach with the chin on the floor and the arms by the sides.

This helps balance the sexual energy and draws the prana to balance apana so that the kundalini energy can circulate to the higher centers in the following exercises.

8) Shoulder Shrugs. Sit in Easy Pose with a straight spine. Hold the knees with the arms straight. Lift both shoulders up towards the ears on the inhale and immediately drop them back down on the exhale. Move rapidly and rhythmically for **1-2 minutes** with Powerful Breathing.

TO END: Inhale, exhale, and relax.

This balances the upper chakras and opens the hormonal gate to the higher brain centers.

9) Neck Rolls. Remain in Easy Pose with a straight spine. Inhale, lengthen the spine a bit more, then exhale, letting the chin slowly lower forward. Inhale and begin to roll the head to the side and back, exhale and continue rolling to the other side and front, keeping a long neck throughout. Continue in a slow and smooth motion. The shoulders remain relaxed and stable. The neck should be allowed to gently stretch as the head circles around. Continue for **1-2 minutes,** then reverse the direction and continue for **1-2 more minutes.**

TO END: Inhale at the center and relax.

10) Sat Kriya. Sit on the heels in Rock Pose with a straight spine and a light Neck Lock. Interlace the fingers with the Jupiter (index) fingers pointing up and the thumbs crossed. For working with masculine, projective energy, place the right thumb over the left. For working with feminine, reflective energy, place the left thumb over the right. Keep the ribcage lifted and the shoulders down; the shoulder blades are drawn down and wide. Chant **SAT** and pull the Navel Point in and up. Chant **NAAM** as you release it. Continue rhythmically for **3-7 minutes.**

TO END: Inhale, apply Root Lock, and squeeze the muscles tightly from the buttocks all the way up the spine. Suspend the breath briefly as you concentrate on the area just above the top of the head. Mentally allow the energy to flow through the top of the skull. Exhale completely. Inhale, exhale, suspend the breath for **5-20 seconds,** and apply all three locks, the Great Lock (Root Lock, Diaphragm Lock, and Neck Lock). Inhale and completely relax. Ideally, the relaxation is twice the length of time that you practiced Sat Kriya.

Sat Kriya circulates the kundalini energy through the cycle of the chakras, aids in digestion, and strengthens the nervous system.

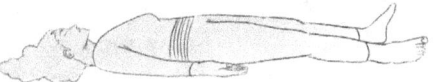

11) Relaxation. Deeply Relax in Corpse Pose.

Deep relaxation allows you to enjoy and consciously integrate the mind/body changes that have been brought about during the practice of this kriya. It allows you to sense the extension of the self through the magnetic field and the aura and allows the physical body to deeply relax.

Comments: This easy kriya is excellent as a tune-up. It systematically exercises the spine and aids in the circulation of prana to balance the chakras.

◊

Sit in Easy Pose with a straight spine and a light Neck Lock.

Mudra: Make fists with the Jupiter (index) and Saturn (middle) fingers extended and the other fingers held down with the thumbs. With the elbows on the sides of the body, raise the forearms forward and up 30 degrees from the vertical with the hands facing forward and fingers pointing up. Press the shoulders and elbows back firmly.

Eye Focus: Third Eye Point.

Breath: Long Deep Breathing.

Mantra: Mentally chant **SAA TAA NAA MAA.**

Mental Focus: Pulse the sound of the mantra rhythmically from the Third Eye Point out to Infinity.

Time: 11-62 minutes.

TO END: Inhale deeply, exhale completely. Repeat **2 more times**. Open and close the fists a few times.

Comments: This practice opens the heart center and the feelings of the positive self. It is a gesture of happiness. It has a great history and is said to have been practiced by many great and wise spiritual leaders, including Buddha and Christ. The hand mudra became a symbol for blessing and prosperity. Try it for 40 days. During that time, eat lightly and speak only the truth directly from your heart. Saa is Infinity. Taa is Life. Naa is Death. Maa is Rebirth/Transformation. This describes the cycle of life. This kriya brings a total mental balance to the psyche. The entire mantra means, "I meditate on Truth, Truth that I am."

◊
_____

Sit in Easy Pose with a straight spine and a light Neck Lock.

Mudra: Place the upper arms next to the body and raise the hands at the level of the torso with the palms facing up and fingers pointing forward. On each **HAR**, circle the hands outward, for an approximately 12-inch (30 cm) diameter circle, keeping the palms facing up. Forcefully bring the upper arms and elbows down to hit the ribs on the sides of the body as the circle is completed. Synchronize the sounding of the mantra, the pulling of the navel, and the circling of the hands until they are a single flow.

Eye Focus: Not specified.

Breath: Not specified.

Mantra: Chant steadily as you pull in the Navel at a pace of one **HAR** per second.

Time: 11 minutes.

TO END: Inhale deeply, suspend the breath, exhale. Repeat **2 more times**.

◇

Sit in Easy Pose with a straight spine and a light Neck Lock.

Mudra: Relax the upper arms at the sides of the body. Extend the forearms forward at a 90-degree angle from the upper arms, with hands facing each other at the level of the navel. On each **HAR**, move the hands in towards each other for approximately 6 inches (15 cm) and then back out. The movement is quick, forceful, and precise. Hold the hands still on the "Gobinday," "Mukunday," "Udaaray," "Apaaray," "Hareerung," "Kareeung," "Nirnaamay," and "Akaamay."

Eye Focus: 1/10th open, looking down the nose.

Breath: Not specified.

HAR HAR HAR HAR GOBINDAY
HAR HAR HAR HAR MUKUNDAY
HAR HAR HAR HAR UDAARAY
HAR HAR HAR HAR APAARAY
HAR HAR HAR HAR HAREEUNG
HAR HAR HAR HAR KAREEUNG
HAR HAR HAR HAR NIRNAAMAY
HAR HAR HAR HAR AKAAMAY

Mantra: Chant the Guru Gaitri mantra with 4 **HAR**.

Time: 31 minutes.

TO END: Inhale deeply, tighten the forearms, hands, and fingers, focus at the brow, and exhale powerfully through the mouth. Repeat **2 more times**.

◇

EMPTY YOUR MIND — SHUNIYA

We usually understand emptiness as a quality in something that used to be filled but no longer is, like a bowl or water bottle that no longer contains liquid. The emptiness I am describing here is not a concept of space at all but a type of consciousness — an absence of concepts, the natural absence of any meaning in an object. Buddhism considers emptiness the essential nature of reality, and this understanding also contains the realization that nothing is inherently good or bad. When you no longer label everything in the world as good or bad, including yourself, you liberate yourself from these identifications and associated suffering.

The more I meditate, the more I understand how we see the world in concepts. You can do that as well. Try to think of the complete absence of all concepts in your perceived world. For example, when we look at a beach sunset, most of us immediately compare it to a mental concept. I'd say we almost always have some idea of reality in our minds that stands between our sensory reception and the actual reality, and that's how we move through life. Can you imagine the lightness that would come with the absence of all these concepts? The sublime emptiness that remains when all the ideas, concepts, and expectations you have of reality are gone?

In this pure mind without prefabricated concepts, reality is created anew at every moment. With emptiness inside, you set the stage for newness. There are no concepts, no judgments, and no mind activities that are already holding a certain reality in place. The space is void to create a brand new reality. Cultivating emptiness is like preparing a garden for a new season, getting it ready for you to plant new seeds. One key to manifestation is to bring your mind to emptiness, then plant your desires in the open space and use your imagination to build inside the emptiness the reality that you want. This requires a receptive quality of the mind, just like the dirt in the garden must be ready to receive the seeds. According to Osho, the peace derived from deep concentration, particularly the receptivity that arises from it, serves as the foundation for powerful next steps. Just like emptiness gives us peace, it can also be a new beginning, a clean slate for our own manifestations.

There are plenty of meditations from various traditions to help you empty your mind. Some might even call this technique a basic meditation practice. Here are just two examples from Kundalini Yoga.

November 3, 1994

PART ONE

Sit in Easy Pose with a straight spine and light Neck Lock.

Mudra: Bend the elbows and keep them relaxed by the sides. Raise the forearms up and angle them slightly out. The hands are relaxed, with the palms facing up. Sit calmly and quietly. Do not move. Give yourself up.

Eye Focus: Closed, looking at the Moon Center (the chin).

Time: 5 minutes. Immediately begin Part Two.

PART TWO

Maintain the posture.

Breath: One Minute Breath (20-second inhale, 20-second suspend, 20-second exhale).

Eye Focus: Closed.

Time: 5 minutes. Immediately begin Part Three.

PART THREE

Maintain the posture.

Breath: Inhale through the nose and exhale through the mouth. Breathe long and deep.

Time: 5 minutes. Immediately begin Part Four.

PART FOUR

Maintain the posture.

Breath: Inhale deeply and totally relax into shuniya, nothingness. Breathe in and out as you please; be absolutely thoughtless.

Time: 10 ½ minutes.

To End: Inhale and hold the shoulders tightly. Twist left as much as possible, hold the posture for a moment, return to the center, and exhale. Inhale, twist right as much as possible, hold for a moment, return to the center, and exhale. Inhale deeply, suspend the breath, and raise the hands up, with the fingers wide and tight like steel. Stretch the spine as much as possible for **15 seconds.** Exhale and relax.

Comments: In the emptiness of *shuniya*, you find fullness. After surrendering yourself, there is no longer a difference between everything and nothing. Your life becomes bountiful and complete.

◊
_____

June 12, 1990

Sit in Easy Pose with a straight spine and a light Neck Lock.

Mudra: Place the hands on the knees in Gyan Mudra, touch the tip of the thumbs with the Jupiter (index) fingers, and keep the other three fingers extended straight.

Eye Focus: Closed.

Breath & Mental Focus:
a) Drink the breath in a single, deep, long sip through a rounded mouth. Close the mouth and exhale through the nose slowly and completely. Continue for **14 minutes.**

b) Inhale and suspend the breath comfortably. As you suspend the breath in, meditate on zero, *shuniya*. Hypnotize yourself and mentally repeat, "I am zero, my disease is zero, everything is zero." Zero applied to your thoughts and feelings of doubt and insecurity results in zero. Meditate on all negative, emotional, mental, and physical conditions and situations. As each thing crosses the mind, bring it to zero — a single point of light, a small, insignificant non-existence. Exhale and repeat. Breathe into a comfortable rhythm. Continue for **7-11 minutes.**

c) Think of the quality or condition you most desire for your complete happiness and growth. Summarize it in a single word like "Wealth," "Health," "Relationship," "Guidance," "Knowledge," or "Luck." It has to be one word. Lock on that word and thought. Visualize facets of it. Inhale and suspend the breath as you beam the thought in a continuous stream. Lock onto it. Relax the breath as needed. Continue for **5-15 more minutes.**

Total Time: 26-40 minutes.

To End: Inhale and move the shoulders, arms, and spine, then stretch the arms up, spread the fingers wide, and breathe deeply a few times.

Comments: After clearing the mind of other distracting thoughts and attachments, it has tremendous capacity and creativity when focused and beaming. Use that beaming faculty. Become still and project the mind to create your future and your relationship with the world. The best way to practice this is on an empty stomach with only liquids taken during the day.

◊
_____

CHAPTER 13
New Spiritual Techniques For Manifesting In Our Times

NEXT-LEVEL MANIFESTATION FOR YOURSELF AND OTHERS

The majority of the teachings on manifestation we discussed in this book focus on individuals manifesting on their own, and this book has been consistent with that approach up to this point. In this chapter, I aim to introduce ideas that go beyond individual manifestation. To the best of my knowledge, they haven't surfaced anywhere else yet, but I believe they are a logical next step and a natural evolution of our current knowledge.

We've discovered that yoga is a technology for connecting with the entire universe, and manifestation is how this reality is applied. After all, you engage the entire universe to manifest your desires! It's simple to overlook the fact that these infinite connections include every human being on the planet. Let's include people's connections as a crucial part of our manifestation efforts and aim for the betterment of all.

Everyone agrees that we must explore new ways of working together globally to address environmental healing, climate change, and a wide range of social issues, including inequality and mental health, for the survival of our planet. Many attempts are made, but most discussions about solutions only reach an impasse, and actual solutions are progressing too slowly to ensure the survival of life on Earth.

For instance, let's begin with the question: Can you be like the spiritual masters of the past? The answer is a solid yes. You have the potential to be like spiritual masters, such as Buddha and Jesus, and they all affirmed that reaching enlightenment is possible for everyone. Every spiritual tradition shares a common goal: the aim of awakening individuals to their true essence and powers and enabling them to live in harmony with the universe. Put simply, the goal is to attain the same level of enlightenment as the ancient spiritual teachers, including the founders of religions, sages, and yogis who recognized the unity of self and the divine. All genuine sacred texts transmit a code for awakening your authentic self, your inner Buddha, Christ, or God, regardless of the label. For example, it is well known that Buddhism teaches that every individual has the potential to achieve enlightenment, or Nirvana. In Hinduism, it is believed that every soul *(Atman)* has the potential to attain *moksha*, liberation. And in Sufism, there is a belief in the potential for spiritual union with Allah for everyone. Yet, many religions still grapple with maintaining hierarchies and placing God and clergy at the apex, despite the fundamental truth that these teachings convey: the inherent equality and oneness of all beings.

"Greater works than these that I do, shall you do." – Jesus Christ

Yogi Bhajan, who spread Kundalini Yoga in the West from the late 1960s up to his death in 2004, told his students several times during his lifetime to aspire to be ten times greater than he was. I've always felt that it was his genuine wish for everyone to evolve like that and surpass his level of mastery, and I've thought a lot about it and also discussed the idea several times with older teachers. I found that if they hear that question from a younger teacher, they suspect arrogance, disrespect, and, most of all, ego. They look at me and seem to think, "Ten times greater? It ain't you, my friend." And they're right; I'm the first one to admit that I'm no yoga master and hardly masterful at anything. So what is the point of asking if anyone can surpass the masters? Isn't it challenging enough to reach even one-tenth of their level? If so few even reach enlightenment, then why reach for even more elusive heights?

My answer to this is that evolution only happens with evolving visions, and we need new visions as much as we need to move forward. Our ideas of mastery always exist in context, and our context is different now than ten, a hundred, or a thousand years ago. In a new context, the need and the potential for becoming greater than anyone before make more sense, and one change in our context is certainly a newly connected world through technology and globalization. Our potential to be together as one global people is greater than ever before, yet we barely tap into it. Let's try this moving forward.

The pronoun "you" has always been used to address both a person and persons, singular and plural. Maybe the potential for being ten times greater, or even twice as great as any master who has ever lived, is not the potential of another individual, but the potential of a group, a community, or all mankind. After all, isn't that what the Aquarian Age is all about? Now, more than ever, our true strength lies in working together, and maybe we can be ten times greater than the yogi masters that came before us by no longer going it alone.

Creating through group consciousness could very well be the next step in our evolution as yogis and human beings. And one step in expressing this unified consciousness is combining our powers of manifestation to create a new world. That is why I am promoting group manifestation as a next step, and I say to all your yoga teachers, studio owners, event organizers, and practitioners: I encourage you to embrace this idea. If you find group meditation effective, try group manifestation next. Choose a goal that everyone can agree on in a general way, then meditate together and see the collective desire fulfilled. It won't matter what each individual sees, but the collective focus on the same general goal might just move mountains.

WHEN TALKING NO LONGER WORKS

In the era of globalization, markets and cultures are easily accessible worldwide, and East and West converge in areas like commerce, medicine, philosophy, and spirituality. At the same time, it's getting harder for people and groups to reach consensus and make peaceful decisions. The vision of a unified, peaceful world becomes more distant as conversations are dominated by opposing viewpoints, self-centered goals, and persistent egos. Discussions at any level frequently devolve into never-ending debates with little consensus, leaving problems unresolved.

Is there a way beyond talking that brings greater unanimity to a group or groups of people on a subject where everyone seeks a solution but hardly anyone agrees on the steps towards it? I'll say that the process of group manifestation is one way. Remember, you can manifest by stating your wish, then seeing and feeling the wish fulfilled. We decide on what, then, the universe handles the how. That's good news for creating on a group level, for any situation in which there is consensus on the goal but not on its details.

Let's use climate change as an example. In any debate about the topic, all participants who recognize the negative impact of environmental pollution on Earth have the same fundamental goal. The common goal is this: an environment free of fossil fuel pollution, clean and renewable energy sources, and healthy air and food for everyone. While there is much more to say about the complexity of climate change, let's remember to keep our goal general. The more general the statement, the greater the likelihood of agreement. If everyone in the debate can agree that what they want is a clean environment and healthy natural climate systems, we have defined our goal, and the group manifestation process can begin.

KRI KUNDALINI RESEARCH INSTITUTE

GROUP MANIFESTATION PRACTICE TO TRANSCEND POLARITY

Group manifestation is equal to group meditation, and group meditation can unlock the same manifestation powers we've discussed and multiply them through the group energy. Group meditation techniques are already used in many professional settings today. They are becoming increasingly popular because they work, and more people every day understand the benefits of mindfulness and expanded consciousness in any group situation. My goal for group meditations is the same that I've been advocating for the entire book — to merge it with manifestation and create a synergy that brings a whole new set of results from meditation practice. The following technique is a group meditation based on manifestation techniques. The basic process is always the same, but you can adjust your instructions and explanations to the needs and consciousness of the group.

1. Preparing a group for group manifestation. In theory, any group can engage in group manifestation as long as all members are on board. The easiest way, of course, is to organize a group meeting for the sole purpose of manifestation as a group. Naturally, yoga and meditation classes and workshops are ideal for an in-depth session, and one of the easiest ways to put a willing group together is to announce a group manifestation event and invite people. You might find that this topic opens up many new possibilities for classes and workshops. However, with the right preparation, you can incorporate group manifestation into most group meetings and classes as long as you communicate the process clearly and adjust it to the level of the group's consciousness and experience. For example, a group manifestation in a yoga setting can include a full physical yoga set and take an hour or more, while group manifestation as part of a business conference would have to be much shorter, most likely just a few minutes, and doable while everyone sits on chairs. Again, communication is key.

2. Agree to meditate together and state the goal. You'll need a goal that is unequivocal and general. Let's continue the example of climate change solutions, as it's easy for a group to agree on the most general level: everyone wants a clean and healthy environment. The goal could be this: a clean Earth where everyone can enjoy fresh air, clean water, and healthy nature. That's good enough. Remember, the details are not your responsibility, and mentioning details like specific solutions for fighting climate change might only polarize the group and scatter the groupthink.

3. Lead the group into meditation. Instruct the group to see the goal realized in their mind's eye. For climate change, ask the group to see and feel what it's like to breathe fresh air without fear, drink clean water with no danger, and move through nature that is pristine. Everyone will have different details in their minds, but the vision on a general level is the same. It's important to allow everyone their own vision of the desired outcome during the first part of the group meditation. After that, guide them to a more inclusive and expanded vision in their minds, i.e., by asking them to see other people, or more people in their vision, benefiting from the desired outcome. In a group meditation for a cleaner environment, for example, an individual might start by seeing and feeling themselves in a pristine part of nature, and from there, through your guidance, they include their loved ones, neighbors, their whole country, and ultimately the whole planet in their vision. This is expansion, and expansion increases the effectiveness of meditation and the results of manifestation.

4. End the meditation with a moment in which everyone integrates their visions into their long-term projections. Ask them to hold their vision as long as possible and activate it whenever they can, especially whenever they remember the need for a cleaner Earth, e.g., when reading the news or observing the effects of climate change in their environments.

The beauty of this technique is that everyone can participate without conflict. Everyone's personal vision is contributing to the greater goal. Union happens through engagement on the spiritual level, not through words or other actions. This practice has the potential to change the world, and it is truly yogic in that we are all connected and use our connection consciously.

MANIFESTATION AS INVESTMENT FOR OTHERS

You can think of stating your desire to the universe as equal to a pitch, in which you promote your ideas to the elements to engage and flesh out your idea into physical reality. Neville Goddard, in his book *The Power of Awareness,* even calls the application of your consciousness for manifestation an investment. A greater investment can yield a greater profit, and this is true for spiritual processes as well. How do you increase your investment in the manifestation process? By including others in the benefits of the fulfilled desire. Your manifestations are much more meaningful if you include others as beneficiaries. And if stating your desire is equal to pitching the universe, then pitching the universe a manifestation that benefits many is more likely to get funding, just like most "real-life" projects are more interesting to investors when you can show that many benefit and not just one. There is nothing wrong with wanting the best life for yourself, but whenever you expand your efforts to help others, everything becomes expanded, and the universe is all about expansion and will align itself agreeably. There is also nothing wrong with considering your own benefit when you serve others, and many will argue that no act is ever selfless, especially when you consider that everything in yoga begins and ends with the self, and that includes helping others. One way or another, your consciousness and experience are at the center of any act for yourself and others. My main point is that you should go right ahead with any manifestation plans that truly come from your heart and mean no harm to anyone but benefit yourself and others. But why not design all plans from the start to include others as much as possible? All spiritual teachings point to the blessings that come from heart-centered actions for the good of the people around you. The translation of this simple fact for manifestors is: expect better results through more support from the universe when your goals include others.

> "The Buddha of Compassion, His Holiness the Dalai Lama, often says that cherishing others is the best way of cherishing ourselves... By cherishing others, refraining from giving them harm, offering them all benefits, all our wishes for happiness, both now and in the future, will be fulfilled." Lama Zopa Rinpoche[95]

Lama Zopa Rinpoche makes clear in the above quote that compassion is the primary key, and you can inject compassion into every step of the manifestation

---

95 Lama Zopa Rinpoche, *Virtue & Reality*, (n.p.: Lama Yeshe Wisdom Archive, 1998), 14.

process. It's easy to add an extra piece in the definition and then elaborate on it during your projections. For instance, a lake house with many guest rooms; a commercially successful artist with a six-figure income from transformative and educational exhibitions, etc. Lama Zopa, in the same book, also gives advice for keeping the feeling of compassion switched on all the time, which is exactly what we do for effective manifestation, the constant holistic projection of the fulfilled desire, complete with feelings.

> "If you never let compassion leave your mind, if you constantly keep in mind the thought of benefiting others, everything you do becomes work for the welfare of others... Your life itself becomes like gold — pure, rich, extremely meaningful, and highly beneficial. Your mind becomes a wealth of merit and good karma, the cause of every happiness."[96]

Incorporate the happiness of others into the 3D movie of your manifested desire, project it as continuously as possible, and see the benefits multiply for everyone. As Lama Zopa puts it, "the purpose of our life is to be of use to others, to benefit other sentient beings, whether it be one or many."[97]

---

96 Rinpoche, *Virtue & Reality*, 42.

97 Rinpoche, *Virtue & Reality*, 24.

The following meditation is from the book *Lovingkindness* by Sharon Salzberg[98], a book I highly recommend for beginners and anyone interested in Buddhist meditation and philosophy. The original goal of loving-kindness meditation is to "dissolve the concepts of separateness that have ruled our lives by practicing metta for all beings without exception" and therefore highly yogic and union-focused. It not only helps us to experience our connections to others but also to love those connections and beings. We also develop an attitude of abundance and generosity, which is a wonderful underpinning for all your manifestation efforts and can simply make you happier overall.

You sit in a meditative pose and begin by conjuring the feeling of "metta" for yourself. Metta can be described as the feeling of benevolence, gentleness, kindness, and hospitality. Sit for a few minutes until this warm cocktail of feelings flows inside of you. From there, transition the projection from yourself to others, directing metta to others or all beings. Salzberg writes: "Traditionally, this is first done by formulating different categories that convey to you a sense of the boundlessness of life, the immeasurable nature of sentient existence." You'll see examples of what she means below, and you can create your own. Please note that you can use inclusive terms like "all beings," "all creatures," "all humans" and combine them with "metta phrases" that express your well-wishing.

"May all living beings be free from danger. May they have mental happiness. May they have physical happiness. May they have ease of well-being."

"May all living beings be free from danger. May they have mental happiness. May they have physical happiness. May they have ease of well-being."

"May all living beings be free from danger. May they have mental happiness. May they have physical happiness. May they have ease of well-being."

"May all living beings be free from danger. May they have mental happiness. May they have physical happiness. May they have ease of well-being."

---

98 Sharon Salzberg, *Lovingkindness: The Revolutionary Art of Happiness* (Boulder: Shambhala, 2002), 170.

Repeat these phrases, or your own variations, for several minutes or until you feel thoroughly connected and that your good wishes are received across the universe. This can be a wonderful meditation experience in an expansive and loving space. It can also be an excellent preparation for a manifestation session afterwards, especially for group manifestations and for those desires that include others or the entire world.

◊
_____

◊ Buddhist Meditation Sympathetic Joy Meditation

A practice similar to the one above is a Sympathetic Joy meditation. As in the previous meditation, you start with one person and then expand to others. First, meditate on someone close to you whom you love. You focus on the good things in their life and wish for their happiness to continue. This helps reduce negative feelings and judgment you might carry for others. From there, extend these positive feelings to other people, including friends, then people you feel neutral about, like neighbors, and eventually to people you don't like so much, even enemies. Finally, project your well-wishing to everyone.

◊

IDEAS ON WHAT TO GROUP-MANIFEST FOR A MORE BEAUTIFUL WORLD

If our thoughts create realities, then the importance of creating positive thoughts and visions for the world is obvious. There can only be an advantage in cultivating optimism for the future, especially since pessimism is clearly prevalent. Just look at popular culture: Many more movies, novels, and TV shows are about a dystopian future where worlds have turned into deserts and people are in constant battle with each other or other menacing outside forces. Just look at the sheer number of shows with zombies in them, set after some apocalyptic event in the near future. While I can't provide exact figures, it's generally safe to assume that most fictional futures are negative to catastrophic. Let's use our imagination and creative powers to install positive visions in the cosmic field. Below are some ideas I like to think about for the positive development of humanity. You can use all of these as inspiration for your group manifestation sessions or create your own:

» The environment is entirely free from pollution, and the glory and beauty of healthy nature are all around us.

» People live in cities and communities designed to mimic natural cycles, free of pollutants, with architecture and technologies seamlessly integrated into nature.

» Materials are eco-friendly, and massive trees provide comfortable living spaces akin to the movie Avatar.

» Cities resemble forests with towering residential trees interspersed with roads, lakes, agricultural facilities, and commerce, creating an adored living environment.

» There are no borders or authoritarian governments; people can move freely and live and work where they prefer.

» There is no exploitation of people, and there are no disadvantages based on race, background, or possessions.

» Financial wealth is no longer the primary motivator for innovation and change or a qualifier for social standing.

» Access to natural food, healthcare, and fresh air is everywhere.

Here are more ideas for a future from the mind of Yogi Bhajan, excerpts from his 2001 lecture "The Self-Sensory System of the Aquarian Age." The lecture is notable for its prescient quality, as some of his predictions are already coming true.

His visions are an uplifting reminder of humanity's potential for prioritizing grace, spirit, and love over status, insincerity, and greed. Each paragraph is an excellent introduction for group discussion, followed by a group manifestation session for taking human behavior to a higher vibration. By the way, the Aquarian Age mentioned in the title of the lecture is a term that refers to the current astrological period in the Earth's cycle when the sun enters the constellation of Aquarius. Many believe that a new era has begun, characterized by spiritual awakening, connection, community, innovation, and the pursuit of greater harmony and understanding among humans. At the very least, the idea of the Aquarian Age serves as one explanation for the massive changes we are currently experiencing on all levels of life. Below, I have selected a few excerpts from the same lecture to help us envision a better and brighter future.

"There will be no need for cosmetic makeup. People will be open, straight, and, simple, and their beauty will be internal, not external. Man and woman are going to reach out with such dignity, such devotion, such an elevated loftiness of self that the beauty of the human character will be so bewitching. Not only the one who is willing will be enjoying and realizing, but their realization will be so profound that no destructive temptation by another person will work."

"You stop searching; you start practicing. The oddness in you becomes even, and your flow becomes as vast as the Universe — and sometimes beyond the Universe. You have the authentic reach to yourself. I don't want anybody because I want everybody. This concept is very difficult. I don't want to be "I"; I don't want to be "we." I want to be 'just as it is.' And my run is with the flow of the psyche of the Universe as it takes me, as it moves me, as it desires me. Man will stop cutting corners and come into a real existence. And it's not long from now."

"Now the time has come that you will have a meditative mind to wait and see what comes to you. Your mind will direct you to work towards the right channels. You will meet the right people. Our future is now, and our presence is our purity. We don't have to purify ourselves — we are pure. We simply have to not make it ugly by diversion, by concoctions, by stories, by creating meaningless romance and fantasy, and by imagining things that are zero."

"We'll master ourselves through our service, through our character, through our commitment, and the most powerful thing that people have — our grace. Our individual grace is the most wanted today. And our projection, which will give us satisfaction, fulfillment, and exaltation, is our nobility. We will act noble, gracious, kind, and compassionate. These are our essential features."

"Our creativity will be our sensory system. And through this sensory system, we will be overflowing with energy, touching the hearts of people, feeling their feelings, and filling their emptiness. We will act great, and our flow will fulfill the gratefulness in the hearts of others. It will be a new relationship. We will create a new humanity that will have a new sensory system, and thus we will establish the Age of Aquarius. This is the fundamental character you have to learn by heart."

CHAPTER 14
CLOSING CONSIDERATIONS: POSSIBLE SELVES

There is more and more scientific research that proves the benefits of various yoga practices, but it might be a while until we have a study that shows the benefits of yoga for manifestation. However, there is one study that relates directly to the argument for manifestation techniques. In a 2006 study called "Possible Selves and Academic Outcomes," published in the Journal of Personality and Social Psychology, 91, 188-204, three social psychologists investigated the mechanism by which imagined future states of self influence academic outcomes. The researchers called these imagined states "possible selves" and defined them as the images individuals have about their future selves that can influence their behavior and decision-making. It's important to note that possible selves can be positive or negative. A positive self is a version of yourself you'd like to be, and a negative one is a version you don't want to be or fear becoming.

The study took place at a midwestern university in the United States and involved 338 undergraduate students. The researchers collected data through surveys and measured three things: the students' possible selves related to academic achievement, their motivation and commitment to academic goals, and their actual academic performance. The findings revealed that students who had positive thoughts about their academic future (such as "I see myself as a successful student") were more likely to do well in school. Conversely, students who had negative thoughts about their academic future (such as "I don't think I can do well in school") were more likely to experience academic difficulties. The authors write:

> "One is more likely to engage in strategies to attain a possible self when the possible self and the strategies feel congruent with one's important social identities (e.g., racial-ethnic, gender, social class). Otherwise, the possible self itself or working on attaining the possible self will feel like it conflicts with the rest of who one is. For example, if boys believe that only girls

raise their hands to participate or do their homework or stay after class for help, they are less likely to engage in these activities, even if they believe that these strategies would help them attain school-focused positive possible selves."[99]

I want to finish this book with this study building a bridge between modern science and manifestation, on top of everything we presented before. If you passionately practice or teach yoga and believe in its magical effects, you may have encountered resistance when trying to convince friends and family to try it. The resistance others feel toward yoga could just be a lack of interest, or they are simply not ready for the liberating effects of the practice. There may also be skepticism and unease regarding the spiritual aspects of yoga and meditation, especially when it comes to engaging with the energies of the universe and one's formless self. I think many instinctively feel that this is part of yoga, and it makes them very uncomfortable. If you know what I mean, you understand the need for the kind of bridge that science can be. Either way, I understand resistance to yoga and meditation well. I used to have a similar perspective on spiritual and religious practices. However, my level of interest drastically changed almost 20 years ago during a spiritual awakening. Suddenly, I began seeking something that I didn't realize was missing in my life. The search led me straight to yoga and meditation. There was less research on yogic practices back then, but it didn't matter to me. My experience was enough to qualify my practice.

A similar awakening occurred again a few years ago when I took a serious look at manifestation techniques. Over the past few decades, science has increasingly validated yoga and meditation, and while these practices have become mainstream, manifestation techniques still live on the fringe. However, new research in areas like mind power and quantum science is now supporting the concept of humans possessing an inherent ability to manifest.

Your experience and success with manifestation, enhanced through yoga and meditation, will inspire more research, wider acceptance, and new ways to manifest for a better world. I hope more people discover the powers of yogic manifestation, and I thank you for joining me on this pioneering path toward greater skill in this inherent human ability. I hope you have a wonderful time ahead, manifesting a new, fulfilling, and abundant life with the help of yogic techniques.

99 D. Oyserman, D. Bybee. & K. Terry, "Possible selves and academic outcomes: How and when possible selves impel action," *Journal of Personality and Social Psychology*, 91, 2006), 188-204.

KRI

– EST. 1972 –